D1745351

AS Level for OCR

Applied
Business

Rob Dransfield • Dave Needham

www.heinemann.co.uk
✓ Free online support
✓ Useful weblinks
✓ 24 hour online ordering

01865 888058

Inspiring generations

Heinemann Educational Publishers
Halley Court, Jordan Hill, Oxford OX2 8EJ
Part of Harcourt Education

Heinemann is a registered trademark of
Harcourt Education Limited

Copyright © Rob Dransfield, Dave Needham, 2005

First published 2005

10 09 08 07 06
10 9 8 7 6 5 4 3

British Library Cataloguing in Publication Data is available
from the British Library on request.

10-digit ISBN: 0 435401 15 7
13-digit ISBN: 978 0 435401 15 3

Copyright notice

All rights reserved. No part of this publication may be reproduced in any
material form (including photocopying or storing it in any medium by
electronic means and whether or not transiently or incidentally to some other
use of this publication) without the written permission of the copyright owner,
except in accordance with the provisions of the Copyright, Designs and Patents
Act 1988 or under the terms of a licence issued by the Copyright Licensing
Agency, 90 Tottenham Court Road, London W1T 4LP. Applications for the
copyright owner's written permission should be addressed to the publisher.

Edited by Rosalyn Bass
Designed by Lorraine Inglis
Typeset and illustrated by Saxon Graphics Ltd, Derby
Original illustrations © Harcourt Education Limited 2005
Cover design by Wooden Ark Studio
Printed in Great Britain by The Bath Press Ltd
Cover photo © Getty
Picture research by Ginny Stroud-Lewis

Acknowledgements

Every effort has been made to contact copyright holders of material
reproduced in this book. Any omissions will be rectified in subsequent
printings if notice is given to the publishers.

Websites

Please note that the examples of websites suggested in this book were up to
date at the time of writing. It is essential for tutors to preview each site before
using it to ensure that the URL is still accurate and the content is appropriate.
We suggest that tutors bookmark useful sites and consider enabling students to
access them through the school or college intranet.

Contents

Acknowledgements   iv

Introduction   v

UNIT 1   CREATING A MARKETING PROPOSAL   1

Introduction   1
1.2.1   Marketing objectives   2
1.2.2   Functional areas of a business and their supporting role   10
1.2.3   Market research   13
1.2.4   The marketing mix   33
1.2.5   Presentational skills   49
1.2.6   How to judge potential success   51
Resources   53

UNIT 2   RECRUITMENT IN THE WORKPLACE   55

Introduction   55
2.2.1   Job roles   56
2.2.2   The recruitment process   59
2.2.3   The selection process   73
2.2.4   The induction process   80
2.2.5   Employee motivation   84
2.2.6   The legal dimension   93
2.2.7   Research   94
2.2.8   How to judge effectiveness   96
Resources   99

UNIT 3   UNDERSTANDING THE BUSINESS ENVIRONMENT   101

Introduction   101
3.2.1   Business ownership   102
3.2.2   Sources of finance   109
3.2.3   Budgeting and budgetary control   114
3.2.4   Break-even analysis   120
3.2.5   Cash-flow forecasts and statements   126
3.2.6   Importance of accurate record keeping and technology   130
3.2.7   Analysis of the current market position   137
3.2.8   Economic conditions and market conditions   142
3.2.9   Ethical, legal, social, political and environmental factors   148
3.2.10 Stakeholders   153
Resources   163

Glossary   164

Index   168

Acknowledgements

The authors and publisher are grateful to those who have given permission to reproduce material.

Every effort has been made to contact copyright holders of material in this book. Any omissions or errors will be rectified in subsequent printings if notice is given to the publisher.

Text Acknowledgements

Dibb, Sally et al., *Marketing Concepts and Strategies*, Boston: Houghton Mifflin, 2001 – page 33

Euromonitor International – page 139

Microsoft Powerpoint® is a registered trademark of Microsoft corporation in the United States and other countries – pages 50, 58

Nielsen Media Research – page 42

Research Machines plc – page 36

Shipley, D., *Pricing Objectives in British Manufacturing Industry*, Journal of Industrial Economics, vol. 29, no. 4 – page 36

The Sunday Times – page 85

Tesco – page 151

World Advertising Research Center/DIMS – page 43

Crown copyright material is reproduced under Class Licence No. C02W0005419 with the permission of the Controller of HMSO and the Queen's Printer for Scotland.

Photo Acknowledgements

Alamy – pages 134, 138

Alamy Images/ACE STOCK LIMITED – page 58

Alamy Images/Allan Ivy – page 4

Alamy Images/David Hoffman Photo Library – page 86

Alamy Images/David Moore – page 45

Alamy Images/Peter Arnold Inc./Oldrich Karasek – page 41

Alamy Images/Photofusion Picture Library – page 15

Alamy Images/Popperfoto – page 89

Alamy Images/Robert Harding Picture Library Ltd/Glynn Genin – page 101

Alamy Images/The Photolibrary Wales – page 105

Art Directors and Trip/Peter Kaplan – page 49

Empics/PA – pages 7, 156

Getty – pages 24, 75, 147

Getty Images/The Image Bank – page 88

Rosabeth Moss Kanter – page 92

Ginny Stroud-Lewis – pages 8, 108, 92, 139

Introduction

Welcome to your GCE Applied Business course. The term 'Applied Business' is used to describe your course because it is focused not just upon learning about business organisations but also upon finding out and investigating how people within such organisations behave and make decisions. The OCR qualification aims to 'encourage candidates to develop skills, knowledge and understanding in realistic business contexts, such as discovering problems and opportunities faced by local businesses and/or developing an enterprise activity'.

Your learning will involve using theory and finding out how that theory relates to all of the decisions and activities that are taken by people within organisations at a variety of different levels. You will undertake a range of investigative portfolio activities that enable you to apply your understanding and use of theory to problems, issues and activities that make your course both theoretical and practical. This provides you with a first-hand opportunity to learn within and outside a classroom about many of the important activities and functions that people in business are involved with by undertaking many of these functions yourself. In this way your course is closely 'work related' and is designed to give you a much deeper and more meaningful understanding of the sort of activities that people in business are involved with, so that you gain both knowledge and experience.

The OCR Applied Business qualification is flexible because it provides you with a real choice about which parts of the qualification you want to undertake. Just like the more traditional A levels, the Applied GCE adopts the AS and A2 structure of GCEs.

The *AS Single Award* comprises three units which must be taken. These are:

Unit 1: Creating a Marketing Proposal (Portfolio)
Unit 2: Recruitment in the Workplace (Portfolio)
Unit 3: Understanding the Business Environment (Externally Assessed).

In this course you will complete both external and internal assessments in the form of portfolio work. The external assessment will relate to a business scenario to provide an appropriate context for the vocational element of your studies. For the internally-based portfolio assessments you will be asked to undertake realistic activities that relate to a vocational scenario, each of which you will be able to undertake in tandem with your learning within each unit. Following the dialogue and undertaking the activities in this book will help you to prepare for all of your assessment activities.

Teachers should refer to the OCR specifications for full details on the requirements for internal and external assessments. There is also sample assessment material available from OCR.

Throughout this book key words or concepts are highlighted in bold. These are also listed in the glossary at the back of the book.

Enjoy your Applied Business course. By succeeding with your course you are opening up avenues so that you can either go into the workplace or go into higher education following your course.

Dave Needham
Rob Dransfield

UNIT 1

Creating a marketing proposal

This unit contains six elements:

1.2.1 Marketing objectives

1.2.2 Functional areas of a business and their supporting role

1.2.3 Market research

1.2.4 The marketing mix

1.2.5 Presentational skills

1.2.6 How to judge potential success

Introduction

If you have been stopped in the shopping mall 'just to answer a few questions' or heard a TV advertisement which says 'nine out of ten **customers** preferred...', you have seen some aspects of **marketing**. You may have wondered how a supermarket decides which products to promote or place on the top or bottom shelf. These are all very visible parts of a highly skilled and sophisticated marketing process which interacts with all the other functions of a business.

It is very easy to take our lifestyle and the range of products and choices that we see or think about every day for granted. When we go into shops there is a huge variety of goods on view and we have to make a range of decisions that relate not just to our needs but also our income. At the same time, we are constantly offered a range of service

opportunities to match our lifestyle. It is clear that all of the people and organisations offering so many different opportunities not only show a good understanding of us as **consumers** and how our thoughts, perceptions and minds work, but they must also have undertaken widespread and precise **market research** to find out about our needs.

At the heart of this process of understanding customers is the need for organisations to find out what their customers require, make appropriate **investments** and bring **resources** together to provide goods or services for their customers. This whole process requires considerable preparation and planning, the starting point of which is the creation of a marketing proposal.

As you study this unit, you will produce a marketing proposal to launch a new product or service of your choice within the context of your chosen business. The proposal will be presented to an informed audience in the form of an oral presentation.

Your oral presentation will focus on your proposal of a **marketing mix** for your new product or service based on your own research and analysis of gathered data.

Finally, you will show evidence of reasoned judgements as you discuss the likely success of your marketing proposal for your new product or service.

1.2.1 Marketing objectives

Marketing is about understanding the customer and ensuring that products and services match existing and potential customer needs. Marketing is also about looking at ways of influencing the behaviour of customers.

Marketing is essential to the success of any business. Its primary aim is to enable businesses to meet the needs of their actual and potential customers, whether for **profit** or not. If a business's marketing is to be successful, it must:

* understand consumer needs
* understand and keep ahead of the competition
* communicate effectively with its customers to satisfy customer expectations
* co-ordinate its functions to achieve marketing aims
* be aware of constraints on marketing activities.

One of the key components of marketing, therefore, is understanding customer wants and needs. Marketing is the process through which Jaguar is able to identify the kinds of cars

people will want to buy in the near future and the features that should be built into those cars. Marketing helps Reebok anticipate changes in consumers' preferences for trainers, and helps digital television formats such as Freeview and Sky Television to identify the types of channels viewers will want to watch in the future.

Marketing objectives are an essential part of the **marketing plan** as they provide direction for activities to follow. Without clear objectives it is difficult to evaluate what a marketing plan is trying to achieve or whether a plan has been successful. It is usual to translate marketing objectives into quantifiable 'result areas', such as **market share**, market penetration or growth rate of sales. Some of these may be further broken down into specific sales volumes, value goals or geographical targets. Marketing objectives may have a time frame and direction. They also provide a basis for evaluation. Marketing must ensure that organisational activities are co-ordinated in such a way that marketing objectives are met.

When an organisation makes a mission statement it is setting a direction for everything that the business does. It is from this mission that decision-takers around the organisation set their own objectives for their particular area of activity. So, if an organisation has a mission to become a global player in aromatherapy oil, marketers within the organisation will know and understand that when they set their business objectives they need to set objectives that help the business to become a global player.

Marketing objectives create a direction for marketing activity. In this way marketing objectives are a starting point from which marketing activities follow. Before an organisation participates in any activity its owners and managers must think about what their marketing objectives will be. It is from these objectives that activities across the whole organisation will develop.

For example, as a business evolves, managers across the organisation need to know how their part of the business is serving the needs of customers. So, somebody involved in operation management or human resources will want to know how well their activities are helping the business to meet the needs of customers or keeping the business ahead of the competition. If they are involved in operations they will want to know that the quality of products is high enough to meet customer needs. Human resource managers will want to know whether staff are trained well enough to carry out activities that help the business stay ahead of the competition and so on.

When writing marketing objectives it is possible to use the SMART approach to writing objectives. This is that marketing objectives must be:

SPECIFIC – the objectives need to relate to the issues and markets in which the organisation is involved.
MEASURABLE – this helps managers to evaluate whether they have been successful in achieving marketing objectives.
ACHIEVABLE – marketing objectives must be realistic. For example, setting sales targets that are too high would create too many pressures upon a business and might damage rather than help the business.

REALISTIC – objectives must relate to the business and its activities and not be too fanciful.
TIMELY – planning for objectives involves identifying when and how they may be achieved.

The following marketing objectives help us to understand how organisations pursue *business activities*.

Understanding consumer needs

It is important to discover the needs of consumers to ensure that quality goods and services are produced. Being human, all customers are different, but only a few businesses (a tailor, for example, or a firm of architects) can provide products specifically designed for each individual customer. Most marketing activities are therefore designed to meet the needs of groups of customers within a market.

Theory into practice

Think of a product on offer that is all about technology and is not focused sufficiently upon meeting the needs of customers. Are there still some of these products around? Think equally about products that are all about sales and perhaps lack some market orientation. Finally, think of products that you feel are really well marketed and are clearly focused upon customer needs. Why is this so? What makes them so unique?

piling high and selling cheap

Selling low-value products cheaply and in volume

CASE STUDY
Marks & Spencer

For many years, Marks & Spencer had been a British institution, supported by their faithful customers. The products were a benchmark of British quality – dependable and decent – and stood as a British emblem. However, people increasingly started to think that a lot of their merchandise was dull and out of touch with changing fashions.

During the 1980s, M&S were probably propped up by good fortune. Men's and women's fashions in the 1980s were based on the older styles of the 1940s and, as more women entered the workforce, the ready-made meal became accepted as a comfort food. At the time, the alternatives to M&S were probably not attractive enough, but then George at Asda, designers at Debenhams, Zara,

Next and Gap changed the fashion world with new merchandise every three weeks instead of M&S's twice-yearly collections. The most fashion conscious of women suddenly became those women in their thirties and forties. They had money, knew about fashion and wanted to make an effort.

During the 1990s, M&S, emphasised 'value' rather then price, and this provided them with an enviable position in the high street. However, it was during this time they also got so hung up on quality they forgot about style and fashion. With inappropriate styles, sales fell and even their food halls lost customers.

In recent years M&S have got into branding, including the launch of their Per Una fashion brand which was formed as a joint venture between M&S and George Davies, the designer.

The future of M&S largely depends upon how well their designers are able to push through improvements to core products and win back the confidence of the British public. It is argued today that M&S's biggest problem is public perception, and their solution to change such perceptions is through the process of branding.

1 **To what extent were the problems encountered by M&S a failure to understand their customers?**
2 **Describe how M&S could use their marketing objectives to improve the way in which they operate. In order to answer this, cross-reference your answer to the marketing objectives within this section.**

Understanding and keeping ahead of the competition

As organisations develop their marketing proposal, senior managers need to think about how to understand their customers and keep ahead of competition. All organisational activities take place in an environment where there is some element of risk. For example, last year a firm might have sold 40,000 fridges to a market in Italy. Who is to say that they will sell the 50,000

they plan to sell this year? They may suddenly find new competitors in this market with a much better product than they currently produce, and which is being sold at a lower price. Italy may go through a cold spell or there may be problems in the economy that reduce the likelihood that people will change their fridge.

A key objective for many organisations is to use market research to provide an invaluable source of information to help organisations make decisions and develop new and existing products

CASE STUDY

Connecting the washer to the Web

Ariston have developed a washing machine that can communicate with the Internet using its own mobile phone. The margherita2000.com washing machine will be able to send breakdown reports for repair and download new washing cycles from its own website. The householder will also be able to control the washing machine remotely either by using a mobile phone or by logging on to the machine's own website.

The key achievement of this machine is that it is the first of a range of web-connected devices in the home that will be able to talk to each other using a new open communications system called – WRAP – WebReady Appliances Protocol. In the first years of the new century Ariston hope to follow up the launch of the washing machine with a dishwasher, fridge and then an oven.

1 **To what sort of audience might the margherita2000 appeal?**
2 **What sort of market research questions might product planners ask before launching this type of product?**
3 **What sort of marketing objectives would marketers have had for Ariston's new washing machine?**

to enable them to keep ahead of their competitors. For example, it could help them to:

* identify their competitors
* improve their knowledge of consumers and competitors so that changing trends can be identified
* use trends to forecast activities
* monitor their market position and develop plans
* improve their competitive advantage.

The need to be innovative and enterprising when identifying opportunities

Marketing is a discipline that involves all of the activities that an organisation engages in. As managers create their marketing proposal, they will be concerned about how to appear innovative and enterprising as well as how to develop new business opportunities for their organisation.

A new product may be one which:

* replaces an old product
* opens up a new market
* broadens an existing market.

It may involve an innovation, a technological breakthrough or simply be a line extension based upon a modification. It is often said that only about 10 per cent of new products are really new. In fact, in order to be enterprising and meet marketing objectives, it is often possible to turn old products into new products simply by finding a new market for them.

There are six distinct stages in the development process for new products. These stages illustrate that by introducing new products organisations are being innovative and enterprising. They are:

* Step 1: Ideas
* Step 2: Screening of ideas
* Step 3: Marketing analysis
* Step 4: Product development
* Step 5: Testing
* Step 6: Launch and commercialisation.

As new products go through each of these stages there is a mortality rate (see Figure 1.1).

Step 1: Ideas

All new products start from ideas. These ideas may be completely new or simply be an update of an existing product. Ideas may come from:

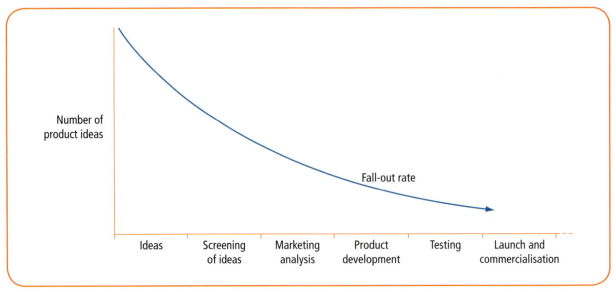

FIGURE 1.1 *Mortality (fall-out) during the new product development process*

Research and development – product development and market research working together. Technological breakthroughs and innovations from research are very important.

Mindstorming – involving a few people developing ideas from words and concepts.

Suggestions box – case incentives may encourage employees to contribute their own ideas.

Sales force – working close to customers, the sales force understands their needs and requirements.

Forced relationships – sometimes one or more products can be joined together to form new product concepts. For example, shampoo and conditioner.

Competitors – monitoring the actions of competitors may provide a rich source of new ideas.

Step 2: Screening of ideas

Once ideas have been generated it is important to screen the ideas likely to be successful and reject the rest. Considerations may include how well the product fits in with others in the product range, the unique elements of any idea that make it competitive, the likely demand for the product and whether or not it could be manufactured economically.

Step 3: Marketing analysis

Once the ideas have been screened, further marketing analysis begins. This involves a thorough analysis of the product's market potential. This type of research helps to identify the market volume (units that could be sold) as well as the value of sales expected. It may also help to identify market potential.

Step 4: Product development

Having come through the test of marketing analysis it is now time to translate the idea or product concept into a product. Design, innovation and the uses of technology are very important in product development. An assessment of packaging and branding may also be involved.

Step 5: Testing

Testing is a vital stage in the product development process. It may involve identifying valuable information through further market research which helps to fine-tune the venture. Test marketing may comprise testing on part of a consumer market or trialling the product to ensure that it meets the required standards.

Step 6: Launch and commercialisation

The launch is the most important day in the life of a product – it is finally revealed to customers. A common technique is to provide sneak glimpses of new products before they are launched.

CASE STUDY
Segway Scooter

The C5 electric tricycle

You probably need to be in your thirties or at least your late twenties to remember the antics of Sir Clive Sinclair, inventor of the fabled C5 electric tricycle. When it was unleashed on an unsuspecting public in 1985, the Sinclair C5 was the last word in futuristic transport and caught the attention of all of the British press. Ten months and £6m of investment later it was consigned to the commercial scrap heap.

Any of you who have been to the United States recently may have seen the revolutionary Segway scooter, another pioneering new personal transporter. The Segway is the brainchild of American inventor Dean Kamen and has been compared to the C5 for presenting a solution to getting around congested cities. Sinclair, having tested the new Segway, has announced news of a follow-up to the C5, called the C6.

Sir Clive is remaining tight-lipped about his new project, describing it only as a 'new product designed for getting people around town'. It is being developed in tandem with a British-based engineering company which specialises in compact electric motors and drive systems. He is convinced there is a gap in the market for his new invention, since he declares the Segway to be unsuitable for British streets.

1 **What are the risks involved with launching innovative new products?**
2 **How might Sir Clive test the market before launching the C6?**
3 **What would be the objectives for such a product if it were launched within the UK?**

Communicating effectively with customers to satisfy their expectations

From the very beginning, human beings have used hand signals, vocal patterns, symbolic drawings and facial expressions for the purpose of communicating some form of message to one another. Today, the exchange of information is a sophisticated process that produces subtle messages and that uses emerging technologies, such as the Internet and digital television.

An effective network of communications is essential for any form of promotional activity. It enables an organisation not only to communicate with its customers and satisfy their expectations but also to build an image with the world at large. Such an image will help others to form a judgement about what the organisation stands for and will influence their dealings with it.

For marketing purposes, communication of products and services contributes to the persuasion process which encourages consumers to avail themselves of whatever is on offer. The various tools used to communicate effectively with customers to satisfy their expectations fall within 'the promotional mix'. The promotional mix might include:

* Advertisements – messages sent via the media which are intended to inform or influence the people who read them.

* Direct mail – personally addressed advertising sent through the mail.

* Public relations – non-personal communications using the media.

* Sales promotions – techniques designed to increase sales, such as money-off coupons, samples and competitions.

CASE STUDY
Special K

One way of communicating with customers is through the process of branding. Special K is a brand with a unique heritage. Over many years it had evolved as a stand-alone product and Kellogg's had not attempted to create any variants or develop the product further. However, over a period of time products reach the maturity phase of the product life-cycle, and in order to keep the brand fresh it may be necessary to revitalise it and extend the growth phase by looking for opportunities to do so.

The solution for Kellogg's was to invest in a series of variants that would support the values of the brand and extend sales of the product. To do this Kellogg's launched cereal bars and also use berries and other variants to provide different taste opportunities for the core product. For Kellogg's this represented low risk and offered a good rate of return.

1 To whom does Special K appeal?
2 What values does the Special K brand communicate?
3 Does such a brand meet Kellogg's marketing objective and communicate such values to customers?
4 Why have Kellogg's invested in a series of variants?

* Sponsorship – the financing or partial funding of a project, event or activity in order to gain consumer awareness or media coverage.

* Product presentation – improving a **brand**'s visibility through packaging, the use of labels, merchandising and branding.

Theory into practice

1 Working in small groups think of a new product idea.

2 If you were to commercialise this idea, what would your objectives be for the first year?

3 How would you measure whether or not you were achieving these objectives?

4 Explain why market share is an important marketing objective for many organisations.

5 Why might improving market share be easier in rapidly changing rather than static markets?

6 Provide two examples of organisations that seem to have improved their market share in recent years.

* Direct selling – making sales with an emphasis upon the importance of salesmanship.

Dealing with internal / external constraints that may hamper marketing activities

Internal constraints

Internal constraints relate to the resource capabilities of an organisation, such as costs. For example, an organisation might identify potential customers, but how capable is it of meeting their needs? It might not have the resources to do so.

For example, in recent years Coca-Cola has developed a global presence. It has been able to do this by ploughing more money into long-term investment. Coca-Cola invests 70 per cent of its profits and achieves a staggering rate of growth.

When a company wants to develop new products or services it needs the resources to finance expansion. The bigger the scale of the development projects, the more resources are required. Sometimes companies finance expansion by selling off existing assets, for example, ICI has moved into higher value-added chemical products, such as components for lip-glosses and eye shadow. To finance this move it sold off a number of its existing heavy chemical plants which had no long-term profit potential.

In addition to financial resources, business organisations need the skills and know-how for a range of marketing activities. Increasingly, companies rely on buying in expertise from outside the organisation.

External constraints

External constraints involve a series of factors, within the business environment in which an organisation operates, that limit its activities. These will include:

* Consumers – if an organisation is not market-focused or if consumers are not interested in a product, then it will be difficult to market.

* Competitors – it may be difficult to market a product for which a competitor already has an advantage.

* Economy – in a period of economic recession when consumers have falling incomes, it may be difficult to market a luxury product.

* The law – there may be a number of laws that constrain the activities of a business and make it difficult for it to do well.

CASE STUDY

Scenario

Daniel and his younger brother George are experienced market traders, working in various markets across south-east London. They are self-motivated entrepreneurs whose main aim in life is to become millionaires. As small businessmen, they do not always find life easy!

Dan was recently offered the opportunity to buy some of the latest videos, which were claimed to be 'kosher'. This is a big opportunity to expand the business, with an up-to-date consumer product that will bring the customers in. The great benefit would be that if customers were interested in the videos, Daniel could offer them a deal with some quick-boiling kettles he bought a few months ago that he has had trouble getting rid of. The kettles look smart but take 15 minutes to boil.

Daniel's problem is that neither he nor George has the money to buy the videos. He is wondering about selling off the van to provide him with the capital, but that would mean buying an alternative form of transport such as 'company mopeds', although this might have the alternative benefit of allowing them to start some courier work.

Another idea Daniel has to expand the business is to use George's expertise in

information technology to set up training courses. Although George was very good with computers, he has not used one for five years and feels that if Daniel is going to do this, they need to buy in help from another person.

1 **What a) internal, and b) external constraints make life more difficult for Daniel and George?**

2 **What might be a better business plan for them?**

The market-focused company will fully research all of these constraints and try to find solutions that enable it to turn weaknesses into strengths and threats into opportunities.

1.2.2 Functional areas of a business and their supporting role

Functional areas

An organisation needs to be sure about its capability, a key part of which is not just the marketing systems and activities, but also the support provided by the functional areas across the business to the process of marketing. For example:

Having appropriate marketing objectives. Organisations need to identify marketing objectives that realistically provide them with opportunities to meet the business plans that they have developed.

Structuring the organisation to support marketing objectives. It is important that the functional areas of an organisation enable marketers to achieve their business objectives.

Organisations depend upon their departments to support marketing activities. By developing and focusing upon marketing objectives each part of an organisation is brought together through a process of interdependence to work to meet the same ends. Even though many of the departments do very different things, they are still working on the same objectives.

Departmentalisation is the process by which certain activities or sections of an organisation are grouped logically and assigned to managers. The way in which this is done depends on the aims of the organisation. Departments are the most usual way in which organisations break down into structures that perform particular tasks

Theory into practice

Find out how your school or college is structured. Discuss how each part of the organisation is designed to meet the needs of its customers.

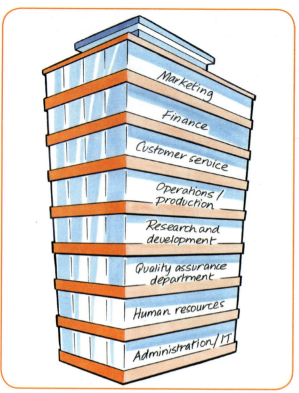

Structuring an organisation to meet its marketing objectives

within an organisation. It is important that they work closely together to co-ordinate the different ways in which they meet customer needs. The departments/activities which an organisation engages with will vary from one business to another.

Marketing

The marketing department is responsible for identifying, anticipating and satisfying consumer requirements profitably. Marketing is not just about sales, promotion or market research. As we have seen it has an important role in setting objectives that create a base for an organisation's business plan, which then affects all of the organisation.

Marketing, like all departments, will have a **budget** to work to, and will work closely with research and development to ensure that new product offers match customer needs and requirements. Marketing must also work with production and operations to ensure that the variety, choice, needs and requirements of customers are met. It needs to ensure that the finance department invests in promotional activities and other activities that help to communicate products and services to customers. Customer service is part of the product offer available for customers, and needs to be co-ordinated alongside other marketing activities.

Finance

The Finance department keeps records of events as they occur and will be responsible for producing the annual financial accounts. Management accounts will be responsible for co-ordinating plans across business organisations, including budgets and targets for achievement. In meeting customer needs they will have a vital role in ensuring that each department within the business organisation has the resource capability to meet customer needs. For example, operations need the capability to manufacture or produce goods or services to meet the number of orders coming from customers. In order to support the activities across the organisation, decisions taken by the finance team would involve allocating budgets to support the activities of each department. Marketing departments must work within the budget specified by the finance department and this can often dictate the type of marketing activities a company will use. The amount of money allocated to marketing a product may depend on the amount of **revenue** a product is likely to generate. For example, Coca-Cola may spend millions on sponsorship, television and radio to promote their products while a smaller company may only spend thousands to market their orange juice. At the same time, finance must be involved with investment decisions that are taken for new products and services.

Customer service

Customers are the most important people for any organisation and are the natural resource upon which an organisation depends. Increasingly, organisations are becoming more customer focused and adding more value to their goods by focusing upon developing relationships with customers through the quality of customer service they provide. Customer service helps to provide repeat business and provides the base for an organisation to achieve its marketing objectives.

In many ways the actions of those involved in customer service are part of the product on offer from an organisation.

Customer service needs to provide feedback to the marketing and production functions to ensure that customer needs are fully met. Those involved in customer service will find out about quality issues and be able to report back to quality assurance who in turn will work with production. Customer service will have a budget that enables it to undertake a range of activities focused upon customer needs.

Operations / production

Operations/production involves the activities necessary to produce a good or service that satisfies a customer. It is often argued that this part of the business is the most difficult to carry out. It involves getting the quality of the good or service just right and it usually employs the largest amount of capital, assets, labour and other factors of production.

Operations have to be customer focused. Although ideally it would be easier for those involved in operations to provide customers with fewer choices and less added value with their own timescale, this would directly conflict with marketing objectives that focus upon meeting customers needs.

It is sometimes said that operations is the 'sharp end' of a business organisation. They are there to ensure that customer needs are met through the quality of goods or services they provide. This might mean 'overtime' for staff during a particular week to ensure that goods are delivered on time or rescheduling production lines to provide for greater variety and choice. To meet the demands put upon this part of the business, operations needs to be appropriately financed with a budget that enables it to do so.

Research and development

New products and innovations taking place around an organisation must match information from market research and be focused upon customers if they are to be successful. Research and development can be very expensive and, while it is going on, the products that are being researched are not generating income. For example, Sony and Nintendo are competitors in the highly lucrative games market. Millions of pounds are invested in research and development and testing with key markets before a games console can be produced and sold to consumers. Research and development needs considerable support from finance to ensure that good quality development can take place. Researchers also need to work with operations to find out whether new product developments can be manufactured at an efficient cost as well as meeting customer service requirements.

Quality assurance department

Some people argue that quality is one of the most important factors in determining demand for many goods and services as consumers often search for quality rather than value. The quality assurance department has a huge influence upon how well marketing objectives are met, by trying to ensure that the quality of products or services meet customer expectations. If quality is not good, the reputation and 'how customers think' about the organisation will dip. This could influence an organisation's market position and cause it to lose business to competitors.

Human resources

Within the **human resources department**, managers will be responsible for **recruitment** and for training staff across the organisation. The success of this recruitment and training process will determine that the right people are in appropriate positions and are able to deal with customer-focused situations within their professional lives. For example, customer service individuals need to understand customer needs and be able to deal with queries on a day-to-day basis.

Human resource management will also be involved in keeping employees focused upon the tasks of the business. This includes keeping individuals motivated so that they feel happy with their role.

Administration and ICT

Information and communication technology have a huge impact upon how well customer needs are met. If a major system goes down, it may be difficult for the organisation to process a payment or provide a customer with appropriate access to information. Increasingly as e-commerce and e-business activities have a larger influence upon supplying goods and services for customers in the right place at the right time, information and

The potential impact of poor customer service upon marketing objectives

communication technology activities have become all the more critical.

All of the above departmental activities are likely to be linked in more than one way through a range of information technologies. For example, they may all be accessing the same systems and be able to see what orders are on the order book and how that relates to operational needs over the next few weeks. For human resources this might mean employing more people; for operations it could mean greater variety and choice in meeting customer needs; and for quality assurance it might mean looking at procedures that help operations produce larger batch runs with greater efficiency and with better quality.

1.2.3 Market research

Business activities are competitive, with producers constantly entering and leaving the market and consumer preferences providing signals for the development of different products and services. Whereas some organisations will succeed and achieve or surpass their marketing objectives, others will inevitably not perform as well.

Market research is that vital link in the chain between buyers and suppliers. It enables those who provide goods and services to keep in touch with the needs and wants of those who buy the services.

The American Market Research Association defines market research as:

Key terms

Systematic – using an organised and clear method or system.

Gathering – knowing what you are looking for, and collecting appropriate information.

Recording – keeping clear and organised records of what you find out.

Analysing – ordering and making sense of your information in order to draw on relevant trends and conclusions.

Problems related to marketing – finding out the answers to questions which will help you to understand better your customers and other details about the marketplace.

Theory into practice

It has been said that 'a problem well defined is a problem half solved'. How might this relate to the context of market research?

Theory into practice

Imagine that your school or college wanted to develop two new courses that would either encourage new students to enter or persuade existing students to stay longer. What information would be helpful before any decisions are made? How might they go about collecting this information?

The systematic gathering, recording and analysis of data about problems related to the marketing of goods and services.

Defining a market

A market is made up of actual or potential buyers of a product and the sellers who offer goods to meet buyers' needs. The market for computers is composed of existing owners and prospective buyers of computers, as well as companies such as Apple Macintosh who manufacture them, Microsoft who develop software and Time who distribute them within the marketplace. A market requires a process of exchange between buyers and sellers.

Interaction between buyers and sellers is based upon the notion of the marketing mix. The marketing mix provides a useful way of looking at the marketplace for products. As we shall see later in this chapter, organisations need to create a successful mix of:

* the right product or service
* sold in the right place
* at the right price
* using the most suitable form of promotion.

FIGURE 1.2 *Process of exchange between buyers and sellers*

Positioning a product or service in a segment within the market

Remember that the simplest and most important principle of marketing is that marketing and its related activities should be designed to serve the customers. Serving customer needs with goods and services that do so more precisely than those of an organisation's competitors has become more important than ever. Whereas in the past, in many markets, all customers were treated to a similar diet of goods and services, organisations now recognise that groups of consumers have different needs, wants and tastes, for example, not every person likes the same make of motor car or has the same taste in clothes.

Instead of trying to serve all customers equally, an organisation may focus its efforts on different parts of the total marketplace. Within the total marketplace it is possible to group customers with similar characteristics and divide the market into parts. This is known as market segmentation. **Market segments** are groups of customers with similar needs and characteristics. The task is to produce and supply different products to suit these segments.

Mass marketing

If you attempt to market a single product to the whole population, this is sometimes called **undifferentiated** or **mass marketing**. A single marketing mix is offered to the whole marketplace. In other words, all potential customers are treated as if they have similar characteristics. This may be a relatively cheap way of tackling marketing, but its weakness is that it ignores individual differences.

Theory into practice

Does any market today exist where segmentation does not take place?

Niche marketing

When it is not possible to satisfy all of its customers' needs with a uniform product, an organisation will use market segmentation to divide consumers into smaller segments consisting of buyers with similar needs or characteristics.

Market segmentation uses differentiated marketing plans to tailor separate products to different sectors of the market. For example, the market for cars has many segments such as economy, off-road, MPV, luxury, high performance, etc. This approach recognises that in order to be successful and hit consumer needs, it is necessary to understand the needs of different groups of consumers and meet them in different ways (see Figure 1.4).

In fact, some organisations simply exist to serve highly specialised market segments. They deliberately choose to compete in one segment and develop the most effective mix for that market. This is known as concentrated marketing. For example, Morgan serves the specific needs of customers who like a car from the past, and Jaguar cars are associated with luxury market segments. Similarly, quality fashion retailers today increasingly use brand names to position themselves in particular parts of a market. A disadvantage is that if sales of a product decline in that segment, the lack of diversification means that this may affect the performance of the organisation.

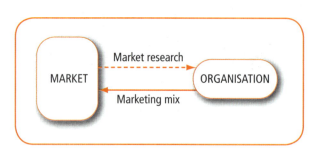

FIGURE 1.3 *Undifferentiated marketing*

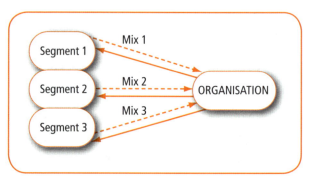

FIGURE 1.4 *Niche marketing*

CASE STUDY

The World Wide Web

It could be argued that one of the great things about the World Wide Web is that it allows small organisations to identify and reach niche markets, sometimes almost as well as large organisations. Most marketers know that 20 per cent of buyers consume 80 per cent of product volume. If you could identify that key 20 per cent and find others like them, you could sell much more product with less effort. The Web enables organisations to do this and makes it easier to enter markets that are well segmented.

Even large companies have embraced niche marketing, by continuing to refine and target their product offerings to more specific buyer groups. For example, we only have to look at the car market to see how many different models are offered by large organisations and the huge number of variants they offer both in terms of the extras they put on them as well as colours and options.

1 **How does the Web provide business opportunities for smaller organisations?**
2 **What is niche marketing?**
3 **To what extent has marketing become increasingly focused upon niches?**

There are three elements to segmentation:

1 *Market segments*. Market segments are groups of customers with similar needs and characteristics. The task is to produce and supply different products to suit these segments.

2 *Targeting*. Once segments have been identified, organisations have to identify one or more segments which has a need which can best be met by the organisation. This is known as **targeting** and may involve mass, niche or concentrated marketing.

3 *Positioning*. Even though parts of the market are divided into segments and organisations have worked out which ones to target, buyers within each segment will not have identical needs. The position is how the product is perceived in the minds of customers. Repositioning involves moving the product away from its current position in the market to another part of the market, where it might compete more effectively. Perhaps the most famous example in recent years is Skoda, who have moved away from a low-cost, low-reliability position in the market to become a well-respected high-value brand.

Investigating consumer attitudes

Consumer attitudes are their beliefs, and they represent how they view the world. It is important to understand such attitudes as there is a relationship between consumer attitudes and their behaviour. For example, by understanding consumer attitudes it is possible to develop products or services that consumers are more receptive to and positive about. It is also possible to advertise or promote goods or services to individuals in a way that encourages them to be receptive.

Market research in action on the high street

FIGURE 1.5 *Buyer behaviour may be influenced if consumer attitudes are known*

Interviewing is one way of finding out about consumer attitudes. It is then possible to link consumer attitudes with the products and services they buy.

Different attitudes can be categorised under the following headings:

Stability of attitude. Some individuals constantly change their attitudes, which results in unstable buyer behaviour patterns.

Conflict of attitude. More than one attitude may be applicable in a certain situation, so the resulting consumer behaviour might need a compromise between conflicting aims.

Strength of attitude. The strength with which an attitude is kept may determine behaviour, with strongly-held attitudes less likely to change.

Elapsed time. Since attitudes are dynamic, the longer the time between the measurement of the attitude and the behaviour, the more likely it is that the relationship between the two will break down.

Situational factors. In some cases the situations individuals find themselves in may preclude action, e.g. they have no money or the retailer is not open.

Monitoring usage

Having anticipated customer needs and attempted to meet them, it is important to verify how well-satisfied customers are. Organisations want happy

Key terms

Customer service might be defined as a reactive approach to resolving problems. It takes place after sales and is intended to solve any problems that occur in an efficient and customer-friendly way.

Customer care is a collective approach to resolving potential problems before they occur. It attempts to anticipate problems and deal with them before they happen, within the context of the notion that 'prevention is better than cure'.

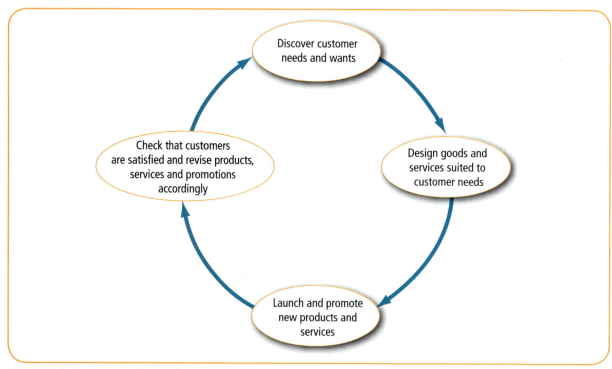

FIGURE 1.6 *The marketing cycle*

customers who will return to them and buy the goods or services again, and even recommend products to friends. Marketing is a cyclical process that starts with customers and ends with customers.

A key function of market research is to audit levels of customer satisfaction. A distinction should be made between customer service and customer care.

There are a number of ways for organisations to monitor and audit levels of customer satisfaction. These include:

* post-sale surveys identifying levels of satisfaction and finding out how sales staff deal with customers
* suggestions boxes to provide an opportunity for customers to make suggestions as to how the buying process could have been improved
* analysing complaint handling.

Forecasting needs

The real benefit of market-research information is determined by how much it improves the marketer's ability to make decisions. Good quality information will enable decisions to be made which satisfy the needs of the target market and also help the organisation to achieve its goals.

The use of market research represents a change from problem-solving by intuition to decision-making based on scientific gathering and analysis of information. The great advantage is that market research systematically provides information upon which managers may base product decisions. For example, many years ago Sir Clive Sinclair invented the C5, a small battery-powered motor vehicle. He saw it as revolutionising how we transport ourselves around. Sadly, his market research was not good. Instead of transforming markets the C5 flopped like a stone. If only he had undertaken market research in order to forecast needs!

Market research by forecasting needs helps not just to reduce business risks. It also helps to create business certainty. Earlier we saw how all of the departments within an organisation work together to meet marketing objectives. With better information it is easier for managers within a business organisation to work together and make decisions that are appropriate for the particular part of the business they manage.

CASE STUDY

DaimlerChrysler (DCS)

DaimlerChrysler have been working with an agency, Maven, to help them to understand their customer needs more fully and guide them in their service provision. Their aim is to improve their customer retention.

The research findings enable DaimlerChrysler to identify key processes and assess where they are performing well and which areas should be the focus for development. The interaction between the dealer and the customer impacts on their business, so it is vital that the needs of both parties are considered.

The research involves identifying the expectations that both customers and dealers have of an ideal finance supplier as well as feedback on the service levels they experienced. The results are used to identify relevant priority areas for improvement, and to set attainment targets in terms of customer satisfaction levels.

The surveys have been designed to cover customers at all stages of their finance contract, from those at the very beginning through to those whose finance contracts have finished, to enable DaimlerChrysler to pinpoint differing needs at various stages of the contract. The research has aided DCS in understanding which types of customers are likely to re-use them and how performance in satisfaction and loyalty could be maximised.

1 **Why do DaimlerChrysler need to understand the experience they provide for their customers?**
2 **How were the results used?**

CASE STUDY

Australian Tourist Commission (ATC)

Established in 1967 to promote Australia as an international tourism destination, the ATC has a clear mission:

'We promote Australia internationally as the world's best tourism experience – for the benefit of all Australians.'

Two of the principle objectives of the ATC are to:

* increase the number of visitors to Australia from overseas
* maximise the benefits to Australia from overseas visitors.

Having conducted an extensive process of market research, the ATC have used this information to provide a range of services to help travellers plan their trip to Australia. The ATC's key activity has been the promotion of 'Brand Australia' – a brand that positions Australia as a colourful, friendly, welcoming, vibrant, free-spirited, informal and optimistic tourist destination. As well as promoting Australia as a desirable travel destination around the world, and emphasising the diversity of holiday opportunities such as snorkelling on the Great Barrier Reef, visiting the National Parks to see a diverse range of wildlife or Uluru (Ayers Rock), finding out about Aboriginal culture and walking and

hiking, the ATC works with a number of partners both within and outside the tourist industry.

It is generally recognised that marketers cannot appeal to all buyers in all markets. Research revealed a real potential for travelling to Australia from the following three market segments:

* backpackers aged 18–24
* independent adventurers aged 25–34
* independent adventurers aged 45–65.

Backpackers are often single students who make their own travel arrangements. Many are on a 'gap year' and travel either on their own or with friends. Backpackers value the experience and see themselves as travellers rather than as tourists. Products that appeal to backpackers tend to have low prices, and might include hostel accommodation, bus passes, sporting activities and Aboriginal experiences in the outback. The use of market research alongside a variety of different experiences and opportunities for these groups has transformed the market to Australia.

1 Why did the ATC undertake market research?

2 How was the market research used by the ATC?

Planning market research

Setting objectives

Just as marketing needs its own objectives, so does market research and the objectives need to be SMART (see page 3). It is important for marketers to think about:

* the groups they intend to target with research activities

* the costs of the market research

* the techniques used to find out the requirements of potential customers

* the sources of information they intend to use

* the timescales for the completion of the research.

In order to meet these objectives market research should:

1 Identify who are the potential consumers and their requirements.

2 Identify possible sources of information, both **primary** and **secondary**.

3 Decide which method of research to use to collect information.

4 Estimate and set a timescale for the completion of the market research.

Identify who are the potential consumers and their requirements

Market research will assist in identifying potential consumers and their needs by focusing upon each part of the potential market. Research is also made into market trends in order to forecast future customer needs and customer preferences, for example, behaviours, lifestyle and aspirations.

Identify possible sources of information, both primary and secondary

Primary information comes from research which is usually carried out to determine a response from the market to a new product. Secondary information comes from research that has already been conducted for another purchase. For example, BMW may make use of **secondary research** regarding the number of cars purchased by consumers last year, but may conduct **primary research** to discover how consumers feel about their brand and what expectations the market may have of a new BMW. Market research is an expensive business and it is important to ensure that investment in research is well spent.

Decide which method of research to use to collect information

There are a number of different methods that can be used to collect primary and secondary data. The method of research chosen is often dependent upon the cost of conducting the research and the time frame allowed for it. Primary data is often more expensive to obtain but it can be collected by conducting personal interviews face to face or on the phone, by running **focus groups**, and by mailing **questionnaires** to your target audience. Secondary data is often obtained from government statistics, research carried out by specialist agencies and occasionally from news reports and trade journals.

Using appropriate methods is particularly relevant as it may be inappropriate to collect data in a particular way. Not all research is good research, and if the market research has not been well planned or uses the wrong data the results could be biased.

Estimate and set a timescale for the completion of the market research

Market research needs to work hand in hand with product development, operations, human resources and all of the other departmental resources. A timescale for market research should be developed alongside these other important elements, and enough time should be allowed for effective market research. Research may often dictate the way a product is developed or the direction it should take, so it is essential in the development of new products. It should follow other developments across the business in a way that allows appropriate and timely business decisions to be made.

Think it over...

Wembley National Stadium Limited has sold season tickets and corporate boxes worth £200 million for the new national stadium that it is building in London. This means that the project has almost broken even before a ball has been kicked or a concert sung.

Theory into practice

Look at the market for one particular type of product, for example, cars, electricity, confectionery or even beer. Comment upon how organisations within this market behave. What sorts of decisions have some of them recently made? What type of information would they have had available before they made these decisions?

Research into a market

Primary research

Any information that is original and is obtained outside an organisation is referred to as primary data. It is obtained by research conducted by or on behalf of the organisation, is specific to its needs and will involve a range of methods such as observation, discussions, questionnaires and surveys, and testing through pilots and field trials.

Observation

This involves looking at how consumers behave in the shopping environment. Information like this can help marketers to make decisions about packaging or influence the choice of point-of-sale materials designed to attract the attention of shoppers. It may also help to make decisions about where to place particular products in a shop. This is particularly important in the retail trade. The process of putting products in a store in the right place at the right time is known as merchandising.

Experiments

Market researchers may want to identify that changes in one variable are caused by changes in another. For example, they may be able to demonstrate that increased sales (the dependent variable) are the result of changes in the packaging of the product (the independent variable). This will involve changing the packaging of the product and observing the consumer reactions.

Laboratory experiments

Laboratory experiments are artificial experiments, but are useful because the researcher is in complete control of all of the relevant variables. Sometimes, whole mock-up-stores are created

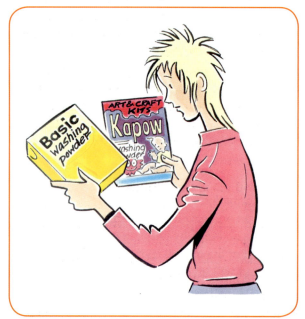

Making on-the-spot decisions in a retail environment

and customers' reactions are observed within them. Such experiments might be used to judge the response to new forms of advertising or changes in the design of either the product or its packaging.

Field experiments

Field experiments test products in real environments, in order to develop an accurate picture of what might happen. These may include:

✴ in-home placement tests where a sample group is given the products to use in their homes and asked to report back

✴ store tests where a variety of retail stores are selected to stock the new item, and customer reactions in terms of changes in sales patterns are noted over a period

✴ test-marketing which involves selecting a specific geographical area and launching a product there with full promotional support. The results are used to predict how sales will

---

CASE STUDY

Costco

Costco, better known for bulk consumer goods, have started test-marketing coffins in its store on the North Side of Chicago. Each of the six models from the Universal Casket Co., in colours including lilac and Neapolitan blue, is priced at $799.99, made of 18-gauge steel, considered medium weight for coffins, and can be delivered within 48 hours.

Shoppers checking out the new coffin kiosk seemed to like the idea that the same store where they buy so many things for this life was branching into the afterlife. Many liked the idea of being able to shop for the coffin long before a loved one's death. Those involved in arranging funerals were not as enthusiastic about discount retailers moving in on their business. Costco's brochure says buyers can cut their overall funeral costs by more than 30 per cent.

1 What is test-marketing?
2 If the test-marketing is successful, what might Costco do next to market their coffins?

go when it is launched generally, and as a result of this the product or promotional plan may be amended prior to the full launch.

Surveys and questionnaires

Many of the market research methods above depend upon the use of a questionnaire as part of a survey. A questionnaire is a systematic list of questions designed to obtain information from people about:

* specific events
* their attitudes
* their values
* their beliefs.

The quality of the questionnaire is linked with the survey. A good questionnaire will result in a smooth interview, giving the interviewer a precise format to follow and ensuring that he or she obtains exactly the information required in a format that is easy for the researcher to analyse later.

Questionnaire design is critical. Although it is easy to make up questions, it is very difficult to produce a good questionnaire – and a badly-designed questionnaire may lead to biased results.

Another problem can be that very few completed forms are returned, or that those returned are only partially completed. In addition, if the questionnaire is being administered by a number of interviewers, there is always the danger that some may misinterpret questions and introduce their own personal bias in a way that prompts certain answers from respondents.

If you were asked to write a questionnaire, where would you start? The starting point would be to think about the focus of your questions. For example, what information do you require and why do you need it? You would also need to think about the target audience that you wish to examine. It would be important to question all of the people who are likely to have relevant opinions or information.

When people give up their own time to answer the questions on a questionnaire, it is useful to tell them who you are and why you are undertaking this research. This is not only polite but will also put the respondent at ease and may facilitate co-operation.

A good questionnaire will:

* ask questions which relate directly to information needs
* not ask too many questions
* not ask leading or intimate questions
* fit questions into a logical sequence
* use the language of the target group
* not use questions that are confusing or ambiguous
* avoid questions relating to sexuality, politics and religion unless they are very relevant.

Sequencing the questions logically is very important. It may be useful to start with a few factual questions that are easy to respond to. Some form of multiple-choice questions may follow these before introducing questions that require the respondent to think about some of the issues being researched. The questionnaire may be closed with 'filter questions' about the background of the respondent, which help to locate them in the sampling frame, i.e. filter questions are used to find out more about the respondent. The answers to these questions might show that it is inappropriate to interview them. The sampling frame is the list of names of respondents before sampling takes place. It is the complete list of everybody within a market.

There is no point including questions that do not relate to the main purposes of the research. The questionnaire should be kept as short as possible. More than 40 questions could put off respondents or cause them to provide hasty replies to questions.

Open and closed questions

The questions in a questionnaire may be 'open' or 'closed'. **Open questions** allow the person answering to give an opinion and may encourage him or her to talk at length. You have to be careful though. Asking questions such as 'What type of music do you listen to?' could lead to such a variety of answers that analysing them would be very difficult. **Closed questions** usually require

Please indicate with a tick which types of music you listen to regularly (tick all that apply):

- [ ] Classical
- [ ] Easy listening
- [ ] Jazz
- [ ] Blues
- [ ] Golden oldies
- [ ] Popular
- [ ] Heavy metal
- [ ] Punk
- [ ] Indie
- [ ] Rap
- [ ] Dance
- [ ] Swing
- [ ] Hip Hop
- [ ] Other (please specify) _ _ _ _ _ _ _ _ _ _ _ _ _ _

FIGURE 1.7 *Extract from a sample questionnaire using closed questions*

an answer picked from a range of options (which may be simply yes/no). Most questionnaires use closed questions, so that they can be answered quickly and a decision has to be made within a range of choices so the answers are easier to analyse (see Figure 1.7).

Rating scales

Sometimes it is necessary to judge the degree of the respondent's feelings on a subject. The best way to do this is to use a rating or response scale.

Likert scales

Likert scales show how strongly the respondent agrees or disagrees with a statement (see Figure 1.8).

Rank order scales

Rank order scale questions ask the respondent to put a number beside various items in order to

These are all considerations when choosing where to buy a new computer. Put them in rank order with 1 by the most important, 2 by the second most important and so on down to 5 against the least important.

Wide choice   2

Helpful sales staff   3

Value for money   1

After-sales service   4

Quick delivery   5

FIGURE 1.9 *Extract from sample questionnaire using a rank order scale*

Put a cross in the box that shows how strongly you agree or disagree with each of the following statements:

	Strongly agree	Agree	Neither agree nor disagree	Disagree	Strongly disagree
The AS course has prepared me well for work		X			
The lecturers at college are well prepared			X		
The lecturers at college are interesting	X				
I was well prepared for my assignments				X	

FIGURE 1.8 *Extract from sample questionnaire using a Likert scale*

put them in some sort of order of preference, as in Figure 1.9.

Intention-to-buy scales

An **intention-to-buy** scale asks respondents to indicate by ticking a box how likely it is that they will buy some items in the future.

If a textbook was available covering this unit / module, I would:

Definitely buy	Probably buy	Not sure	Probably not buy	Definitely not buy
1 ☐	2 ☐	3 ☐	4 ☐	5 ☐

FIGURE 1.10 *Extract from sample questionnaire using intention-to-buy questions*

Semantic differential scales

Semantic differential scales use two words describing the opposite ends of a scale, with a series of points highlighted between them. The respondents are asked to indicate where on the scale their opinion lies. For example:

Place a cross on the scale below to show what feelings you have about Frosty's ice creams:

Frosty's ice creams are:

Good value	| | | | | |	Poor value
Tasty	| | | | | |	Tasteless
Well packaged	| | | | | |	Poorly packaged
Satisfying	| | | | | |	Unsatisfying

FIGURE 1.11 *Extract from sample questionnaire using semantic differential scales*

Theory into practice

Use the questionnaire below to discuss your feelings about one product which you regularly purchase (Product A):

Total performance of Product A (including product, sales, support, price, etc.):

Dissatisfied ☐ ☐ ☐ ☐ ☐ ☐ ☐ ☐ ☐ ☐ **Very satisfied**
  1   2   3   4   5   6   7   8   9   10

Compared to one year earlier, is Product A's total performance:

☐ Better   ☐ Worse   ☐ Same

Why?

What one thing can _____ do to improve the performance of Product A in meeting your total needs?

1 Explain how the answers you have provided for this brief questionnaire might be used.
2 What information has it provided?
3 Comment upon the structure of the questions.
4 How easy is it to analyse and interpret the information it has provided?

Think back to any questionnaire or form which you have recently filled in, for example your course enrolment form. What was the purpose of the form or questionnaire? Was it simple or easy to understand? Do you feel that it was well designed? If not, why not?

Prompt cards

To help interviewers operate a questionnaire, a prompt card is sometimes used. This means that, if several or all of the questions in the questionnaire have the same range or set of answers, these can be numbered and then the respondent's answers can be recorded as numbers.

Relevant questions

Some questionnaires are designed so that respondents can concentrate on the questions that are relevant, and skip over the questions which do not relate to them (see Figure 1.12).

> Question 6 **Do you have a bank account?**
>
> ☐ YES
>
> ☐ NO
>
> If your answer is **NO**, proceed to question 20

FIGURE 1.12 *Extract from sample questionnaire using relevant questions*

Focus groups

Focus groups are an inexpensive method of obtaining useful qualitative information from consumers. Under the guidance of a chairperson, a group of users of the same product may be invited to provide opinions on its use. Members of a focus group might be members of the public who have opinions on certain products and services. They may be drawn from a certain market segment or from an industry. They are very good at testing customer reactions to new developments or proposals.

A good leader is essential for a focus group. He or she will introduce key topics for discussion, keep order and ensure that every group member has the opportunity to make a contribution. The main benefit of such groups is that new ideas and opinions can be 'bounced off' each group member to refine them and prompt further creative

Focus groups need a good leader

CASE STUDY

Vauxhall

Like other car manufacturers, Vauxhall has to cope with a rapidly changing world. To keep pace it begins planning the next model even as the wraps are coming off a new launch.

This begins with a series of 'clinics' where the reaction to a new shape is tested out on a number of pre-selected motorists. These motorists are recruited by an outside agency from owners of cars in the target group together with a small number positioned above the group (who may be persuaded to trade down) and below the group (who may be persuaded to trade up). They will be people who have no connection with the motor or advertising industries.

Confidentiality is very important at this stage, so the respondents are not told which manufacturer is conducting the clinic. This also avoids any personal prejudices.

1 **Why do Vauxhall use focus groups or clinics?**
2 **What sort of issues are they likely to raise at such groups?**
3 **Who might be targeted to attend such groups?**
4 **How is Vauxhall likely to use this information?**

thought. A focus group requires a note taker and may also be audio or video-taped.

Secondary research

Secondary marketing information is effectively anything that has previously been published. It can be built from both internal and external sources.

Internal sources of secondary data

Internal data is information already held within the organisation, usually in databases. A database is a large amount of information stored in such a way that it can easily be found, processed and updated. Users may access the database across an organisation.

Information on existing customers will form the core of the database, with sales invoices probably being the most valued source of data. The invoice is created for financial purposes but it contains a considerable amount of customer data that can be made immediately available for others. For example, it might contain information such as:

* **Customer title** — gender, job description, other forms of identification
* **Customer surname** — ethnic coding
* **Customer address** — geographic coding
* **Date of sale** — tracking purchase rates and repurchasing patterns
* **Items ordered** — product category interests
* **Quantities ordered** — heavy/medium/light users
* **Price** — value of customer
* **Terms and conditions** — customer service needs

CASE STUDY

Customer database

An electricity distribution company may set up a customer database by giving each customer a customer reference number and attaching the following information to each entry:

* Tariff type. The price a customer pays for electricity can vary according to whether they are a home or a business, a large or small customer.
* Consumption. The company can then track the amount of electricity a customer uses, and when.
* Method of payment. Some customers prefer prepayment rather than credit, while others prefer to pay monthly rather than quarterly.
* Change of tenancy. The company knows when customers move out of and into a property.
* New buildings. The company knows when and where new buildings that use electricity are being erected, because an electricity supply is applied for.

From such information it is possible to obtain answers to an almost endless list of questions such as:

* What is the size of the market?
* What type of user uses the most / least electricity?
* How do customers prefer to pay?
* What is the average credit period?
* How many new users are coming on-stream?
* How many users is the company losing?
* What is the average consumption per user?
* What is the profitability for each type of customer?
* How does the use of electricity vary during the day?
* Where is the market expanding / contracting?

1 How will answers to these questions improve the way the electricity company manages its business?
2 What other questions might be answered from this type of database?

Tesco loyalty card

Loyalty cards

One way in which organisations in the retail industry keep and analyse data from customers is by the use of loyalty cards. By using loyalty cards, it is possible to match the postcode of the customer with the nature and type of purchases they might make, and then to use this information as a base for making product and merchandising decisions within a store.

External sources of secondary data

External data exists in the form of published materials, collected by somebody else. It can be used to enhance existing knowledge, for example, postcodes may help to group customers geographically. By identifying and labelling certain characteristics of a customer, a company may be able to make assumptions about their needs. Two examples of useful external sources are:

* *Domestic socio-economic data.* Customers are classified according to their house type, the assumption being that a certain lifestyle is associated with that type of house.

* *Industrial classification.* Organisational customers can be classified according to the nature of their activities. Certain types of organisations can then be expected to have predictable demands for services.

External information can complement an organisation's own information by providing

Theory into practice

Imagine that you are the owner of a small shop selling sports equipment in your local neighbourhood. What sort of information might give you a better understanding of the purchasing decisions you have to make?

direct comparison with competitors, by putting performance within the context of the economy as a whole and by identifying markets offering potential.

Government statistics

These are principally supplied by the following:

* Office for National Statistics (ONS) www.ons.gov.uk

* Department of Trade and Industry (DTI) www.dti.gov.uk

* Department for Education and Skills (Dfes) www.dfes.gov.uk

* Government Statistical Service (GSS) www.statistics.gov.uk

* Organisation for Economic Development and Co-operation (OECD) www.oecd.org

Some of the key publications include:

* *Monthly Digest of Statistics* – summary information on many economic trends.

* *Regional Trends* – regional profiles, households, labour, living standards, etc.

* *Labour Market Trends* – topical articles, hours worked, sickness, training, vacancies, disputes, earnings and unemployment.

* *Social Trends* – trends in labour markets, incomes, spending by item and by region.

* *Family Spending* – details on who earns and spends what.

* *New Earnings Survey* – earnings listed by industry, area, occupation etc.

* *National Food Survey* – expenditure on and consumption of food by income group and region.

* *Population Trends* – family statistics including births, marriages and deaths, etc., in regions.

* *Annual Abstract of Statistics* – population, social conditions, production, prices, employment.
* *Bank of England Quarterly Bulletin* – articles on financial trends.
* *General Household Survey* – social and socio-economic issues.
* *Consumer Price Index* – changes in prices across the country.
* *Census of Production* – data about production by firms in all industries.
* *Eurostat Publications* – a variety, covering economic, industrial and demographic changes across Europe.
* *Indicators of Industrial Activity* – production, employment and prices across a variety of industries and compared worldwide.
* *Business Monitors* – statistics concerning output in different business sectors. *The Retailing Monitor* is of particular interest, covering what is being bought by region.

Media

Another useful source of information is the media. It is unlikely to provide detailed data but may present a series of stories about key market sectors or larger organisations. Sources normally include:

* *Newspapers* – broadsheets such as *The Times* and *The Financial Times* are authoritative sources. However, the value of local papers and local circumstances should also be taken into account.
* *Magazines and trade journals* – the obvious ones are *The Economist* (www.economist.com) and *The Grocer*.

Theory into practice

Choose a product, market or industry in which to research. Visit the reference section and the periodicals section of either your school or college library or your local public library. Identify which sources would help you with this research and produce a short report. Use the Internet to support your final analysis.

* *TV and radio* – these include specialist news and current affairs programmes.
* *Teletext* – this provides a variety of current information across many topics.

Business directories

There are many business directories that provide general information about industries and markets. These include Kompass Register (www.Kompass.co.uk), Who Owns Whom and Key British Enterprises.

Trade associations

Trade associations publish information for their members concerning their particular fields. There are associations for almost all trades.

The Internet

The Internet has rapidly become an invaluable research tool providing a rich resource for information from a multitude of sources. As a resource it is predicted to continue to grow rapidly and become much more central to the workings of organisations not just in terms of 'Internet Marketing' but also as a business resource. Try visiting the research agency MORI at www.mori.com.

Many organisations such as Boots (www.boots-plc.com) and Nestlé have their own intranet. Unlike the Internet which is available to all, an **intranet** is a data-sharing facility within an organisation.

Commercial market research companies

There are a number of commercial market research companies offering a range of services including selling data that they acquire from a variety of sources. Mintel (www.mintel.co.uk) is a commercial research organisation which, in return for a fee, provides a monthly journal containing reports on consumer markets such as bread, alcoholic drinks and financial services. Information includes areas such as market size, main competitors, projected growth, market share of main competitors, advertising spend of main competitors and other trends. Mintel also produces in-depth reports on certain markets.

The types of reports produced by agencies include:

1 *Retail Business Market Surveys*. These are published monthly and each carries details of certain industries. It is important for those involved in market research to be able to access those relevant to their particular field. Each copy will carry an index of industries investigated. For example, there will be details on market size, market sectors, price trends, sales abroad, advertising and promotion, consumption, distribution, branding and prospects for the industry.

2 *Key Note Reports* carry even more information with specific information upon each industry.

3 *Retail audits* collect data of retail sales through supermarkets and larger chains and then sell the information to organisations wishing to buy it. These figures enable producers to work out their market shares, the sales of different products and the effects of any recent price change or promotional campaign.

CASE STUDY

Applying to be a market researcher

Market researchers organise the collection of public and business opinion about products, services or organisations. They may also conduct market research interviews and test new questionnaires.

Role

The duties of a market researcher may include the following:

* discussing information with clients
* designing surveys and questionnaires
* organising and managing surveys
* liaising with field workers and their supervisors
* supervising survey staff
* conducting interviews
* undertaking secondary research.

Skills

Market researchers need good research skills and the ability to think logically so that they can design good surveys and questionnaires. They need mathematical and statistical ability and computer skills to analyse and interpret their data. Organisational and time-management skills are also important in this work as well as good written and oral communication skills.

Knowledge

Market researchers should know about questionnaire design, survey methods and marketing techniques. They should also know how to interpret statistics and they need to be aware of different sampling and interview methods. It is important for market researchers to have some knowledge and understanding of the businesses or industries they research.

Personal qualities

Market researchers need to be able to work well under pressure, and juggle many tasks within a project. Accuracy is important, and they should be culturally sensitive when designing questionnaires and managing survey projects. They should be team players, and honesty and the ability to manage tasks and take responsibility are important for this job. Market researchers must also be able to keep information private.

Appearance

As market researchers spend a lot of time dealing with people such as clients, respondents and other professionals outside the organisation, their appearance is important.

1 Using the information from this case study, draft a person specification for a market research post.
2 Look at the above requirements for market researchers. Think about how you might or might not fit the bill for such a post. Draft a letter of application for the post of a market researcher at an organisation you have some knowledge of or interest in.

Interpretation of market research information

Having gathered marketing data for your marketing proposal you need to be able to make sense of it. Information needs to be summarised, classified and presented in a way that aids understanding, interpretation and presentation of results. It is important that marketers have access to information that is clear and provides a basis for decisions to be taken.

Arithmetic mean

One way of summarising information is to use basic statistics through the use of averages. An average is a measure of central tendency that is used to find the number which is representative of a group of numbers, that is, the middle value. Average is also referred to as the arithmetic mean.

To illustrate how the arithmetic mean is calculated, we can use the following information:

15 people were timed assembling an exercise machine and they took, 7, 8, 9, 9, 10, 10, 11, 11, 11, 12, 13, 13, 14, 15 and 16 minutes.

The **arithmetic mean** is calculated by totalling the sum of all the numbers in a group and dividing them by the number in the group. (See box at the bottom of the page).

Median

The **median** is the value of the middle number and is found by arranging the numbers in order and selecting the middle number from the list. In essence it is the value that divides the distribution into two. It is particularly useful when there are

---

The position of the median

$$= \frac{n + 1}{2}$$

where n is the number of values.

In our example:

$$\text{Median} = \frac{15 + 1}{2}$$

(that is the 8th number in the list which is 11)

---

extreme values in a series of numbers that would otherwise distort the arithmetic mean.

Mode

The **mode** is the most frequently occurring item in a list of numbers. In our example, 11 occurs three times and is the mode.

Theory into practice

The following list represents the number of phone calls made to a customer service department within July. Work out the arithmetic mean, median and mode from the data.

Describe how summarising such data could be useful in asking key questions about products and services.

5	6	8	9	9	9	10	11	11	12
12	12	12	16	18	18	19	20	20	20
20	20	22	28	31	33	34	34	35	35
41									

Arithmetic mean	=	$\dfrac{\text{Sum of all values}}{\text{Total number of values}}$
	=	$\dfrac{7+8+9+9+10+10+11+11+11+12+13+13+14+15+16}{15}$
	=	$\dfrac{169}{15}$
	=	11.3

Percentages

One series of marketing information that we are constantly faced with is that of **percentages**. Organisations use percentages to describe their sales. We see percentages on literature designed to sell us products. Percentages simply mean an amount out of every 100. 100 per cent is therefore 100 out of 100 which might mean full marks for a test or 100 per cent reliability.

To increase an amount by a specified percentage you need to calculate the percentage and add it to the original figure. For example, to increase £20 by 15 per cent you need to calculate 15 per cent of £20 which is £3. By adding £3 to the original amount you are increasing the amount by 15 per cent.

An alternative way of increasing £20 by 15 per cent is to make the assumption that we now need to know what 115 per cent of £20 is. If we divide 115 by 100, this equals 1.15 and then multiply this by the original figure of £20, it will give you the same answer of £23.

To decrease an amount by a specified percentage simply calculate the percentage and subtract it from the original figure. For example, to decrease £20 by 15 per cent, calculate 15 per cent of £20 which is £3, and reduce the £20 by £3, to make £17.

To find one quantity as a percentage of another involves calculating the percentage one figure is of another and then dividing the first by the second and multiplying by 100.

For example, to calculate what percentage 60 is of 3000: Divide 60 by 3000 which equals 0.02 and then multiply this by 100 which equals 2 per cent.

Theory into practice

You are in the process of re-pricing goods within your store. Work out the following:

1 You want to take 25 per cent off the original price of men's jackets which are usually sold for £80.

2 You want to increase suit prices that sell for £125 by 15 per cent.

Forecasting

If we remind ourselves that the purpose of market research is to collect information that enables us to identify and anticipate customer requirements, we are able to see that the outcome of market research is a prediction of consumer behaviour. A significant amount of expenditure might be risked on the basis of these predictions. For example, organisations make huge investments in new products and new product developments. If they get the market research wrong, this could involve wasting many millions of pounds.

When large-scale risks are taken, then managers are clearly interested in the degree of accuracy of their predictions of customer behaviour. The likelihood that predictions will be accurate is termed **probability**. Complex statistical techniques can be applied to calculating probabilities.

Sales forecasts are usually based upon previous sales results. Many factors can affect sales, for example, competition and consumer trends and their likely effects need to be identified and taken into account within forecasts. One way of dealing with this is by moving average totals (see Figure 1.13).

At the end of December we can see that the total sales for the year is £2,930. By deducting the earliest value in the year (Jan 2004) of 250 and adding the latest value in January 2005 of 240, we can see that the moving average total of sales has dropped from £2,930 to £2,920 because of the impact of a recent value. The moving average therefore takes into account later and more recent values in indicating average sales over a period.

From the figures above it can be seen clearly that sales grew during June, July and August, but levelled off towards the end of the year, reverting to the static sales pattern at the beginning of the year. On this basis, all things being equal, a marketing manager might conclude that the increased advertising during June to August might have resulted in the increased sales growth during the following months which fell back when advertising was reduced to previous levels.

Understanding the needs of customers and anticipating their future needs is vital to success

Year	Jan	Feb	Mar	Apr	May	June	July	Aug	Sept	Oct	Nov	Dec
2004	250	200	160	150	240	310	420	430	280	130	100	260
MAT												2,930
2005	240	210	140	160	260	350	490	570	320	140	100	270
MAT	2,920	2,930	2,910	2,920	2,940	2,980	3,050	3,190	3,230	3,240	3,240	3,250

MAT = Moving average total

FIGURE 1.13 *Moving annual total sales of Fizzy cola 2005*

in today's dynamic markets. Increasingly sophisticated market research systems provide more and more detailed consumer information on which to base forecasts. When assessing that information and making decisions to use expensive resources, marketing managers need to question the validity of the data presented. For example, how reliable is the data? Are they based upon a representative sample size? Is there an element of bias in the results? How strong are the correlations between factors? All these play a part in gauging the probability and the accuracy of the forecasts.

PEST model

One useful way of analysing an organisation's external environment is by grouping external forces neatly into four areas by using a **PEST analysis**. PEST stands for Political, Economic, Social and Technological influences, all of which are external.

Carrying out a PEST analysis involves identifying the key factors external to an organisation which are in a state of flux and are likely to have an influence on the organisation in the coming months and years.

Whereas identifying these factors is relatively easy, assessing their ongoing impact and effect is more difficult. An effective PEST analysis will be based on detailed research using all of the latest journals and publications. For example, if certain taxes are likely to be lowered, how much are they likely to be lowered by? What will be the impact on the sales of each product? If interest rates are expected to go up, how much will they go up? How long will they be raised for? What will be their impact upon sales and costs?

Political, legal and fiscal factors. Business decisions are influenced by political, fiscal (taxation) and legal decisions. For example, although in recent years many people have been encouraged to become self-employed, there has been a feeling by many of these people that they are over-regulated. These influences might include:

* changes in the tax structure
* privatisation
* the influence of unions
* changes in the availability of raw materials
* duties and levies
* regulatory constraints such as labelling, quality, safety.

Economic factors. Though the economic environment is influenced by domestic economic policies, it is also dependent upon world economic trends. Rates of economic growth, inflation, consumption patterns, income distribution and many other economic trends determine the nature of products and services required by consumers, as well as how difficult

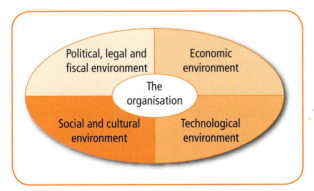

FIGURE 1.14 *PEST analysis*

it becomes to supply them. Influences might include:

* inflation
* unemployment
* energy prices
* price volatility.

Social / cultural factors. To understand the social and cultural environment involves close analysis of society. Demographic changes such as population growth, movements and age distribution will be important, as will changes in cultural values and social trends such as family size and social behaviour. Factors might include:

* consumer lifestyles
* environmental issues
* demographic issues
* education
* immigration/emigration
* religion.

Technological factors. In marketing goods and services, organisations must become aware of new materials as well as developments in manufacturing and business processes. At the same time organisations have to look at the nature of their products and, in particular, their cost-effectiveness as well as their performance in relation to competition. Factors might include:

* new technological processes
* energy-saving techniques
* new materials and substitutes for existing materials
* better equipment
* new product developments.

Forces external to the organisation are rarely stable, and many of these forces can alter quickly and dramatically. It is important to recognise that while some of these forces will be harmful to marketing efforts, others will create new opportunities.

Theory into practice

Choose an organisation which you are going to use as the centrepiece for a PEST analysis. If possible, arrange a meeting with an employee of the organisation to discuss each of the PEST forces influencing the business and use this information as a starting point for your analysis. Use the Internet and a reference library to find out more to support the points made throughout the interview. Present your findings back to the class, and then discuss the impact that all of these external forces have had upon the decisions made by the organisation over recent years.

SWOT analysis

A particularly useful approach to examining the relationship between an organisation and its marketing environment is a **SWOT analysis**. A SWOT analysis sets out to focus upon the Strengths, Weaknesses, Opportunities and Threats facing a business or its products at a given moment. It includes both an internal and an external element. The internal element looks at current strengths and weaknesses of the organisation. The external element looks at the opportunities and threats present in the environment in which the organisation operates.

Carrying out a SWOT analysis requires research into an organisation's current and future position. The analysis is used to match an organisation's strengths and weaknesses with the external market forces in the business environment.

As a result of carrying out a SWOT analysis, an organisation should go on to develop policies

Inside the organisation (internal)	Outside the organisation (external)
Strengths (positive)	**Opportunities** (positive)
Weaknesses (negative)	**Threats** (negative)

FIGURE 1.15 *SWOT analysis*

Inside the organisation	The external environment
Strengths +	Opportunities +
Weaknesses −	Threats −

FIGURE 1.16 *The planning balance sheet*

and practices that will enable it to build upon its strengths, minimise its weaknesses, seize its opportunities and take measures that will cancel out or minimise threats. The SWOT is thus sometimes called 'the planning balance sheet' (see Figure 1.16).

A simplified SWOT analysis might show, for example, that a business organisation has the following:

Strengths
* good product
* good relationship with customers
* good management team.

Weaknesses
* operates on a small scale
* regular cash-flow problems
* deals in a limited market.

Opportunities
* new and rapidly growing markets
* changing tastes of consumers
* could diversify into a number of product lines.

Threats
* growing competition from rivals
* recession leading to poor demand in the economy
* development of foreign competitors.

1.2.4 The marketing mix

The marketing mix provides us with a useful way of looking at the marketing of products. Organisations need to create a successful mix of:

* the right product (or service)
* sold in the right place

Theory into practice

Make a study of consumer choice for a particular type of product which is sold in a supermarket. How many different types and brands of the product are on sale? How do the types and brands compete against each other? To what extent do consumers benefit from having this choice? Identify the different segments for this type of product. Does variety lead to increased quality? What are the other benefits of variety? What are the drawbacks of having so much choice?

* at the right price
* using the most suitable form of promotion.

The marketing mix is therefore a series of controllable variables that an organisation can use in order to best meet customer needs and ensure that an organisation is successful in the markets in which it serves.

Product / packaging

The product is the most important element in an organisation's marketing mix. According to Sally Dibb et al (1994):

A product is everything, both favourable and unfavourable, that is received in an exchange.

Brands

Many mass-produced products are almost identical. For example, most washing powders are similar, as are different types of margarine. These goods tend to be produced by two or three large companies who encourage sales by creating a brand that differentiates the products in the minds of consumers.

A **brand** can be a name, a symbol or a design used to identify a specific product and differentiate it from its competitors. Brand names, designs, trademarks, symbols, slogans and even music can be used to distinguish one product

Key terms

A **brand** is a part of a particular product and includes characteristics that identify it with a particular producer.

from another and allow an organisation to distinguish its products from competing ones.

The business of creating a brand is a particularly important function of marketing. Often people will buy the brand name as much as the product itself. You will see people in supermarkets pick up an item (which they have not seen before) and say, 'this must be a good one because it is made by...'

There are three different types of brands. These are:

1   *Manufacturer brands*. Examples of these include Kellogg's Cornflakes, Nescafé Coffee and Heinz Baked Beans. These manufacturer brands associate the producer with the specific product, and the producer will be heavily involved with the promotion of the product.

2   *Own-label brands*. Examples of these include Tesco, St Michael (Marks & Spencer), Farm Foods (Asda) and Sainsbury's own label. These brands are owned and controlled by retailers.

3   *Generic brands*. Such products are extremely rare in the modern competitive market, and those that exist are usually at the lower end of the market with respect to price and quality. These products have no identifiable name or logo. Examples may include plain T-shirts or bin-liners if they have no branded packaging or labels attached that identify the originator.

Organisations seek to create a portfolio of individual products which support the image of a brand. Well-known brand names will therefore emphasise quality throughout the organisation. A brand which is held in high esteem is worth a lot of money to an organisation. There is a well-known saying in business that, 'an organisation can afford to get rid of its other assets, but not its brand image!'

Theory into practice

Identify two or three brands of products in a particular market. To what extent could these brands be further developed in a way that represents the image of each brand?

Product features

Customers do not buy features, they buy what those features can do for them – the problems they solve, the money or the time they save, etc. A product is really a bundle of benefits. A key aspect of marketing is to make sure that products create the benefits that a consumer desires in a particular product and that the product offering is better than those of competitors. Associated with this is the need to make sure that the market fully understands the range of benefits on offer, through strong communications.

When we understand the benefits that customers are looking for in a product, we are best placed to know why they will buy it – and hence focus our marketing accordingly. For example, in buying toothpaste the benefits that customers may be looking for include:

✳ flavour and product appearance

✳ brightness of teeth

✳ decay prevention

✳ price/value for money

✳ appealing brand name and confidence in brand.

Knowing that these are the benefits the consumer requires enables the organisation to focus its efforts on creating products that will produce one or more of them, and then promotion can be used to highlight the organisation's ability to create these benefits.

There are often clear and **tangible** features (things you can touch and see) associated with a product. Tangible features might include shape, design, colour, packaging and size.

Intangible features are not so obvious. These include the reputation of an organisation, the brand image, after-sales service, availability of spare parts, service centres and so on.

It is also argued that products provide advantages for customers through three different dimensions:

1   *Generic dimensions*. These are the key benefits of a particular item. For example, shoe polish should clean shoes.

2 *Sensual dimensions*. These have an impact upon the senses. They might include design, colour, taste, smell and texture. The sensual benefits are frequently highlighted by advertisers. This is clearly the case when advertising food and drinks with words such as 'smooth and creamy', 'the amber nectar' and so on.

3 *Extended dimensions*. A wide range of additional benefits are included here. Examples are servicing agreements, credit facilities, guarantees, maintenance contracts and so on.

With any group of products there is a distinct mix of items. They may include:

Product item

A product item is a specific model, brand or size of a product that an organisation sells, for example, a 2kg box of Uncle Ben's Long Grain Rice.

Product line

A product line is a group of closely related product items, with similar characteristics and/or applications, for example a line of Uncle Ben's Rice items, including short grain, long grain and pudding rice.

Product mix

A product mix is all of an organisation's product lines, e.g. including rice, flour, sugar, pickles and other lines. Any product mix can be described according to its width, length, depth and consistency.

Width

Width is the number of different product lines on offer. For example, Coca-Cola produces quite a narrow range of soft drinks including Sprite, Fanta and Coca-Cola. In contrast, a company like Unilever has a wide range of products from Walls ice cream and Birds Eye frozen foods to many different types of soap powders and cleaning agents. Having a narrow range of products enables the consumer to benefit from **economies of large-scale** production whereas breadth enables an organisation to benefit from diversification. Broadening a line to create breadth means extending it beyond its current range.

Length

Length is the total number of items on offer. The decision on the number of lines to offer is very important. Too many lines and you may overstretch yourself, and even start to compete against your own lines. Line stretching involves increasing the product line, either by moving into higher-quality items or moving downmarket. When the car manufacturer Volkswagen bought a 31 per cent share in Skoda in 1991, the leading Skoda model was the downmarket Favorit. Not only were substantial changes made to the Favorit, but in 1995 a new, more upmarket Felicia was added to Skoda's lines with great success. The process of line filling involves filling in gaps in product lines. For example, confectionery manufacturers regularly develop new chocolate bars to fill perceived gaps in their range of products. Line rationalisation involves cutting out lines that are not central to the organisation's major focus of interest, or those that have lost popularity.

Depth

Depth is the number of variants of each brand, for example, the number of different sizes, models or flavours within a product line. Detergent companies like Procter & Gamble or Unilever offer many different sizes of soap powder boxes as well as lots of different kinds of soap powder, all targeted at slightly different groups of customers. It makes sense for a large company to offer a product for all occasions in order to aim for a position of leadership. However, it is important not to cannibalise the sales of your own products. Deepening a product would mean adding more lines within your existing range. Line pruning means cutting the depth of a product line by reducing the number of alternative sizes, models of flavours in the line.

Consistency

Consistency is the closeness of the relationship between each product line.

Theory into practice

Examine the annual report of a well-known public company, for example Cadbury Schweppes. Comment on the width, depth and consistency of their product mix.

CASE STUDY

Research Machines (RM plc)

Founded in 1973 by Mike Fischer and Mike O'Regan, RM plc is the UK's leading provider of commercial education services and a pioneer in the application of technology to education. The Group's first educational microcomputer was launched in 1977 and schools, colleges and universities have become the main market for RM since then. In recent years RM has expanded its range of products and services to include interactive whole-class teaching services, teacher training, ICT-based needs assessment and school management information systems.

According to RM, *'In the 1990s it became clear that the educational community was looking for more from their suppliers than simple technological expertise. RM rose to the challenge. Looking beyond the* technology, the Group formed long-term partnerships with both educationalists and other learning technology companies. These partnerships allow us to deliver genuine learning productivity. It is a strategy that has worked as our market leadership shows. RM's passion is education and its aim is to explore and exploit the potential of IT to improve educational standards. Today, RM is expanding its relationships with customers further by providing a diverse range of education services.'

1 **What makes RM different from many other IT organisations?**
2 **In marketing terms describe how it has developed the products it offers.**

Creating the optimum product mix means having the right balance in terms of width, depth, length and consistency An effective product mix should yield a balanced profit contribution from a number of lines – although there will always be some products that are the highest yielders.

Organisations need to decide whether they have the right mix at any one point in time while having an eye on future changes. Key concerns are: Should we stick to the narrow range of lines in which we are successful? What are our current strengths and weaknesses? What are the opportunities and threats of diversifying? How can we avoid competing with ourselves?

Pricing and the techniques of pricing

Price is the only element of the marketing mix that directly generates income – other elements of the marketing mix are costs. The importance of price in the marketing mix varies. In low-cost, non-fashion markets price can be critical (for example, in the sale of white emulsion and gloss paint). In fashion markets, such as clothing, it can be one of the least relevant factors. Certain products are designed to suit a particular segment (e.g. economy family cars), while others perform a specific function regardless of price (e.g. sports cars). For consumers with limited budgets, price is a key-purchasing criterion, while for those to whom 'money is no object' price is less important.

The first pricing task is to create an overall pricing goal for an organisation which is in line with the marketing aims, and then determine objectives for each of the product lines.

Researcher D. Shipley found the following principal pricing objectives of firms:

Pricing objectives	Percentage of firms
Target profit or return on capital employed	67%
Prices fair to firm and customers	13%
Prices similar to those of competitors	8%
Target sales volume	7%
Stable sales volume	5%
Target market share	2%
Stable prices	2%
Other	1%

FIGURE 1.17 *Firms' pricing objectives*

Once pricing objectives have been established, organisations need to establish an appropriate pricing model.

Penetration pricing

Penetration pricing is appropriate when the seller knows that there are many competitors within a market. Penetration pricing enables an organisation to 'penetrate' a market with an artificially low price in order to gain market share away from other competitors. A low price is therefore required to attract consumers to the product. Penetration pricing is normally associated with the launch of a new product for which the market needs to be penetrated (see Figure 1.18).

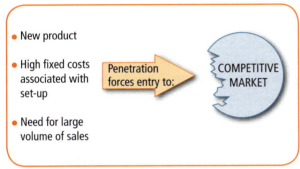

- New product

- High fixed costs associated with set-up

- Need for large volume of sales

Penetration forces entry to: COMPETITIVE MARKET

FIGURE 1.18 *An environment appropriate for penetration pricing*

As the price starts low, even though a product will be developing market share, the product may initially make a loss until consumer awareness is increased. For example, a new breakfast cereal or a product being launched in a new overseas market would be launched with a relatively low price, coupled with discounts and special offers. As the product penetrates the market, sales and profitability increase and prices then creep upwards.

Penetration pricing is particularly appropriate for products where economies of scale can be employed to produce large volumes at low unit costs. Penetration pricing is also common when there is a strong possibility of competition from rival pricing.

Skimming

At the launch of a new product, there will frequently be little competition in the market. Consumers will probably have little knowledge of the product. Skimming involves setting a reasonably high initial price in order to yield high initial returns from those consumers willing to buy the new product. Once the first group of customers has been satisfied, the seller can then lower prices in order to make sales to new groups of customers. This process can be continued until a larger section of the total market has been catered for. By operating in this way, the business removes the risk of underpricing the product.

The name 'skimming' comes from the process of skimming the cream from the top of a milk product (see Figure 1.19).

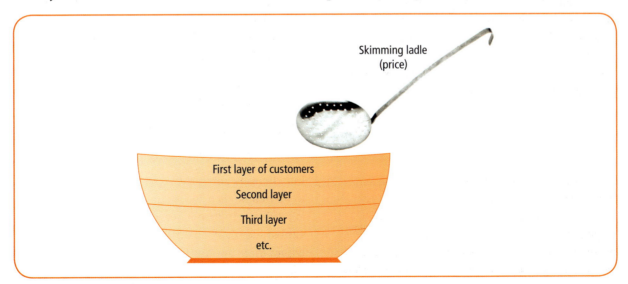

Skimming ladle (price)

First layer of customers

Second layer

Third layer

etc.

FIGURE 1.19 *Skimming*

Cost-plus pricing

Information about costs is usually easier to piece together than information about other variables such as likely revenue. Firms will often simply add a margin to the unit cost or mark-up each item sold by a certain percentage, for example, fashion items are frequently marked up by between 100 and 200 per cent. The unit cost is the average cost of each item produced. For example, if an organisation produces 800 units at a total cost of £24,000, the unit cost will be £30.

The process of cost-plus pricing can best be illustrated in relation to large organisations where economies of scale can be spread over a considerable range of output. For a large organisation, unit costs will fall rapidly at first as the overheads are spread over a larger output. It is therefore a relatively simple calculation to add a fixed margin (e.g. 20 per cent) to the unit cost. The organisation is able to select an output to produce and to set a price that will be 20 per cent higher than the unit cost of production (see Figure 1.20).

Although cost-plus pricing is very popular, there are many dangers associated with it. If the price is set too high, sales may fall short of expectations and if the price is set too low, then potential revenue is sacrificed. However, the greatest danger of cost-based pricing is that it indicates a production-orientated approach to the market. Emphasis on costs leads to tunnel vision that looks inwards at the company's product rather than outwards at the customers' perception of the product.

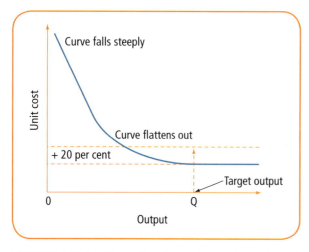

FIGURE 1.20 *Adding a fixed margin to the unit cost*

Theory into practice

Why is the margin for luxury goods such as designer goods and fashion accessories likely to be higher than for cigarettes or newspapers?

Value and price

There is a strong link between value and price. Delivery of value is an important ingredient of an exchange. In the longer term, the success of organisations will depend on their ability to provide customers with value for money through the exchange process.

Some customers are value orientated and want to pay low prices for acceptable quality whereas some buyers want high quality and are willing to pay more for it. Many of today's retailers are using emphasis upon 'value' as a form of competition. Instead of focusing simply upon price, they provide customers with a better value package – more for the same price – than other competitors in that segment of the market.

It is therefore important to price according to the nature of customers in the marketplace. On the one hand you may lose customers by charging too high a price where customers feel that they are not getting value for money. On the other hand you may lose custom from charging too low a price as potential customers may feel that the low price indicates lower quality than they are seeking.

Theory into practice

Compare two products or services for which roughly similar prices are charged. Explain which product or service represents a better value proposition.

Competition-based pricing

In extremely competitive situations, costs have to be treated as a secondary consideration. This is particularly true when competing products are almost identical, customers are well informed and where there are few suppliers.

If a product is faced by direct competition, then it will compete against other very similar products in the marketplace. This will constrain pricing decisions so that price setting will need to be kept closely in line with rivals' actions. An individual organisation might try to insulate itself against price sensitivity by differentiating its products from those of rivals.

In contrast, when a product is faced by indirect competition (i.e. competition with products in different sectors of the market) then there will be more scope to vary the price. For example, a firm might choose a high price to give a product a 'quality' feel. In contrast, it might charge a low price so that consumers see the product as a 'bargain'.

Markets are sometimes classified according to the level of competition that applies. For example,

FIGURE 1.21 *Competition*

an extreme level of competition is termed perfect competition. The other extreme is monopoly where a single firm dominates a market. In the real world, most markets lie between these extremes and involve some level of imperfection.

Where organisations seek to reduce competition and make their products better than their rivals, the development of monopolistic powers enables them to push up prices and make larger profits. The level of competition is a key determinant of price. Where there are many close competitors, there is little scope to charge a price which is above the market price. Organisations in such markets are **price takers**. In a situation where there is no competition, the seller can often charge a relatively high price. In other words they are a **price maker**. However, the seller cannot charge more than the consumer is prepared to pay as consumers can spend their income on alternative products.

Promotion

Promotion includes all of the techniques that an organisation uses to communicate with other individuals and organisations. Organisations are the senders in the communication process and consumers are the receivers. A sender will put information in the form that a receiver can understand. This might involve oral, visual, verbal or written messages to transmit the ideas. This process is called **encoding**. The sender will also choose a particular medium to use to send the message to the receiver (e.g. television, radio, newspapers). If the consumer interprets the message as required, it should have the impact that the seller wished for.

Though the message flows through to the receiver there is no guarantee that the receiver will either receive the full message or understand it. This is because the process may be subject to some form of interference, which affects the flow of

---

Theory into practice

Categorise the following examples into:

✳ penetration pricing

✳ skimming

✳ cost-plus pricing

✳ value-based competition

✳ competition-based pricing.

In each instance explain why you have chosen a particular category.

1 A new book comes onto the market in hardback form at £25, two months later it comes out in paperback at £15, the following year it comes out in a 2nd edition at £10.

2 In order to improve its competitive position in the high street, a major retailer creates a series of sub-brands designed to improve the way in which its customers view its products.

3 A breakfast cereal manufacturer introduces a new type of cereal at a low price in order to attract customers to buy the product.

4 A garden centre sets a margin of 30 per cent on all of its stock.

5 A company launches a revolutionary piece of software.

6 In a fiercely competitive market, a business simply looks at the price charged by others before setting its own price.

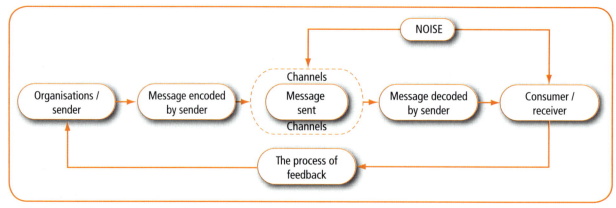

FIGURE 1.22 *The communication process*

information. This is known as noise and may lead to the downfall of the message. It will take the form of any barrier which acts as an impediment to the smooth flow of information and may include linguistic and cultural differences between the sender and the receiver. For example, one leaflet put through your door may be lost amongst a sea of direct mail from other organisations.

To increase the chances of a message getting across, an organisation needs to think carefully about the target audience. For example, it is important to channel the message through the most appropriate media. It might also be necessary to repeat the message several times rather than rely on one transmission.

Once the audience has been identified the communicator also needs to think about the sort

Theory into practice

Competition in the market for personal computers is fierce. Imagine that you work for a small organisation selling machines by mail order and you wish to target 'first-time' purchasers of PCs, particularly the over-60s. Explain what you would do to build your communication planning around the purchasing process.

of response required. If, for example, the final response required through the communication process is purchase, there may be six phases to the buyer-readiness process (see Figure 1.23).

It is important, therefore, that the promotion mix takes into account each of these stages with different types of promotional activities.

Advertising

Advertising is a method of communicating with groups in the marketplace in order to achieve certain objectives. Advertisements are messages sent through the media which are intended to inform or influence the people who receive them (see Figure 1.24).

It can be defined as a paid-for type of marketing communication that is non-personal, but aimed at a specific target audience through a mass media channel.

Advertising messages may be sent through a variety of media forms, such as TV, radio, cinema, posters, billboards, flyers, transport advertising and the press. For more information about advertising look at the World Advertising Research Center website on www.warc.com.

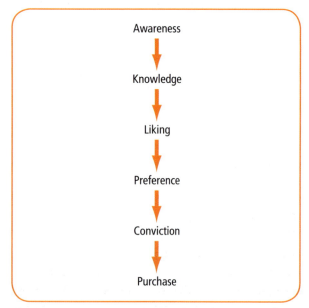

FIGURE 1.23 *Buyer-readiness phases*

Informative	Persuasive (influencing)

'The Shopping Centre
is closed on
25 December.'

PRIZES

'Come to the Shopping
Centre where you will
find bargains galore.'

FREE GIFTS

SALES

PROMOTIONS

OFFERS   COMPETITIONS

FIGURE 1.24 *Advertisements can inform or influence people*

Advertising must be a directed communication at a targeted market, and should draw attention to the characteristics of a product, which will appeal to the buying motives of potential customers. The ultimate purpose of advertising for organisations is to enhance buyers' responses to its products by channelling their desires and preferences to their products ahead of their competitors.

Within this purpose there may be a range of advertising objectives. For example:

* Promoting goods and services
  – to assist with selling
  – to increase sales
  – to develop awareness of new products or developments to existing products
  – to provide information that may assist with selling decisions
  – to encourage a desire to own a product
  – to generate enquiries.

* Developing the image of the organisation
  – to provide information for a target audience
  – to soften attitudes

  – to assist with public relations activities
  – to change views
  – to provide a better external environment
  – to develop support from a community.

Advertising is often classified under one of three headings:

* *Informative advertising* conveys information and raises consumer awareness of the features and benefits of a product. It is often used in the introductory phase of the **product life-cycle** or after modification.

* *Persuasive advertising* is concerned with creating a desire for the product and stimulating purchase. It is used with established and more mature products.

* *Reinforcement advertising* is concerned with reminding consumers about the product, and is used to reinforce the knowledge held by potential consumers about the benefits to be gained from purchase.

Theory into practice

Compare and contrast two advertising campaigns, where one is clearly trying to promote goods and services and the other is trying to improve an image by developing public support for its activities. Comment upon how their approaches to advertising are a) similar, and b) different.

Advertising plan

The starting point for an advertising campaign is to produce an advertising plan. This will involve allocating a budget to a range of activities designed to meet advertising objectives. There are seven steps in an advertising campaign. These are:

Step 1: Identify the target market.

Step 2: Define advertising objectives.

Step 3: Decide on and create the advertising message.

Step 4: Allocate the budget.

Step 5: Develop the media plan.

Step 6: Execute the campaign.

Step 7: Evaluate the effectiveness of the campaign.

At all stages in the advertising process it is important to assess how effectively advertisements have contributed to the communication process. In order to measure objectives DAGMAR has become a fundamental part of good advertising practice. This stands for: *Defining Advertising Goals for Measured Advertising Results*. In other words, before any advertising campaign is started, an organisation must define its communication objectives so that achievements can be measured both during and after the campaign.

Printed media

Printed media make up by far the largest group of media in the UK. The group includes all newspapers and magazines, both local and national, as well as trade press, periodicals and professional journals. There are about 9,000 regular publications in the UK which can be used by the advertiser. They allow the advertiser to send a message to several million people through the press or to target magazines of special interest such as *Business Education Today*, which allows the advertiser to communicate with people in the teaching profession. As a result, the media allows for accurate targeting and **positioning**. Analysing readership profiles identifies types of customers.

The benefit of printed media is that long or complex messages can be sent and, as the message is durable, may be read repeatedly. If an advertisement appears in a prestige magazine it may take on the prestige of that particular publication.

Broadcast media

Broadcast media includes commercial television and commercial radio. Television is the most powerful medium – reaching 98 per cent of

CASE STUDY

Advertising expenditure
The following table lists the top six advertisers in the UK in 2003 and their allocated advertising expenditure

Rank	Company	Total	TV %	Radio %	Press %	Other %
1	Unilever UK Ltd	205,249,905	60.1	4.5	15.0	20.4
2	Procter & Gamble Ltd	197,895,564	74.6	6.4	13.8	5.2
3	COI Communications	143,698,612	51.2	16.6	24.4	7.9
4	BT Ltd	96,899,977	53.8	6.0	31.6	8.7
5	L'Oreal Golden Ltd	90,375,244	74.0	0.2	21.9	3.9
6	Ford Motor Company Ltd	79,215,351	48.3	6.3	29.0	16.4

Source: Nielsen Media Research

1 What do the allocations of expenditure tell you about the nature and types of advertising undertaken by each of these advertisers?

2 What forms of advertising might fall into the 'other' bracket?

3 Why do you think the six companies have such a large advertising spend?

4 If you were working for one of these companies, how would you evaluate the effectiveness of such a spend?

households – and viewing figures for some programmes can exceed 20 million. Television advertisements are, however, high cost and advertising messages are short-lived.

Direct mail

Direct mail is personally addressed advertising that is delivered through the post. By using direct mail an organisation can establish a direct relationship with its customers or prospective customers. Direct mail has been the third largest medium for over 13 years and now represents 14.3 per cent of all advertising expenditure in the UK. 5,418 million direct mail items were mailed in 2004 and £2,468.63 million was spent by advertisers on this medium in the same year. It is estimated that consumer direct mail generates nearly £27 billion worth of business every year.

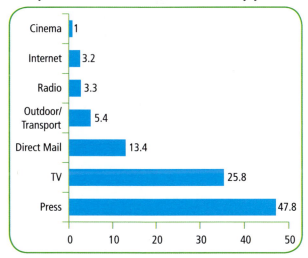

Source: World Advertising Research Center/DMIS

Theory into practice

Over a weekly period collect all of the direct mail entering your home. Try to explain why your family has been the target of such direct mail.

Public relations

The forces in an organisation's external environment are capable of affecting it in a variety of ways. The forces may be social, economic, political, local or environmental and might be represented by a variety of groups such as customers, **shareholders**, employees and special interest groups. Reacting positively to such forces and influences is very important.

Public relations is the planned and sustained effort an organisation makes to establish, develop and build relationships with its many publics (see Figure 1.25).

The purpose of public relations (PR) is therefore to provide an external environment for an organisation in which it is popular and can prosper. Building goodwill in such a way requires behaviour by the organisation which takes into account the attitudes of the many people who come across it and its products.

Whereas many of the other promotional methods are short term, public relations is long term, as it may take a long time for an organisation to improve the way people think about its products and activities. For example, just think about the sort of public relations problems that chemical and oil companies have in a world

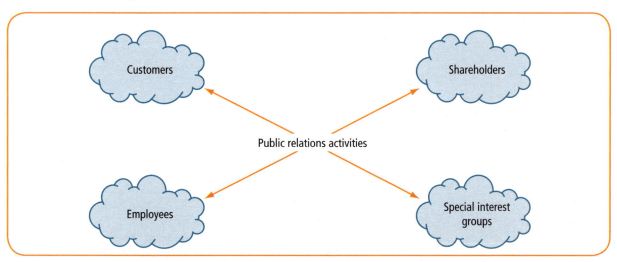

FIGURE 1.25 *Public relations activities*

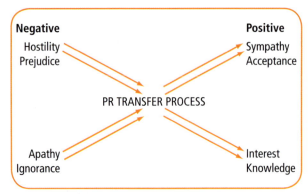

FIGURE 1.26 *The PR transfer process*

where consumers have become increasingly environmentally-conscious.

According to PR guru Frank Jefkins, PR involves a transfer process which helps to convert the negative feelings of an organisation's many publics into positive ones (see Figure 1.26).

There are many different types of public relations activities:

✳ *Charitable donations and community relations* are good for an organisation's image, often provide lots of good publicity and also help to promote and provide for a good cause.

✳ *Hospitality* at top sporting events is a popular method used by organisations to develop their customer relations. For example, there are opportunities to entertain customers at events such as the FA Cup Final, Wimbledon and the Grand National.

✳ *Press releases* covering events affecting the organisation, such as news stories, export achievements, policy changes, technical developments and anything which enhances the organisation's image.

✳ *Visits and open days* are a popular method of inviting people to various events to improve their understanding of what the organisation stands for.

✳ *Sponsorship* of sporting and cultural events is viewed as a useful opportunity to associate an image with a particular type of function. For example, the NatWest Trophy and the Embassy World Snooker Championship.

✳ *Lobbying* of ministers, officials and important people from outside interest groups, so that an accurate portrayal can be made of a problem or a case, may help to influence their views of the organisation.

✳ *Corporate videotapes* have become an increasingly popular way of providing interested parties with a 'view' of an organisation's activities.

CASE STUDY

The Royal Marriage

The marriage of Prince Charles to Camilla Parker-Bowles in Windsor during the spring of 2005, although a great royal occasion, runs in stark contrast to the overwhelming popularity of Princess Diana in his former marriage.

Princess Diana was viewed as the 'people's princess' and was very high profile in her involvement in royal duties, to the extent that she was loved and admired by many. Her tragic death saw a huge outpouring of grief across the nation.

In many ways the marriage to Camilla represents a classic PR problem that has to be dealt with in a variety of ways by Prince Charles. The negative perceptions held by so many, in direct contrast to their feelings about Diana, need to be dealt with sensitively and positively and in a way that transfers such negative images to positive ones. Inevitably, this means that Camilla will have to become involved in a series of public relations activities related to royal duties. As a former mistress to the prince, public relations will be critical in helping the public to identify Camilla with positive virtues.

1 Why is Camilla associated with negative perceptions?
2 How could PR help the public to create positive images of her?

* *Minor product changes*, such as no-testing on animals or environmentally-friendly products may provide considerable PR benefits.

Theory into practice

Search the press for a PR problem. Having found the problem, discuss how you would attempt to solve this problem and the sort of activities which would help to do so.

Sales promotions

Sales promotions describes a category of techniques which are used to encourage customers to make a purchase. These activities are effectively short term and may be used:

* to increase sales
* to help with personal selling
* to respond to the actions of competitors
* as an effective alternative to advertising.

The Institute of Sales Promotion defines sales promotion as follows:

> *Sales promotion is the function of marketing which seeks to achieve given objectives by the adding of intrinsic, tangible value to a product or service.*

The essential feature of a sales promotion is that it is a short-term inducement to encourage customers to react quickly, whereas advertising is usually a process that develops the whole product or brand.

As you walk down a town high street or through a shopping mall, you will see many different examples of sales promotions. Such

Theory into practice

In recent years complaints about sales promotions have soared. This has arisen from a failure to properly observe the legal terms and conditions of prize draws and competitions. This is compounded when companies save money by omitting to have their promotions checked by solicitors.

promotions may serve many different purposes. For example, competitions, vouchers or coupons and trading stamps may be designed to build customer loyalty and perhaps increase the volume purchased by existing customers. Product sampling is often used to introduce new products into the marketplace. Clearance sales of overstocked goods will increase turnover during part of the year in which business might otherwise be slack. Many sales promotions are undertaken in response to the activities of competitors to ensure that an organisation remains competitive. Sales promotions can be divided into two broad areas:

* promotions assisting with the sale of products to the trade
* promotions assisting the trade in selling products to the final consumer.

Selling into the pipeline is an expression used to describe promotions which move products from the manufacturer into the distribution system. Selling out of the pipeline describes promotions which trigger the end-user to make a purchase (see Figure 1.27).

There are many different types of sales promotion:

* *Dealer loaders* are among the inducements to attract orders from retailers and wholesalers. They may include a 'free case' with so many cases bought. For example, thirteen for the price of twelve is known as a 'baker's dozen'.

* *Competitions* may interest dealers and consumers. For dealers they may be linked to sales with attractive prizes for the most successful dealer. Scratch cards, free draws and

FIGURE 1.27 *Selling into and out of the pipeline*

bingo cards are popular promotional methods for consumers.

* *Promotional gifts* such as bottles of spirits, clocks, watches or diaries are considered useful inducements for dealers.

* *Price reductions* and *special offers* are usually popular with consumers. They can, however, prove expensive as many consumers would otherwise have been prepared to pay the full price.

* *Premium offers* may offer extra product for the same price. Coupons which offer money off or money back may also be attractive incentives for consumers. These may appear in magazines, be distributed door to door or appear on the side of a pack.

* *Charity promotions* can be popular with younger consumers, who collect box tops or coupons and send them to a manufacturer, which then makes a donation to charity.

* *Loyalty incentives* are today an increasingly used form of sales promotion. Dealer's loyalty might be rewarded with bigger discounts, competitions and prizes, or they might even have their names published as stockists in advertisements. For consumers, loyalty incentives such as loyalty cards and points may provide 'cash back', free gifts or a variety of other tangible benefits.

Place

The place element within the marketing mix provides the basic structure for customers needs to be satisfied. For example, physical distribution involves getting a product from A to B which is an important part of the place process. In doing so it enables manufacturers and distributors to provide

Theory into practice

There are many different aspects to physical distribution, most of which should be designed to work together as a whole. For example, if this book wasn't available on the shelf of your local bookshop, what processes do you think would take place once you have placed your order?

goods for customers at the right time, in the right place and in the condition required. It may also reduce the time from when a customer first makes an order until the time when that order is delivered.

Physical distribution must balance the need for customer service against the need to minimise costs. To maximise customer service, an organisation may need a lot of stock and warehouse space, efficient staff and rapid transport mechanisms. To minimise costs they need low stock levels, limited storage space, few staff and slower transport. Designing a physical distribution system therefore involves trading off costs against service, or inputs against outputs.

Inputs involve all of the distribution costs such as freight costs, inventory costs, warehousing costs and other service costs. It is important to know exactly what each of these costs is and control the costs in order to minimise waste. This may involve a detailed analysis of labour time, transport time, and other factors spent on each product.

Outputs can primarily be measured in terms of the value of services provided for customers. Distribution can provide a clear competitive benefit in meeting customer needs, for example, by offering a quick and efficient service. Every business must decide how it is going to use distribution and relate this to its competitive advantage. Weaknesses in distribution would clearly need to be compensated for by strengths in other areas of the marketing mix.

The physical distribution system that an organisation selects will largely depend upon the scale of operations and the size of an organisation's market. A business handling a lot of international mail, for example, might locate near a large airport. Key decisions about physical distribution may include the following:

* *Inventory.* A business that wants to maximise customer service will have the highest inventory costs because it needs to hold stock to meet all requests. The key inventory decisions are when and how much to order. The danger of keeping too little in stock is that an organisation could lose custom because of dissatisfaction with the quality of service.

* *Warehousing.* A key decision is where to locate warehouses and how many to have.

* *Load size.* Should units be transported in bulk or broken down into smaller units for delivery? Again, an organisation will have to trade-off customer convenience and the cost of distribution.

* *Communications.* It is important to develop an efficient information processing and invoicing system.

Sales channels

Channels are the networks of intermediaries linking the producer to the market. Direct selling methods do not use an intermediary, but indirect selling methods use one or more channels of distribution through which goods are transferred from the producer to the end user (see Figure 1.28).

Intermediaries such as **wholesalers** stock a range of goods from competing manufacturers to sell on to other organisations such as retailers. Most wholesalers take on the title to the goods

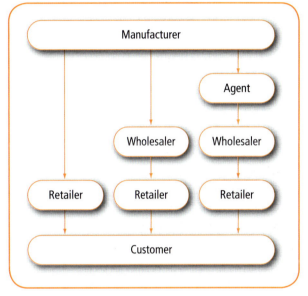

FIGURE 1.28 *Indirect sales channels*

CASE STUDY

Distribution to Sainsbury's stores

Within the M25 area, Sainsbury's has more than 80 branches, each of which requires several deliveries daily. Average traffic speeds in London have fallen to 11 mph over the last decade as traffic densities have increased.

In order to improve their systems of physical distribution, Sainsbury's have consolidated their supplies into fewer, larger loads for final delivery, by using 38-tonne vehicles. This enables goods to be delivered in fewer vehicles, reducing delivery costs, carbon dioxide emissions and congestion. As far as possible, deliveries are made between 10 p.m. and 6 a.m. to reduce congestion.

'Just-in-time' scheduling reduces time that goods are held in the warehouse. The requirements of branches are relayed via computer, with many product lines on a 24-hour cycle (ordered one day for delivery the following day), while others are ordered once or twice a week for delivery 48 hours later.

1 **What problems might be encountered delivering within the M25 area?**
2 **How could such problems be overcome?**

and so assume many of the risks associated, which include:

* *Breaking bulk*. Manufacturers produce goods in bulk for sale but they might not want to store the goods themselves. They want to be paid as quickly as possible. A number of wholesalers buy the stock from them and generally payment is prompt. The wholesaler then stocks these goods, along with others bought from other manufacturers, ready for purchase by retailers.

* *Storage*. Most retailers have only a limited amount of storage space. The wholesaler can be looked upon as a cupboard for the retailer. Manufacturers are able to unload finished goods on the wholesaler.

* *Packing and labelling*. The wholesaler will in some instances finish off the packaging and labelling of goods, perhaps by putting price tags or brand labels on the goods.

* *Offering advice*. Being in the middle of a chain of distribution, wholesalers have a lot more information at their fingertips than either the retailer or manufacturer. In particular, wholesalers know which goods are selling well. With this in mind they can advise retailers on what to buy and manufacturers on what to produce.

The chain of distribution without the wholesaler would look something like Figure 1.30. Manufacturer 1 has to carry out four journeys to supply retailers 1, 2, 3 and 4, and has to send out four sets of business documents, and handle

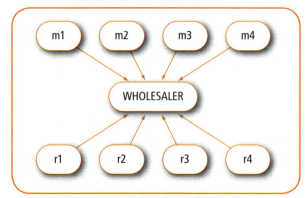

FIGURE 1.29 *The distribution chain with the wholesaler*

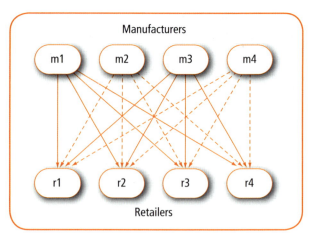

FIGURE 1.30 *The distribution chain without the wholesaler*

four sets of accounts. The same situation applies to each of the manufacturers, so that in total 16 journeys are made and 16 sets of paperwork are required. This is a simplification because, in the real world, thousands of different transactions might be involved!

An intermediary can simplify costs and processes of distribution by cutting down on journeys, fuel and other costs as well as cutting down on paperwork such as invoicing and administration.

By contracting out the process of distribution, a company can concentrate on its core functions.

The French word *retailer* means *'to cut again'*. We have already seen that the wholesaler breaks down bulk supplies from the manufacturer. The retailer then cuts the bulk again to sell individual items to customers. In the modern retailing environment, *the physical environment* for selling to end users has become increasingly complex and in tune with customer focus and needs.

Daewoo, for instance, is distributing cars in the UK without using a traditional local car dealership network. The use of telephone, modem and the Internet as well as fax are also providing the consumer with new ways to view and purchase products. Telemarketing is now being used to sell products such as insurance and pensions, which were previously sold by a one-to-one personal interview. The availability of satellite TV channels has promoted the introduction of home shopping, with the American company QVC launching an English-speaking shopping channel within Europe. Simultaneously, the Internet is increasingly being used for electronic commerce, selling goods to consumers. This new channel of distribution is being investigated by many other organisations such as supermarkets (see e.g. www.tesco.com), who are already involved in the distribution chain. These imaginative approaches to distribution are being viewed as a major new opportunity to meet customer needs within a rapidly changing physical environment.

Theory into practice

Use either your own experience or the experiences of people known to you to discuss the a) advantages, and b) disadvantages of using the Internet for shopping.

Theory into practice

Draw a plan of your local shopping area. Make a list of the different types of retailers in the area.

Theory into practice

Compare and contrast the physical environment of two retailing organisations. Look, for example, at their size, location, number of branches, pricing structure, market position, range of goods, associated services and support for their customers. Carry out a short shopping survey to find out what type of organisation customers prefer to use for a range of different selected products.

1.2.5 Presentational skills

One key element of business life is the need, from time to time, to give some form of presentation to others. Just as in the business world, having prepared a marketing proposal, a marketer would then have to present the proposal to a chosen audience. Presentations are useful because they help to:

* provide a basis for discussion and ongoing analysis by a group of colleagues or for an audience

Involving the audience can be the key to a successful presentation

* help to elicit a variety of perspectives from others, and can provide an active forum that fine-tunes and revises a proposal

* develop a key communication skill which is very important within the business world.

It is important to discuss with your tutor beforehand the sort of criteria they are using to analyse your presentation. Remember that the purpose of your presentation is to communicate the key areas of your assessment proposal. Use the guidelines below to help you prepare your presentation:

1 *Do not try to be too ambitious.* In a talk lasting up to 20 minutes you are not going to be able to make more than a small number of key points, summarising various elements of the marketing proposal. If you try to put too much information into the talk, you will end up having to rush through your proposal or find that you are displaying far too much information for your audience to appreciate. It is more important to discuss the key elements of the proposal and to discuss those key elements well, rather than to get through too much.

2 *Show that you understand marketing principles and practices and can use appropriate business terminology.* Remember that the presentation is an assessment of your own **learning**. Marketing has its own terminology, use of language and ways of operating. Try, within your presentation, to show how well

you understand marketing principles and practices by using terms such as 'targeting', 'segmentation', 'placement', 'product life-cycle' and so on. This will help your tutor to appreciate your depth of understanding of how you have planned to meet your marketing objectives.

3   *Use visual aids and other techniques to engage your audience.* There are a variety of visual aids that you may want to use. For example, you may have a film or video clip that you feel complements and supports some of the points you would like to make. Make sure that you know when to use the clip, that the equipment is working and that you describe and contextualise the clip within the talk by discussing it in relation to your proposal. Whereas in the past many presentations used an overhead projector, increasingly most presentations nowadays rely heavily upon you using Microsoft PowerPoint® to prepare and present your talk.

   In your PowerPoint presentation, apply a background, company name and logo to the master slide to ensure there is a consistency about the appearance of all the slides. Animations, sound effects and flashy graphics may enhance your presentation but be aware of how many you are using as they can also detract from the talk. Make sure that when using PowerPoint an appropriate size is chosen for the text, which should be at least 32-point. Introduce all pages from the same direction and use only one PowerPoint page for every two to three minutes of the talk. Do not prepare too many PowerPoint slides as you will not have time to get through them.

4   *Structure the talk logically to help the audience to appreciate the points you are making.* It is important to work through the proposal itemising the key areas to be following. As you prepare the talk you may highlight the more important areas for discussion, and have extra materials on hand if your talk is finishing too soon. You may wish to repeat the main parts of the presentation and it is always important to summarise the talk at the end.

5   *Talk clearly and feel confident. This helps the listener to appreciate the main points of the presentation.* It is useful to rehearse and practise the talk several times to make sure that you feel confident with the material as well as to ensure that the timings are appropriate. It also provides you with the opportunity to edit and change different parts of the talk. It is possible to reduce nerves although possibly not eradicate them by:

* making sure that you are confident with the materials and know them well

* focusing upon the materials as you talk, thinking about how to make sure that your audience understands them

* relaxing before the talk. Always take deep breaths and don't speak too quickly

* arriving early and making sure that the room and the materials are prepared and ensuring that the technology works

* providing yourself with water or some other form of drink to consume.

As you conduct your presentation, use a watch or a clock to time yourself. Think about how many minutes to allocate to the various phases of the talk and do not start until everybody is quiet and all attention is focused upon you. Sometimes it is useful just to introduce yourself and explain what you hope to achieve and what you hope the audience will learn from your talk. Explain when you want questions, either in the middle of your talk, after key sections or at the end.

   When you speak it is quite acceptable to use postcards as a prompt as they can help you to make sure that your include everything. However, try to make eye-contact with your audience as much as possible and speak clearly and not too quickly. If necessary pause every so often to gather breath. At the end of the talk, sum up all of the points you have made and thank the audience for listening.

Presentation tips

1 Do not talk too quickly.

2 Respect the viewpoints of the questioners.

3 Introduce the talk and sum up the points you make.

4 Try to move logically from one visual aid to the next.

5 Stick to your brief and be careful about improvising on the day.

6 Make eye-contact with your audience.

7 Demonstrate to others that you are enjoying giving the talk.

8 Avoid making the talk unnecessarily complicated.

9 If necessary, provide a handout for your audience.

10 If you are running out of time, do not rush.

11 Make sure that your slides are relevant.

12 Listen carefully when being questioned to make sure that you understand the points being made.

1.2.6 How to judge potential success

Having developed a marketing proposal it is important to audit it. This means that you must try to assess how or whether the marketing proposal would work and what might influence how it would operate. It is essential to evaluate the relative strengths of the market proposal you have developed and then try to think about what would be necessary to fine tune or further develop it. For example, it may be possible to use a SWOT analysis to evaluate the strengths, weakness, opportunities and threats to the proposal.

To evaluate the marketing proposal, you need to consider the following:

* whether the marketing objectives are likely to be fulfilled

* whether the needs of potential customers are likely to be met

* whether the proposal is sustainable over time, both in terms of its potential market position and actions of possible rival competitors

* how the marketing proposal fits with the business's current product-portfolio

* how the marketing proposal impacts upon the different departments and functional areas of the business.

Are your marketing objectives likely to be fulfilled?

Does the mix have the potential to meet the marketing objectives set within the marketing proposal? How well could an organisation meet the objectives that have been identified? Use the SMART framework to consider how the marketing objectives meet each of the SMART categories. You may want to talk to somebody who either runs a business or is involved with marketing to find out how realistic the proposal is. Try to use reasoned judgements and, if possible, supply some form of evidence about the possible success of your approach.

Are the needs of potential customers likely to be met?

You may want to test out particular elements of your marketing proposal by discussing your marketing mix with potential customers. Collecting evidence is important to support your evaluation. Look to see how other organisations meet similar customer needs and try to judge whether your approach is more appropriate.

Is the proposal sustainable over time?

Will your proposal and plans be able to sustain themselves over a period of time and be successful within a market from one year to another? Try and look at similar products in similar businesses and find out about their successes and failures. What is the failure rate within the markets you intend to serve? What are some of the problems and issues affecting this market and how might that affect or influence your particular proposal?

Does the marketing proposal fit with the business's current product-portfolio?

It is important that the proposal matches the aims and objectives of your company. Are they still the same? If they have evolved, your marketing proposal will need to be modified to reflect the current direction of your company.

How does the marketing proposal impact upon the different departments and functional areas of the business?

You may want to interview people who work within different parts of business organisations. Find out how marketing proposals impact upon their activities and how some of their decisions are affected by marketing proposals.

CASE STUDY

Learning from failure

Is it possible to learn from the mistakes of others? According to a New York marketing agency, it is important to analyse why products fail because then it is possible to understand how to develop marketing proposals that might succeed. The agency argues that the main factor behind most product failures is simply the high number of products appearing on the market, and where there are too many products it is just impossible for products to distinguish themselves.

One very difficult market to compete in is the grocery market. The product might be satisfactory, but if it is put in the wrong packaging or in the wrong place in the supermarket its death is assured. Some of the great marketing disasters have involved the

biggest names. Levi's lacked focus upon their customers and let the brand lose its popularity. Burger King went head-to-head to compete with McDonald's instead of identifying their differentiating features. In these instances organisations made decisions about how to market their products in a way that damaged their brand.

1 **What is a marketing failure?**
2 **Why do many products fail?**
3 **Find out more about great marketing failures.**
4 **Evaluate how knowledge of marketing failures helps to reduce some of the problems and issues with your marketing proposal.**

KNOWLEDGE CHECK

1 What is meant by market orientation?

2 Identify the four Ps of the marketing mix.

3 Explain how a finance department helps an organisation to achieve its marketing objectives.

4 Describe the role of 'operations'.

5 What is mass marketing?

6 How does mass marketing differ from niche marketing?

7 Describe what is meant by targeting.

8 What role might a suggestions box have within an organisation?

9 What is a field experiment and how might it be used?

10 Name three attributes of a good questionnaire.

11 How does an open question differ from a closed question?

12 Provide two examples of sales promotions.

13 Why might a market researcher use a prompt card?

14 Explain the purpose of using a wholesaler.

15 What is a moving average and why might a marketer want to use one?

16 Provide two examples of brands.

17 What is a market segment?

18 Provide an example of 'printed media'.

19 What is direct mail?

20 Describe one pricing technique.

Resources

There is a wide range of textbooks to support learning about marketing. Some good sources include:

Needham, D. et al., *Marketing for Higher Awards*, Oxford, Heinemann, 1999

The Advertising Association, *Marketing Pocket Book 2005*, Henley-on-Thames, World Advertising Research Center, 2005

Kotler, P. et al., *Marketing: An Introduction,* Hemel Hempstead, Prentice Hall, 2003

Dibb, S. et al, *Marketing: Concepts and Strategies*, Boston, Houghton Mifflin, 2001

Websites

Some useful websites are listed below. These addresses are current at the time of writing. However, it needs to be recognised that new sites are being launched on the Internet on a regular basis and that older sites may change or disappear.

www.tt100.biz
www.cim.co.uk

www.marketinguk.co.uk
www.dma.org.uk
www.mad.co.uk
www.marketing-society.org.uk
www.brandrepublic.com
www.bitc.org.uk
www.marketingpower.com

TV Choice video

TV Choice (www.tv.choice.com) produces a range of videos related to marketing. Their most topical is called *What is marketing?* This video is a good starting point and shows the impact of TV in the 1950s as well as the consumer boom. It then analyses the classic breakdown of marketing strategies into the four Ps and looks at the promotion of the brand rather than the product and globalisation.

Magazines

Marketing magazine
Marketing Today
Marketing Week

UNIT 2

Recruitment in the workplace

This unit contains eight elements:

2.2.1 Job roles

2.2.2 The recruitment process

2.2.3 The selection process

2.2.4 The induction process

2.2.5 Employee motivation

2.2.6 The legal dimension

2.2.7 Research

2.2.8 How to judge effectiveness

Introduction

It is important to have a good understanding of how businesses acquire one of their key resources – people. Many of you will already be involved in part-time work and a work placement is a beneficial part of the learning process on a vocational course. Studying the processes involved in the recruitment and selection of people to work for a business gives you a better understanding of:

* the various processes that are involved from the business side when recruiting and selecting the workforce

* how you can prepare yourself when applying for jobs and for job interviews.

As you study this unit, you will produce a report with supporting documentation showing how you have set about recruiting and selecting an individual for a particular job role, as well as producing an induction and motivational programme for your chosen job role and successful **applicant**.

Your class peers will adopt the roles of prospective employees applying for your chosen role and will participate in your **selection** process. You will also be expected to assist your class peers in meeting the evidence requirements for this unit by taking on the role of a prospective employee, applying for positions and participating in their recruitment and selection processes for advertised positions. More detailed guidance about the assignment is given at the end of this unit.

Your report will be informed by your research into current human-resource practices used by a range of different businesses and your analysis of the gathered data. Finally, you will make reasoned judgements as you discuss the effectiveness of your chosen approaches to both the recruitment and selection processes and the induction and motivational programmes created for your chosen job role and successful applicant.

2.2.1 Job roles

Before considering the recruitment and selection of individuals to fill new posts, you need to have an understanding of the various job roles and levels of management that can exist in a medium- to large-sized business. These include:

* managers
* supervisors
* IT operatives
* administrators
* customer service operatives.

Manager

A **manager** is someone with responsibility, usually for others, for making decisions and for managing resources. For example, the job description of a marketing manager in a company might state that this person is:

* *accountable* to their marketing director
* *responsible* for staff in the market research function of the company
* *responsible* for planning, organising and delivering market research campaigns

* *responsible* for creating a market research budget and for monitoring that budget each month
* *responsible* for making sure that the company keeps in tune with the changing needs of its customers.

From the example shown above, you can see that management involves responsibility. The level of responsibility depends on the level of management:

* senior managers are responsible for long-term decisions made in a company as well as major resources
* middle managers are responsible for some medium-term decisions and some important resources
* junior managers are responsible for short-term decisions and they have some responsibility for resources.

Supervisor

Supervisors also have an important role to play in an organisation and their responsibilities can be equivalent to those of a junior manager. Supervisors have responsibility for supervising a particular task or group of people.

Theory into practice

The following is an extract from an advertisement for a marketing manager in a clothes manufacturing company based in the East Midlands. Read the advertisement and answer the following questions.

Berkeley Bridal Wear

Marketing Manager

Grantham

Base salary to £25k + benefits
Plus on target bonuses of £10k

An excellent opportunity to join the country's largest independent bridalwear retailer with outlets throughout the UK.

Typically you will be a creative marketing professional with:

- experience of 'high end' clothing or luxury goods
- the ability to develop relationships with leading fashion journalists
- a good knowledge of brand positioning
- experience of internal and external communications
- experience to handle a substantial budget and to manage a team
- experience of marketing websites.

To apply, please send your full CV and covering letter, stating current salary package to recruitment@good.silk.co.uk

1 Do you think the job is classified as a senior, middle or junior management post? Explain why.

2 What evidence is there in the advertisement that the job involves responsibility? List the main areas of responsibility.

Supervisors will often work within fairly tight boundaries. They have responsibility for making sure that:

✷ the right standards are met

✷ time deadlines are met

✷ people or other resources are supervised in an appropriate way.

Just because an employee is not a manager or supervisor does not mean that their work is any less important. Most employees have the potential to become supervisors and managers. Employees have a responsibility to meet legal requirements and the responsibilities of the job set out in a job description. Today many employees are given additional responsibilities because managers recognise that individuals work best when trusted to do fulfilling work.

IT operative

Information technology is very important in modern businesses and most employees need to have some level of IT capability to carry out their work. For example, when you visit a bank the person that serves you over the counter will be using a computer terminal from which they can call up details of your account. Similarly, when you ring up an insurance company to take out a car insurance policy, the person you deal with at the end of the line will be sitting in front of a computer terminal.

Today there is a shortage of IT specialists nationally and as a result the wages of people working with IT are increasing. IT operatives are typically involved with a number of tasks.

Database management

Database management involves creating databases, for example, of customers, or patients in a hospital, by using existing database packages. Usually database management involves creating a number of relevant fields, e.g. creating fields for patients with a certain illness, those seen by a certain doctor, etc. It is then possible to create records for individual customers, patients etc.

Spreadsheet creation

Most businesses process a lot of quantitative information (information that involves numbers) and spreadsheets help organisations to make calculations very quickly. For example, a spreadsheet can be created showing wages paid to particular employees. Deductions can be made from the wage to account for income tax, national insurance and other deductions. IT workers will create a spreadsheet for an organisation or simply enter data into an existing spreadsheet.

Creating presentations

IT specialists may be asked to prepare eye-catching presentations for managers within an organisation. They can then use their expertise with presentation software such as PowerPoint®️ to create exciting presentations.

Setting up IT systems

IT workers are also expected to trouble shoot and set up IT systems within an organisation. This may involve networking (linking together) various computers or setting up the systems for new computers as well as maintaining them. They will also help out employees who are having problems by troubleshooting for them and maintaining virus checkers and other important software systems.

Administrator

Administrators play an important role in modern organisations by creating a range of paper-based and computer-based systems for other employees in the organisation. All large organisations depend on administrators for dealing with tasks such as enquiries, communicating messages and producing documents for the workforce.

Administrators are very important because they service the work of an organisation, although problems can arise when administrators disturb the functioning of an organisation with administrative work that moves the business away from its central objectives.

Many large firms have a central office that is responsible for controlling key aspects of the firm's paperwork. This department might handle the filing of materials, the company's mail, word-processing and data-handling facilities (such as the creation and maintenance of databases).

Office manager

In many companies, each department will have its own clerical and support staff. However, it is common practice to have an office services manager with the responsibility for co-ordinating office services and for offering expert advice to departmental managers.

The work of the office manager will include the following areas:

✳ taking responsibility for and organising the training of administrative staff

✳ advising departments about office layout, office equipment, working practices and staff development

✳ co-ordinating the supply of office equipment and stationery

✳ studying and analysing administrative practice within the organisation in order to develop an overall **strategy** for administration

✳ ensuring the standardisation of administrative work, the layout of documents, letters, etc

✳ providing and maintain a communications system within a company, including phones, mailing systems, computer hardware and other data-processing facilities

✳ reporting to, and providing statistics for, the company board about the effectiveness of existing administrative practice.

Customer service operative

Many of you will have direct experience of the work of customer service operatives as a result of your work experience or part-time work. Most organisations depend heavily on their customer service operatives.

For example, the retail store ASDA believes that its success lies in delivering 'legendary customer service'. Every employee is given training in how to deliver 'legendary' customer service which involves developing knowledge about their job and the products that they sell, as well as other skills in dealing with customers on a day-to-day basis.

Customer service employees must know:

* how to do their job efficiently, e.g. serving customers at the till or greeting customers when they enter a store

* about the products they are selling, e.g. where to find them and the various qualities of different products

* how to give priority to customers, what to say to them, how to talk to them and how to make them feel welcome.

2.2.2 The recruitment process

Businesses must plan to make sure that they have the right number of suitable employees for their needs. When a business is looking to recruit a new employee, it needs to be able to define key roles and responsibilities that will be expected in the new post. You need to understand the ways in which businesses set about this task by creating the following recruitment documents:

* person specification
* job description
* job advertisement
* application form.

Qualities in employees

Businesses need to be clear about the sorts of qualities that they are looking for when recruiting employees in order to attract the most suitable applicants. They will need to consider carefully:

* what they expect applicants to already be able to do

* what applicants should already know
* the skills required
* the attitudes required.

Theory into practice

Examine the job advertisement below.

SUPERIOR INDUSTRIES LTD

Admin Assistant

Due to expansion, Superior Industries require an administrative assistant to help in their Customer Service department.

The successful applicant will possess excellent PC literacy and data entry skills and will be responsible for the management of customer orders for the business.

With an excellent telephone manner, you will be reliable and enthusiastic, well-organised, a self-starter and play a pivotal role in the day-to-day running of this busy but friendly department.

For further information and an application form please call Rosamund Manning on 01457 905549

Although this post is not at a high level in the organisation, the company is looking for a number of qualities.

1 What sorts of existing skills is the company looking for?

2 What sorts of personal qualities are expected of the prospective employee?

3 Why might you be tempted to apply for the post?

4 Why might you not be tempted to apply for the post?

Theory into practice

Select a job that you are familiar with. Make a list of the competencies, knowledge, skills and attitudes that you would expect someone to have to be appointed to your chosen job role.

Reasons for recruiting staff

There are a number of reasons for recruiting new staff:

1 *The growth of the business*
   One example of a growth area is e-commerce, buying and selling through the Internet, which has led to the recruitment of web page designers and other IT specialists.

2 *Filling vacancies caused by job leavers*
   All businesses have a turnover of staff. For example, supermarket chains like ASDA and Sainsbury's constantly need to recruit checkout staff, car park attendants and other employees. There will be a regular stream of people leaving their jobs, e.g. to go to college or university, who will need to be replaced.

3 *Changing job roles*
   Modern work is constantly changing. Next year's jobs will require different skills from those that are required today. Businesses will therefore constantly create new opportunities and new jobs requiring new people.

4 *Internal promotion*
   Most companies encourage their staff to take on more demanding and better-paid posts within the business. New employees are required to replace those moving up the ladder.

Job analysis

In many companies, when creating new jobs or altering existing ones, it is common practice to carry out a **job analysis** before going on to create a **person specification** and **job description**. Organisations need to attract, recruit and retain the best possible people to fill the posts required and thus help a business to achieve its objectives.

The starting point for many businesses that want to recruit and select new employees to fill a job role is to create a job analysis. A job analysis is a study of the tasks that are required in order to do a particular job. Job analysis is very important in creating a clear job description (see page 63). Job analysis involves carrying out a study of the key components of a particular job.

If a job already exists, such as a business studies teacher in a school, a checkout operative in a supermarket or an apprentice hairdresser in a hairdressing salon, the person doing the job analysis

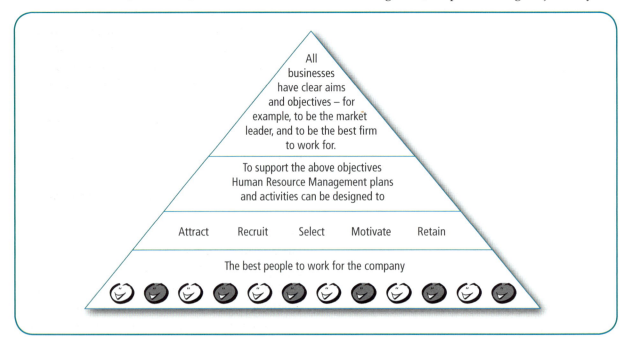

All businesses have clear aims and objectives – for example, to be the market leader, and to be the best firm to work for.

To support the above objectives Human Resource Management plans and activities can be designed to

Attract   Recruit   Select   Motivate   Retain

The best people to work for the company

FIGURE 2.1 *How employees contribute to business objectives*

just needs to carry out a study of the tasks involved in carrying out the same or a similar position. This can be done by looking at various documents describing the current job role or by studying the activities carried out by current job-holders. For example, if you were to study the work carried out by a supermarket checkout desk operative for one evening you would have a good idea of what the job involved.

It is more difficult to carry out a job analysis when a new post is being created in a business. One way to carry out the analysis is to study work carried out by an employee in a similar firm. Alternatively, the job analyst may need to interview people to find out what exactly the job will involve, setting out details such as:

* the key tasks that the person carrying out the job will be expected to do
* the key skills that the job-holder will need to have
* the qualifications that the job-holder will need to have
* the attitudes and manner that the job-holder will need to have.

Theory into practice

Draw up a job analysis for the post of marking business studies assignments in your school or college. What steps would need to be taken to carry out a job analysis for such a post? What would you expect to be the key tasks, key skills, qualifications and attitudes that such an analysis would reveal?

Theory into practice

A large supermarket chain currently does not have enough shop assistants to meet the demands of customers, particularly at weekends. There are long queues at the tills, and it has become impossible to stack shelves neatly or to price all items accurately.

Set out a job analysis for a shop assistant, by answering the following questions:

* What tasks need to be performed?
* What skills and qualities are required?
* How can these skills be acquired?

Person specification

A person specification should set out clearly what attributes an individual needs to have to do a particular job well. The person specification goes beyond a simple description of the job by highlighting the mental, physical and other attributes required of a job holder. For example, a recent Prison Service advertisement specified the following:

> *At every level your task will call for a lot more than simple efficiency. It takes humanity, flexibility, enthusiasm, total commitment and, of course, a sense of humour.*

A personal specification for police recruits might include physical attributes related to having a particular standard of physical fitness or qualifications including Advanced level or equivalents, etc.

Think it over…

Until recently the police force typically asked for a minimum height level among new recruits. However, this is not acceptable today because it is felt to discriminate against certain groups.

Armed with this sort of specification, those responsible for recruiting and selecting someone to do a particular job have a much clearer idea of the ideal **candidate**. At the same time those applying for a job have a much clearer idea of what is expected of them and whether they have the attributes.

The human resources department may set out, for its own use, a 'person specification', using a layout similar to the one shown in Figure 2.2.

Personal attributes and achievements

A person specification is concerned with identifying those people who have the right qualities to fit the jobs you are offering. For example, personal attributes for a member of the Paratroop Regiment might include physical toughness and alertness. The personal attributes of a teacher may include the ability to work well with others and to find out about the learning

Summary of job			
Attributes	**Essential**	**Desirable**	**How identified**
Physical			
Qualifications			
Experience			
Training			
Special knowledge			
Personal circumstances			
Attitudes			
Practical and intellectual skills			

FIGURE 2.2 *Layout for a person specification*

needs of pupils. The personal attributes of a shop assistant might include punctuality and smartness of appearance.

Personal achievement gives a good indication of the existing abilities of given individuals. For example, someone who has achieved the Duke of Edinburgh Awards shows qualities of enterprise and initiative. Personal achievements can be good indicators of qualities such as the ability to work in a team, to help others, to persevere, etc.

Qualifications

Qualifications are another important part of a person specification. For example, when recruiting a new human resources lecturer it would be essential to appoint someone with formal teaching qualifications and some experience of work at an appropriate level in human resource management.

Qualifications are a good measure of prior learning. This has been simplified in recent years by the development of nationally recognised qualifications such as AS and A2 qualifications.

The idea of a qualification is that it prepares you to do a particular job or activity. In creating person specifications, organisations will therefore need to consider the level of qualification required by a job-holder.

Experience

Someone with experience in carrying out a particular post or who has had particular responsibilities should be able to draw on that experience in new situations. For example, an experienced lecturer has already taught, assessed, administered and carried out a variety of other duties in a college. A new lecturer has not had the same opportunities. However, a new lecturer in a college can bring new ideas or transfer their knowledge from experience of working in an industrial setting.

Employers benefit from recruiting experienced staff as they are able to do a range of tasks. This makes them more flexible workers, which in turn increases the output of the business.

Customers often like to deal with experienced employees. For example, customers will often ask for their car to be serviced by a more experienced mechanic or to have their hair cut by a more experienced stylist.

We talk about the learning curve which results from experience. The implication is that the good learner will learn at a progressively faster rate as they draw on their experience. A person specification should therefore set out the required experience for a job-holder.

Competence

Competence is a word that is widely used today. Competence implies that a person has sufficient knowledge or skill to carry out particular tasks or activities. Most people would rather visit a competent than an incompetent doctor, or be taught by a competent rather than an incompetent teacher. Firms therefore benefit from employing more competent employees who are trusted by customers and are more reliable at producing quality outputs.

Person specifications should set out levels of competence required by a particular job-holder. Hairdressers, for example, need to show competence in a range of performance criteria that make up the elements of hairdressing work. A hairdresser would be foolish to take on a new stylist for dyeing purposes who had not first exhibited competence in mixing and applying hair dye.

Competence is an important aspect of work ability

Theory into practice

List ten situations in which you prefer to deal with more competent and better qualified employees. Are you prepared to pay more for the service provided? In each case explain why you think the organisation will benefit from employing more competent and better qualified employees.

Job descriptions

A job analysis can then be used to create a job description. A job description will describe how a particular employee is to fit into the organisation and will need to set out:

* the title of the job
* to whom the employee is responsible
* for whom the employee is responsible
* a simple description of the role and duties of the employee within the organisation.

A job description could be used as a job indicator for applicants. Alternatively, it could be used as a guideline for an employee and/or line manager as to his or her role and responsibility within the organisation.

Job descriptions can be used by organisations to provide information for use in drafting a situations vacant advertisement and for briefing interviewers.

Job title

One of the most important parts of a job description is the job title. The job title should give a good indication of what the job entails. For example, you may hear people in organisations make statements such as: 'She's supposed to be the Managing Director, let her make the decision,' or 'leave the word-processing of letters to the administrator, that's not your job'.

When looking through job advertisements the first thing that job applicants will look for (apart from the salary) will be the job title.

From time to time job titles will change, often to give a slightly different feel to some jobs or to give the job title a new status, for example, the Principal of a College may become a Chief

Job titles help to make employees feel important

Job descriptions provide useful guidance to employees

Executive, a dustbin man may become a 'disposal services officer' or a petrol pump cashier may become a 'forecourt executive'.

Position within organisation structure

A job description will often establish where an individual stands in a particular organisation's structure. This means it shows who the post-holder is accountable to and who is accountable to him or her.

The position within an organisation will also give a clear idea of responsibilities. Job applicants will be interested in locating the position in order to work out whether their previous experience will be broad enough and to assess the kind of commitment they will be expected to make to the organisation.

Duties and responsibilities

A further important aspect of the job description will be that which sets out the duties and responsibilities of job-holders.

Prior to setting out a job description an organisation may carry out an analysis of the tasks which need to be performed by a job-holder and the skills and qualities required.

If this is done carefully, then organisational planners will have a clear picture of how particular jobs fit in with all the other jobs carried

on in an organisation. It also helps job applicants to get a clear picture of what is expected of them, and it helps job-holders to understand the priorities of their work.

Theory into practice

Examine two job descriptions produced by an organisation (perhaps by the organisation that you work for or where you carried out your work experience). Explain why these organisations create job descriptions and who would use them.

Job advertisements

Job advertisements form an important part of the recruitment process. An organisation is able to communicate job vacancies to a selected audience by this means. Most job advertisements are written (or at least checked) by the personnel department, a task involving the same skills as marketing a product. Advertisements must reach those people who have the qualities to fill the vacancy.

Job advertisements take many forms, according to the requirements of the post. Good advertisements include the information shown in Figure 2.3.

Job description	This should highlight the major requirements of the job in a concise format
Organisational activities and market place	There should be a brief description of the environment in which the organisation operates
Location	Applicants need to know the location of the organisation and the location of the job
Salary expectation	Figures are not always necessary, but an indication of the salary level (or a recognised grade) should always be given
Address and contact	This should appear, with a telephone number if appropriate
Qualifications	Certain jobs require a minimum entrance qualification, which should be clearly stated
Experience	This should be made clear as it will have a bearing on the expected salary level for the job
Fringe benefits	The advertiser may wish to mention a company car, health scheme etc.
Organisational identity	This may be in the form of a logo (or simply the name of the organisation)

FIGURE 2.3 *Content of a good job advertisement*

In this unit you are required to recruit and select a candidate for a chosen job role. You can use the table below that we have set out for you to evaluate the effectiveness of the following advertisement for a Director for the New Globe Theatre Company and of other job advertisements that you collect from the national press for a range of jobs.

By evaluating a range of job advertisements you will be best placed to create an effective job advertisement of your own. This work will help you to show evidence of having carried out research and subsequently analysing it.

Does the advertisement give a clear picture of what the job entails?	
Does the advertisement set out clearly where the job is located?	
Do you think the advertisement is focused enough to attract people with the right sorts of qualifications to fill the post?	
What sorts of people do you think are most likely to apply for the post?	
Does the advertisement indicate opportunities for job development and for personal challenges over time?	
Would an applicant know how to apply for the job?	
Would the advertisement in its present form screen out unsuitable applicants?	
What improvements would you make to the advertisement?	

Director

London, Basic £30k + car + bonuses

The New Globe Theatre Company is an established group which will be staging productions in major London theatres. The Director will receive an initial salary of £30,000 but can expect to progress steadily to higher rates as the size of the company increases and the scale of operations expands.

We are looking for someone with extensive experience of theatre production and management who will probably have worked in a similar capacity for at least five years in regional theatre productions.

If you wish to take the opportunity of pioneering this new and exciting venture please forward a letter of application to:

Director of Personnel
The New Globe Theatre Company
1001 The Strand
London WC2 0NG

Telephone 0207 900 1234

The assessment for this unit asks you to produce a report on how you have recruited and selected an individual for a job role. You are also assessed on your research and subsequent analysis. Consult with you tutor on the best way of presenting this information. Make sure it is all kept together in a well-structured portfolio as part of the report that you produce.

A good job advertisement, while providing prospective candidates with helpful information, also helps to deter people who do not have the required qualifications for the job.

Presentation of the advertisement is very important as it gives prospective employees a first impression of the organisation.

Job applications and curriculum vitae

We are now in a position to look at **job applications** and **interviewing**. First examine the two flow charts shown below (Figures 2.4 and 2.5) which show the selection process for a job from the employer's point of view and from the applicant's point of view.

1. The need to recruit an extra member of staff is identified.

2. A new job description is set out, or an existing one is updated.

3. The job specification is reviewed and revised.

4. Advertisements are designed and placed in appropriate media.

5. Job details and application forms are sent to applicants.

6. Applications are sorted out and a shortlist is drawn up.

7. Interview invitations are sent to shortlisted applicants.

8. Interviews take place (and an oral job offer may be made).

9. Referees are invited to comment.

10. If the references are satisfactory, a written job offer is sent.

11. The offer is accepted.

12. A written contract of employment is signed.

FIGURE 2.4 *Job selection – the employer's point of view*

1. Evaluate different career choices, and narrow down your options.

2. Produce and update your curriculum vitae.

3. Ask two or three people to act as referees.

4. Photocopy your examination and other certificates.

5. See an interesting job advertisement and send for details.

6. Find out more about the organisation.

7. Send a short letter or e-mail asking for an application form or apply online.

8. Fill in the form and write a short letter supporting your application. Send copies of certificates and CV. Keep copies of all these documents.

9. If invited for interview, immediately telephone to confirm the arrangements.

10. Verbal acceptance of job.

11. Write a letter of acceptance and return the contract.

12. Make sure you know when and where you are expected to be on the first day.

FIGURE 2.5 *Job selection – the applicant's point of view*

Qualifications and experience

Many jobs require that applicants should have certain qualifications which are necessary to do the job. For examples, doctors need to have completed a degree in medicine and have relevant work experience before they are allowed to practise. The same applies to other professions such as teaching, the law and accountancy, where practitioners are expected to have the relevant qualifications before they can take up jobs. It is not only in the professions where necessary qualifications are required, the same applies to many skilled jobs such as electricians and Information Technology specialists who will typically be expected to have certificates showing that they are qualified to carry out their work.

In addition to qualifications many jobs require previous experience and expertise. For example, when advertising for a job in sales and marketing a company may be seeking to recruit staff who already have experience of doing a similar job.

Sometimes applicants for jobs are expected to demonstrate their skills and expertise by doing tests which measure these skills. For example, an applicant for a teaching job may be expected to carry out a demonstration lesson in front of a class in the school where they are applying for a post.

Letters of application

The following comments relate to how you should go about writing job applications. They are equally relevant in examining what businesses are looking for when they come to choose applicants. All students who are following this course will need at some stage to produce letters of application for jobs and it is important that you get this process right. It is surprising how often there are two students who are almost identical in terms of qualifications, appearance and ability, but one is offered many interviews while the other receives only a few. Usually the difference is in the quality of their letters of application.

A letter should have a clear structure, with a beginning, a middle and an ending. It should state:

* your reasons for applying for the job
* the contribution you can make to the organisation

* how you have developed your capabilities through training and education
* the skills and knowledge you have acquired that would help you to do the job well.

The letter needs to be interesting – you are writing about (selling) yourself. It should contain just enough information to support your application form and CV (see page 71), highlighting the most relevant evidence. You will know that you are writing effective letters if they lead to interviews.

Here are some important rules to remember:

* use good English with accurate spelling – always check in a dictionary if you are unsure of the spelling of a word or use the spell-checker on your computer

Theory into practice

Write a letter of application for the job described below:

* The position: Part-time shelf filler at Strictly Food Supermarket.
* Basic duties: Filling shelves at Strictly Food Supermarket from 6 a.m. to 8 a.m. each morning.
* The company: One of the top ten companies in the UK by turnover and a leading retailer.
* Responsibilities: Shelf fillers are expected to show initiative for displaying goods in ways outlined by supervisors and by training with the company. On completion of training and satisfactory performance you may be required to provide guidance to other trainees.
* Attitudes: New employees are expected to be punctual and co-operative. Good communication skills and willingness to share ideas are desired qualities.
* The training: The initial training will introduce new employees to the values of Strictly Food Supermarket and the nature of the job. Particular attention will be given to teamwork practices and quality presentation of goods.
* Wage: £5.00 per hour rising in increments on the satisfactory completion of training and taking on responsibilities for others.

CASE STUDY

Applying for a job

The following letter was sent by an applicant for the role of trainee accountant with Great Western Trains.

21 Wade Park Avenue
Market Deeping
Peterborough
PE6 8JL

20th February 2005

Great Western Trains Finance Manager,
Room 109
East Side Offices
Bristol
BS3 9HL

Dear Sir/Madam,

I noticed in a national paper that you have a job available for a junior accountant. I am very interested in the post because I see it as presenting a good opportunity for me. I have always been very interested in rail accounts. I am also studing accounts at collage. I understand that on your accountancy training scheme there will be good opportunities for promotion. I am also studying an A2 course in Business (OCR Examinations). This is a very interesting course and I have had good reports from all my tutors on the course. As part of the course I am sing accounts. I have found the accounts to be the most exciting and interesting parts. I am also interested in train spotting.

I am working at the Anglia Co-operative Society. This is a part time post but it involves a lot of responsibility. I have to check the stock and make sure the shelves are well organized. I also have had EPOS training.

I am currently working on my cv and will send it to you next week. Many thanks for your interest in my application.

Yours Sincerly
Charles Lawson

1 **What strengths and weaknesses can you spot?**
2 **If you were to advise Charles Lawson on how he could improve his letter what comments would you make?**

High Street Retailers PLC
Application form • Strictly confidential

What job are you applying for? _____   What is your national insurance number? _____

Have you been employed by this organisation before? _____   Give dates of previous employment _____

Surname _____   First name _____

Present address _____   Post code _____

Telephone number _____   Email _____

Date of birth _____   Have you any relatives or connection by marriage already employed by this organisation? _____

Secondary education

Dates From/to	Name and address of current/last school	Examinations taken (subjects/grades/dates)	Examinations to be taken (date, subject, level)

Further education

Dates From/to	Name and address of college	Examinations taken (subjects/grades/dates)	Examinations to be taken (date, subject, level)

Have you been convicted of a criminal offence which is not legally spent? Yes/No

Work History
Please cover at least your last 5 years' employment, leaving no gaps. Include temporary and part-time posts as well as periods of unemployment.

Exact dates	Employer's name and address	Job – Title/position	Pay	Exact reason for leaving
From To	Present employer Address		Basic pay Regular bonus or commission	Is it your own choice Yes/No Current notice period
From To	Previous employer Address		Basic pay Regular bonus or commission	Was it your own choice Yes/No
From To	Previous employer Address		Basic pay Regular bonus or commission	Was it your own choice Yes/No

If you have additional information about yourself which you think would be of interest, please add it here (hobbies, interests, extra qualifications, languages) _____

Please check the information given before signing. To the best of my knowledge the information on this form is complete and correct.

Signature _____   Date _____

Referees
There is no need to complete this at this stage. If an offer of employment is being considered, you may be asked to give details of two people who have known you for at least two years who are aged not less than 18 years who would be willing to provide a personal reference if needed. Do not give the names of employees, your relatives, or your teachers.

Name _____   Address _____   Occupation _____

Name _____   Address _____   Occupation _____

FIGURE 2.6 *An example of an application form*

- use your own words rather than copying those in the advertisement
- do not try to be too clever by using long words
- keep the paragraphs short
- try not to use 'I' too much
- word-process your work
- follow the correct convention of addressing people – either 'Dear Sir/Madam' and ending with 'Yours faithfully' or 'Dear Mr Chanderpaul' and ending with 'Yours sincerely'
- keep a copy of what you have written.

Application forms

Figure 2.6 is an example of an application form for a position in a retail chain. It should give you some ideas about how you can set out your own application form.

Sending a covering letter

Here is some useful advice about how to write a covering letter and its content when you apply for a job that you have seen advertised.

1 *Put yourself in the reader's shoes.* Before you start word-processing your letter, decide on the benefit to the employer of choosing to interview you.

2 *Be clear about what your purpose is.* Always be clear about your purpose, for example, decide whether your purpose is to get a meeting or a job interview.

3 *Make sure that your first sentence grabs the attention of the reader.*

4 *Be short and clear.* Keep the letter to one side of word-processed A4. Try to use short and punchy words.

5 *Use bullet points and tabulation to make key terms stand out.*

6 *End your letter with a clear and positive request for action.* For example, 'I look forward to hearing from you and meeting you to discuss the job offer in the near future.'

7 *Use good quality A4 white paper, with a clear font.* Don't use too much bold, italics or variations in font size.

8 *Write a new letter for every application you make.* The reader needs to see that you have made an individual application for their job.

9 *Check that all the information you have included is correct.*

10 *Make sure that you sign the letter with a neat and clear signature.*

Curriculum Vitae

A **Curriculum Vitae** (usually called a CV) is a summary of your career to date. There are three stages you should follow when setting out your CV:

- assemble all the facts about yourself
- draft the CV
- edit the document several times.

Remember to keep the 4 Ss in mind:

- Simple
- Structured
- Succinct
- Significant.

At the initial stage you are trying to get together as many relevant facts as possible about your career to date. It does not matter if you put down too many to start with – make a list of all your educational, work-based and leisure achievements, as well as training activities and courses you have been on. Make brief notes about each of these as well as about projects and assignments you have been involved in.

Always use a word-processing package with an impressive, yet conservative, font and never lie. Make sure that you are truthful in the way you set out your CV – there is nothing worse than being caught out telling a lie. Divide your CV into the following areas.

Personal profile

Your personal profile includes your name, date of birth, address and telephone number and it is also an opportunity to describe yourself, your aims and objectives and to sell yourself by introducing the positive aspects of your personality.

Keep this section to no more than 10 lines. Remember, this is your chance to make your mark and get yourself noticed by a prospective employer. Any spelling mistakes in this section will be disastrous.

Education and training

As well as your qualifications from school or college, list other achievements and skills such as:

* any first-aid skills
* computer packages you are familiar with or have used
* keyboard skills – can you word-process at a reasonable speed?
* any language skills
* a driving licence, if you have one.

Remember that the key part of the CV is the career history, so the sections that go before should not be too long. For example, when dealing with training, list only the most important and relevant training courses, and then if necessary include some of the others under 'other information'.

Positions of responsibility

List positions of responsibility you have had:

* at school, for example, form captain, prefect, sports captain
* at 6th form/college, for example, 6th form Head, member of Young Enterprise
* elsewhere, for example, Treasurer of local badminton club or any other positions that show your leadership qualities.

If possible try to give examples of a situation where you may have had to make decisions, to build a team or work as a member of a team.

When you set out your responsibilities and achievements, decide whether it is necessary to put some of them under sub-headings.

Interests and activities

Employers do not expect students to put reading as an interest on their CVs as they expect students to read. Do not put down words like socialising that suggest you spend most of your spare time at the pub! Interests may include the following:

* playing an instrument, for example, piano, guitar
* hobbies, such as cookery, amateur dramatics, foreign travel, rock climbing
* an interest in the theatre/cinema
* participation in any sports, such as badminton, scuba diving, swimming, tennis and any medals or awards achieved
* membership of any clubs/societies.

Work experience and references

It is normal practice to start your career history with your most recent job and work backwards in time, because employers are usually more interested in your recent experience.

Briefly include details of any previous part-time or full-time work experience. Describe in more detail any work experience you found particularly interesting or where you were successful.

If some of your experience is of a technical nature, try to present it in a way that can be read easily by the general reader (rather than only by a specialist).

Try to use dynamic words in your CV. Here are some good examples:

Accomplished	Achieved	Conducted
Completed	Created	Decided
Delivered	Developed	Designed
Directed	Established	Expanded
Finished	Generated	Implemented
Improved	Increased	Introduced
Launched	Performed	Pioneered
Planned	Promoted	Redesigned
Reorganised	Set up	Solved
Succeeded	Trained	Widened
Won	Work	Wrote

Curriculum Vitae

Name	Prakesh Patel
Date of birth	1.3.1986
Address	50 Palmerston Road, Reading, RG31 9HL
Telephone	01604 76321
Education and training	Waingels' Copse School Reading, Sept 1998 – July 2004
Qualifications (GCSEs)	Mathematics (B)
	English (B)
	Business Studies (A)
	French (B)
	Geography (B)
	German (A)
	History (B)
	Technology (B)
	All 2004
Interests and activities	Captain of the school football team, house captain and prefect (2002–2004) Venture Scout, Gold Award Duke of Edinburgh. Member of Woodley Chess Club.
Referees	Mr I. Marks / Waingels' Copse School / Denmark Avenue / Woodley / Reading RG3 8SL Rev R. Babbage / St Jude's / Church Street / Reading / Reading RG4 7QZ

FIGURE 2.7 *An example of a CV*

2.2.3 The selection process

As soon as applications for a particular job role are received, then a business must select the best individuals available. You need to understand that a selection process can be broken down into the following stages:

* shortlisting candidates (you will not be expected to carry out this task)

* writing letters inviting candidates to interview

* preparing interview documentation, such as equal opportunities forms, interview questions, **selection criteria** and interview assessment forms

* designing tasks for interviewees to undertake

* carrying out an interview process

* post-interview taking up references and other security checks

* informing successful/unsuccessful candidates

* gaining the successful applicant's formal acceptance.

Shortlisting procedures

Shortlisting involves drawing up a list of the most suitable applicants from those that have applied for a post with an organisation. Usually a small group of people will be trusted with the task of drawing up this list. Armed with a job description, person specification and other sets of criteria, it is possible to reject candidates who do not meet the required criteria.

Think it over...

It is very important that shortlisting abides by Equal Opportunities legislation. A set of criteria is established usually by using the job description and person specification as a guide.

Theory into practice

Produce an attractively laid-out four-page booklet setting out good practice for recruiting and selecting applicants to fill posts in a specific organisation. You may want to base the work on the organisation in which you have carried out your work experience or had a part-time job. The booklet should consider:

* creating an effective person specification, and job description

* creating a job advertisement

* shortlisting

* interviewing to get the best candidates

* any other areas that you consider relevant.

Once you have developed your material you can use it to evaluate the recruitment and selection processes in different businesses. Using your own experience of being recruited and selected to work in a particular job, evaluate how the process you experienced compares with the good practice guidelines that you have drawn up.

It helps to sort into three piles:

Letters of invitation

Prior to an interview, brief letters are sent out inviting candidates for an interview. These letters set out when and where the interview will take place and any task that the candidate might need to do before the interview. If the advertised job is for an IT specialist, the interviewee might be expected to do an IT-related task to check on their IT skills as well as attending the formal interview.

Preparing interview documentation

It is usual for an interviewer to create forms for use during the interview including a list of questions that the interviewer or panel will ask. Equal Opportunities requirements state that the same questions must be asked of each of the candidates you are interviewing for the job.

A list of criteria judging the effectiveness of each candidate in terms of meeting the required job criteria may also be drawn up.

In preparing to interview other members of your group, the following documentation will be required:

* copies of the interviewees' application forms, curricula vitae, and supporting letters of application.

* copies of the person specification, the job description, and interview assessment schedules showing the criteria which the applicants will be judged against.

It may also be helpful to produce a standardised sheet for the interviewing panel to set out their comments about each of the candidates.

The interview process

Generally speaking, interviewers should try to make the interviewee feel relaxed and comfortable so that the interviewee can show his or her best side. An opening remark might be to ask the interviewee about his or her journey to the

Suitable candidates	Possible candidates	Rejects
Those that meet all or most of the relevant criteria	Those that meet some of the relevant criteria and may show some exciting characteristics that could make them worth interviewing	Those that meet very few of the criteria

Shortlisting – sorting candidates' applications into three piles

A typical job interview

interview on that day: 'Where have you come from?' 'Did you find it easy to get here today?'

When there are several interviewers a starting point might be to introduce the interviewee to each of the panel in turn.

Interview questions

It is important to recognise that the interview is a two-way process and there should be opportunities for both sides to answer questions. Not only is the interviewing panel seeking to find the best candidate for the post, but also the candidate should be seeing if the job is suitable and they want to work for the company. The candidate may ask questions about training, promotion prospects and social facilities.

The interviewee is usually asked a set of predetermined questions. The questions asked

Theory into practice

Create a scoresheet to be used in an interview situation. Relate the requirements to the job specification.

should relate to the person specification and job description. The interviewer will have a copy of the candidate's application form and curriculum vitae and will normally make notes to check how each interviewee meets the job requirements. A scoresheet may be used to record these notes (see Figure 2.8). By using a scoresheet it is possible to compare candidates' responses to questions and their behaviour in the interview situation.

Interviewing requires a considerable amount of intelligence and inventiveness. It is also up to the interviewer to try and ask questions that require a detailed response. Follow-on questions are very important here. Some follow-on questions may be planned in advance, while others may need to be developed on the spur of the moment. For example, an interview for the job of a shelf-stacker in a supermarket may proceed as follows:

Interviewer: Have you had experience of shelf-stacking in a supermarket before?

Interviewee: Yes, I worked at Waitrose doing it for three months.

Interviewer: (Follow-on question). Can you tell me exactly what you were responsible for doing in your shelf-stacking job and why you left your previous job?

Post: Junior Retail Manager

Candidate's name: Linda Booth

Requirements	Score 1–5 1 = poor 5 = excellent	Notes
Tidy appearance	3	Untidy hair
Intelligence	5	Answered questions quickly and with good attention to detail
Punctuality	1	Turned up 2 minutes late for interview

FIGURE 2.8 *Part of an interviewer's scoresheet*

Without follow-on questions an interview can pass very quickly with little being found out about the true strengths (and weaknesses) of job applicants.

Interview tests

Many jobs today involve some form of **psychometric** or **aptitude testing** to find out whether individuals have the right sorts of personalities to carry out particular types of work. A psychometric test is a way of assessing an individual's personality, drives and motivations, either by means of a paper and pencil questionnaire or online test.

For example, one of the dimensions the psychometric test might draw out is an individual's willingness or ability to work in a team situation or to handle stress.

A number of organisations place a great deal of emphasis on these tests because they believe they are reliable indicators of the sociability / personality of individuals, and that they are useful predictors of whether individuals will fit into the organisation.

Aptitude tests are used to find out whether a candidate is suited to carrying out a particular type of work and involve some form of simulation of that type of work. For example, in selecting new pilots a number of airlines will give candidates tests which involve testing their reactions to sudden movements as well as the use of flight simulators to test how quick their reactions are and how they respond to pressure.

Theory into practice

Obtain a psychometric test that is used for selection purposes. Try out the test. What does it claim to show about your personality and disposition? Do you agree?

Using body language

People do not communicate with each other just through words. They also communicate through their **body language**. An interviewer who wants to draw the best out of candidates for a job will use appropriate body language. The interviewer should be seated at the same height as the interviewee with a good frontal or open posture.

The interviewer should not cross his or her arms or make threatening gestures such as pointing a finger or banging a fist down on the table. He or she should smile and use clear eye contact.

Closing the interview

The usual way of closing an interview is that, when the interviewer or interviewing panel have finished their list of questions, they will ask the interviewee if there is anything he or she would like to ask. When this is completed the interviewer will say something like:

> *Thank you very much for coming to the interview, I hope you have a safe journey back. You will be hearing from us by...*

The interviewer will clarify the arrangements through which the interviewee will be informed of arrangements, and explain how any administrative task such as claiming for expenses should be done.

Giving feedback

Often candidates for a post will be given feedback on how they performed in the interview situation. They should be told about their strengths and weaknesses and the reasons why they were or were not chosen for the post. This feedback should be seen as a positive process concerned with the ongoing **development** of the interviewee.

Theory into practice

In groups, carry out mock interviews for a post that you are familiar with from work experience.

Preparing for an interview

There are many ways you can prepare for an interview. You can practise your answers to the questions likely to be asked, possibly with the help of a friend who takes the role of the interviewer.

You may want to try out the clothes that you will wear to the interview beforehand, perhaps by wearing them to some sort of public occasion. There is nothing worse than feeling uncomfortable in the clothes you have chosen for an interview.

Many people like to plan the route they will take to get to the interview, even doing a dummy run beforehand.

Factors	Rating					INTERVIEW ASSESSMENT Remarks
	A	B	C	D	E	
Appearance Personality Manner Health						
Intelligence Understanding of questions						
Skills Special skills Work experience						
Interests Hobbies Sports						
Academic						
Motivation						
Circumstances Mobility Hours Limitations						
OVERALL						
A = Exceptional B = Above average C = Satisfactory D = Below average E = Unsuitable						

FIGURE 2.9 *An interview assessment form*

You may like to prepare yourself by thinking about the kinds of things that interviewers will be looking for in you. Figure 2.9 shows an interview assessment form which gives you some useful indications of the qualities that are looked for in many job-holders.

Interview advice

Showing confidence

It is important to appear confident but not over-confident. You should be confident in your own abilities. One of the most important attributes to have in the interview situation is enthusiasm. An enthusiastic person will tend to radiate confidence whereas candidates who appear timid will be viewed in a poor light, particularly for posts that require some degree of responsibility and initiative.

Body language

At an interview it is important for you to adopt the right body language. Look alert and eager. Look the questioner in the eye, avoid nervous movements, and try not to cross your arms in a defensive position. Try not to threaten the interviewer by pointing your finger or making violent movements. Sit up straight and try to look confident and at ease – not apathetic and too laid back.

Appropriate body language

Answering questions

When you are answering questions, do not give brief one-line answers, but try to expand on your answers so that the interviewer can see you at your best. When you are being interviewed, listen carefully to the questions that you are asked. If you do not understand a question or have not heard it clearly, it may be helpful to say, 'Please could you repeat that question?'

Asking questions

When given the opportunity ask a small number of relevant questions. Don't ask questions that simply involve the repetition of what you have already been told. If you are not sure whether you want the job or not, ask questions that will help you to make an informed choice.

Be clear and concise

Good verbal communication involves asking and answering questions in a clear and concise way.

Think it over...

It is often in the first few minutes of an interview that an interview panel make up their minds about which candidate to appoint. In addition, a recent study reported that the person who is first on the interviewer's list is three times more likely to be hired than the last name on the list. This is often the case because the interviewing panel are usually more alert and interested at the start of a busy interview schedule than at the end of the day.

Theory into practice

Study the following pictures which show three views of one of the people who turned up for an interview for a part-time shelf filler's post – in each case explain why the body language is inappropriate.

DO	DON'T
Find out about the firm before the interview	Be late
Dress smartly but comfortably	Smoke unless invited to
Speak clearly and with confidence	Chew gum or eat sweets
Look at the interviewer when speaking	Answer all questions 'yes', 'no' or 'I don't know'
Be positive about yourself	Be afraid to ask for clarification if anything is unclear
Be ready to ask questions	Say things which are obviously untrue or insincere

FIGURE 2.10 *An interview checklist*

The person who is straightforward, interesting and direct will often sway an interview in a positive way.

The checklist shown above should also be helpful in giving you some useful preparatory advice for interviews.

Interview evaluation

Aspect of performance	Rating				
	Very good	Good	Fair	Weak	Very weak
Eye contact					
Body language					
Appearing confident					
Answering questions					

FIGURE 2.11 *An evaluation form*

After an interview, all interviewers and interviewees should fill in a self-evaluation form which is an opportunity to identify any strengths and weaknesses and improve performance. The types of questions you need to ask are as follows:

* how did you feel about the interview?
* how do you consider the interview went?
* what impression do you think that you gave?
* what do you think of the interviewers'/ interviewees':
  * planning and organisation?
  * preparation for the interview?
  * performance at the interview?

Evaluating recruitment and selection processes

Recruitment and selection can be a very costly process for a business. It takes a great deal of time to set up the process which includes drawing up a job description, advertising the position, sifting through applications, checking which applications best meet the criteria set down for the post, interviewing candidates and finally, selecting the best candidate for the post.

There is considerable scope along the way for waste and inefficiency. For example, when a job advertisement attracts 100 applicants there will be a considerable waste of time and resources when reducing the list down to six. If you get your procedures wrong you may eliminate some of the best candidates right from the start and end up with six who are barely satisfactory. If you end up choosing an unsuitable candidate for the job, the company will suffer from having a poorly motivated person, who may make trouble within the organisation before walking out on the job and leaving the company to go through the expense of replacing him or her yet again.

Post-interview procedures

On completion of the interviewing and selection processes, the best candidate for the post will be selected and approached by the chair of the interviewing panel to see if they will be prepared to take up the post. Often this will take place over the telephone as soon as possible after a decision has been made. If the candidate agrees to take up the post and a formal offer has been made then it becomes legally binding on both parties – referred to in law as formal acceptance. In many situations the employer may want to take up the references before the final offer is made.

Once the 'best' candidate has been contacted, then the chair of the panel can contact unsuccessful candidates informing them of the decision. At this time, the unsuccessful parties may ask and be provided with feedback about their performance in the interview and the sorts of areas that they should work on if they want to secure a similar job.

If the person chosen turns down the job offer, then the chair will quickly move on to ask the second 'best' candidate. It is very important to make an offer and have it accepted soon after the interview, because candidates for the post will quickly feel aggrieved if they are not informed about whether their application has been successful or not. The business should not create a bad impression – after all those candidates that it rejects may be customers or may want to work for the firm in the same or another capacity in the future.

2.2.4 The induction process

Induction is the process of introducing new employees to their place of work, job, new surroundings and the people they will be working with. Induction also provides information to help new employees start work and generally 'fit in'.

Once the successful applicant has been selected and offered the post, the human resources department needs to prepare a suitable induction programme for when the new employee starts work. Typical features of an induction programme include:

* an awareness of the workings and objectives of a business

* an awareness of health and safety issues

* requirements when absent, ill or late

* introduction to management and workmates

* identification of any immediate training needs.

It is important to produce an induction programme that meets the needs of the job role and the successful applicant.

The induction process will vary from company to company but it is important that you have an understanding of the sort of induction activities that you will need to design for your assignment for this unit.

To create an induction package you will need to set out:

* the objectives for the induction programme – what are you trying to achieve through it? Perhaps you could set out some outcomes for the induction – in other words what should the inductee know or be able to do at the end of the induction that they did not know or were not able to do at the start?

* a timetable for the induction. Typically this will cover the induction day/s for the new job-holder and any follow-up induction activities.

* an outline of the main induction activities which they will be involved in – e.g. health and safety induction, introduction to the company and its objectives, introduction to key employees in the organisation, team building activities etc.

The workings and objectives of a business

The general purposes of induction are:

* to make the new employee feel welcome and part of a team

* to make sure that they are aware of important issues such as company policies, their rights and entitlements at work, and above all to make sure that they are familiar with health and safety requirements

* to make sure that they can start working productively for the company as soon as possible.

During the induction therefore, new members of the organisation need to:

* find out as much about the organisation as possible, what it is like, what it does, what it is trying to achieve

* find out about where they fit into the organisation, what they will be expected to do and how they will be expected to work

* be motivated and inspired to feel that they have chosen to work for a company that will help them to flourish and develop themselves

* find out about their rights and responsibilities.

Key terms

Training includes all forms of planned learning experiences and activities designed to make positive changes to performance and other behaviour. You can train an individual to develop new:

* knowledge

* skills

* beliefs

* values

* attitudes.

Learning is generally defined as 'a relatively permanent change in behaviour that occurs as a result of practice or experience'.

Induction can be seen as the first part of the training and development process that takes place when an individual joins an organisation.

Contents of an induction pack

Useful criteria therefore for judging how well you have designed your induction programme is the extent to which – if you were starting work at that company yourself – you would feel that the induction had introduced you to all of the things you need to know and be able to do to start working effectively for the company.

Induction should also consider the initial training needs either on joining a new organisation or on taking on a new function

CASE STUDY

Induction at a financial services company
When Joe started working for a financial services company in Nottingham he had the following induction.

* On the first day, he had a series of talks from important people in the company, including the managing director, the personnel manager and a briefing about health and safety at work from the safety officer. He was given some packs of information and details of how he would be paid, and his various rights in the workplace.

* The second day was spent on team-building exercises with other new recruits at work.

* The rest of the week was spent on IT training.

* The following week Joe worked alongside an experienced employee in the section he was due to work in.

* In the third week Joe started to work independently.

1 **What do you think of the structure of Joe's induction programme?**

2 **How does Joe's induction programme compare with your own work experience or the induction programme you had when you first came to college?**

CASE STUDY

Induction at ASDA

When an employee first starts working for ASDA they are introduced to the following:

1 The aim of ASDA as a business. This includes being the best-value fresh food and clothing store in Britain. They also aim to satisfy the weekly shopping needs of ordinary working people who demand value.
2 The importance of customer service which includes such aspects as:
 * smile when greeting customers and maintain eye contact
 * take customers to a product rather than pointing
 * offer assistance when a customer is struggling
 * listen to customer feedback and pass this on to relevant colleagues
 * recognise and help customers with special needs
 * treat customers as you would like to be treated yourself
 * remember that the customer is always right.
3 ASDA's policy on minimising waste.
4 Working as part of a team.
5 Health and safety responsibilities.
6 Personal safety.

1 Why do you think that Asda's induction programme introduces new members to the aims and purposes of the company?
2 Why do you think so much emphasis is placed on customer service during the induction process?
3 Design an induction activity of your own which would introduce new ASDA recruits to teamwork processes?
4 Prepare an evaluation sheet to find out what the inductees thought of the process.

within it. It should also deal with the structure, culture and activities in the organisation. The new recruit will typically be given an induction pack that introduces him or her to the organisation.

Health and safety

Health and safety is the most essential part of any induction programme. Businesses must ensure the health and safety of their employees and the wider public that comes into contact with the business at all times.

Individuals cannot start work until a proper risk assessment has been carried out of the activities that they will be involved in. This is just as true for work experience as for actual full-time work processes.

All places of work must have a written health and safety policy and it is the responsibility of the safety officer and the directors of a company to ensure safe working practices. Failure to produce a safety policy by a company can lead to extensive fines and up to two years' imprisonment for company officials.

In researching health and safety issues you may be able to examine the way in which your school or college inducts new staff, for example, Administrators in health and safety deal with issues related to using computer equipment (to avoid repetitive strain problems) or staff who deal with harmful substances such as spent computer cartridges, fire drills etc.

Health and Safety at Work Act 1974

The main points of the Health and Safety at Work Act are as follows:

It shall be the duty of every employer to ensure, so far as is reasonably practicable, the health, safety and welfare at work of all his or her employees.

The employer has a duty to ensure:

1 The provision and maintenance of plant and systems of work that are, so far as is reasonably practicable, safe and without risks to health.

2 Arrangements for ensuring, so far as is reasonably practicable, safety and absence

of risks to health in connection with the use, handling storage and transport of articles and substances.

3 The provision of such information, instruction, training and supervision as is necessary to ensure, so far as is reasonably practicable, the health and safety at work of his of her employees.

4 Safe means of access to and from work.

The Act also places a responsibility on employees. The employees' duty is to take reasonable care to ensure both their own safety and the safety of others who may be affected by what they do or do not do.

Other Health and Safety Regulations include:

Reporting of Injuries, Diseases and Dangerous Occurrence Regulations

These regulations state that injuries that result from accidents at work where an employee is incapacitated for three or more days must be reported to the authorities within seven days. Injuries involving deaths must be reported immediately.

Control of Substances Hazardous to Health (COSHH) regulations

Employers must carry out assessment of work tasks that are likely to create risks for the health and safety of employees. Employees should then be given the necessary training for dealing with these substances.

European Union Regulations

In addition there are a number of European Union Regulations such as those relating to noise at work. Employees must be given appropriate training e.g. in the use of ear protectors when they are exposed to potentially harmful noise.

Requirements when absent, ill or late

As part of the induction process it is important for trainers to make sure that employees are aware of procedures involved in employees reporting any difficulties which they may be having which may lead to them being absent or late for work.

Theory into practice

Discuss in class the requirements for absences, illness, or lateness in part-time jobs which members of the group have had.

In planning your induction activities for a new employee you need to set out how inductees will be informed about arrangements for when they are absent, ill or late.

The human resources department is responsible for planning labour budgets (i.e. making sure that they have enough people available to do the tasks required). Absences can lead to problems for the whole team, and adversely affect production in a company. HR will therefore create procedures.

For example, a well-known retailing organisation requires all employees to report to their supervisor at least one hour in advance of a morning shift that they will be absent. They will then need to produce a written note explaining their absence. If they are absent from work more than twice in any given month they will need to have a meeting with their supervisor to explain the cause of the absence.

Similarly if employees are going to be late they must inform their supervisor when they are likely to arrive so that cover can be provided.

In the case of illness, employees will be asked to provide a note explaining the nature of their illness. Should they be away for more than five days they will require a doctor's certificate, because their absence will affect their entitlement to sickness benefits (from the government).

Immediate training needs

As part of the induction process, new employees may be introduced to new processes or software that they are unfamiliar with. The employer should explain each of these processes to new employees, question them about their experience with the processes or software and listen carefully to their answers to gauge their level of experience. For example, an employee may be familiar with the Microsoft Office software package but may not have had extensive experience with spreadsheets. If this is a requirement of the role, then careful

Theory into practice

Judge the effectiveness of the induction programme designed by another member of your group.

questioning will determine the skill level of the employee and the training required to enable them to do their job. Training may be carried out formally through a course or more informally by a colleague or with training manuals. Identifying immediate training needs and implementing training in a timely manner is important to ensure the new employees are equipped with the skills to properly carry out their duties.

2.2.5 Employee motivation

A business needs to motivate its workforce if it is to retain them and remain competitive. You need to understand some of the methods that are commonly employed. These include:

* financial incentives such as:
  * wages, salaries and bonuses
  * profit sharing
  * share options

* non-financial incentives such as:
  * goal setting
  * perks and status symbols
  * **appraisal**
  * meeting training needs.

Pay and financial incentives

From a management view a payment system should:

* be effective in recruiting the right quantity and quality of labour

* be effective in retaining labour over the required period of time – it is expensive to have to keep advertising for and training new employees

* keep labour costs as low as possible in order to maintain the competitiveness of a business

* help to motivate staff and encourage effort (careful thought needs to be applied to

structuring pay systems in a way that encourages motivation and performance)

* be designed to allow for additional rewards and benefits.

The sum paid for a normal working week is termed a basic wage or salary. Many employees receive other benefits in addition to their basic wage, either in a money or non-money form. The main ways of calculating pay are outlined below. Sometimes elements of these methods are combined.

Flat rate

This is a set rate of weekly or monthly pay, based on a set number of hours. It is easy to calculate and administer but does not provide an incentive to employees to work harder.

Time rate

Under this scheme, workers receive a set rate per hour. Any hours worked above a set number are paid at an 'overtime rate'.

Piece rate

This system is sometimes used in the textile and electronics industries, among others. Payment is made for each item produced that meets given quality standards. The advantage of this is that it encourages effort. However, it is not suitable for jobs that require time and care. Also, many jobs particularly in the service sector produce 'outputs' that are impossible to measure.

Bonus

A bonus is paid as an added encouragement to employees. It can be paid out of additional profits earned by the employer as a result of the employee's effort and hard work or as an incentive to workers at times when they might be inclined to slacken effort, for example at Christmas and summer holiday times.

Commission

Commission is a payment made as a percentage of the sales a salesperson has made.

Output-related payment schemes

Output-related schemes are the most common method used to reward manual workers. Most

CASE STUDY

The best companies to work for

In March, 2005, *The Sunday Times* carried out a survey of the best 100 companies to work for in this country. Aspects of good companies that they identified included:

Holidays	Companies offering a minimum of 25 days' annual leave to all employees – 45 of the top 100 companies.
Maternity	Companies offering at least 10 weeks on full pay during the first period of maternity leave (compared with the statutory minimum of six) – 19 out of the top 100.
Childcare	Companies that provide a workplace crèche or nursery and / or vouchers or cash to contribute towards childcare costs – 47 out of the top 100.
Women	Companies where at least 33% of the senior managers are women – 31 out of the top 100.
Long service	Companies where at least 40% of the staff have worked there for more than five years – 33 out of the top 100.
Pensions	Companies offering a final salary pension scheme, non-contributory scheme or one in which the employer contributes at least double the amount contributed by the employee – 49 out of the top 100.
Health insurance	Companies offering private health insurance for all employees, their spouses and dependants – 16 out of the top 100.
Gym	Companies offering either an on-site gym or subsidised membership of a nearby gym – 70 out of the top 100.
Shares	Companies where employees are offered share options – 33 out of the top 100.
Charitable activities	Companies where at least 10% of staff are known to undertake charitable activities – 30 out of the top 100.

Source: *The Sunday Times*, 6 March 2005

The top 10 large companies using these and other criteria were:

1 Nationwide (financial services)
2 ASDA (supermarkets)
3 KPMG (auditing and tax services)
4 The Carphone Warehouse (mobile telecoms retailer)
5 Mothercare (retailer)
6 Cadbury Schweppes (food and drink manufacturer)
7 Compass Group (catering)
8 Pfizer (pharmaceuticals)
9 Severn Trent Water (utility company)
10 WS Atkins (engineering consultancy)

1 Carry out some research of your own into a medium to large company that a family member or friend works for. Does the company give 25 or more days of holiday a year? Does it provide a workplace crèche or similar facility? What percentage of senior managers are women? What percentage of the staff has worked in the company for five years or more? Does the company provide an on-site gym or subsidise employees' gym membership?

2 What do you see as being the most important ingredients of a 'good company to work for'?

Method study sets out to determine what is the most effective way of carrying out particular tasks.

Work measurement takes place in three stages:

1 The time taken to perform a task is measured.

2 The effort of an individual worker or work-group is rated.

3 The work carried out is assessed and compared with the standard rate.

1 Give a brief definition of performance-related pay.

2 Do you think it is appropriate to use performance-related pay in the police force? How would performance be measured?

3 Give examples of jobs where performance-related pay might be appropriate and ones where it definitely would not be appropriate.

schemes involve an element of time-rates plus a bonus or other incentive. Standards are set in many ways, varying from casual assessment to a detailed work study, based on method study and work measurement (see Key terms above).

A standard allowable time is set according to the two stages. The worker's pay is then determined according to the success of the third stage.

Performance-related pay

In recent years, the emphasis in a number of organisations has shifted towards performance-related pay. Performance is assessed against working objectives and 'company goals'. Scoring systems are then worked out to assess performance against objectives, and these distinguish levels of attainment, e.g. high, medium or low.

Managerial jobs are most affected by performance-related pay. Based on **performance appraisal** techniques, such schemes have been adopted in a wide range of occupations, including the police force, universities, insurance and banking. Evidence indicates that up to three-quarters of all employers are now using some form of performance appraisal to set pay levels.

One way of rewarding performance is to give a bonus if certain targets are met. Another is to give increments as targets are met, with the employee progressing up an incremental ladder each year.

Profit sharing

Profit sharing is an incentive tool which involves giving profit related pay to employees or giving them bonuses based on the profit performance of a business. Using this approach, employees are able to see that the success of the company will also lead to personal rewards for them.

Share options

Employees may be encouraged to take up shares in a company, often as part of a rewards scheme. When employees take up these share options they are then rewarded according to the performance of the business. When the business does well so too does the value of their shares and the dividends they receive as a return to shareholders. Dividends are typically paid twice yearly.

Fringe benefits

In addition to financial rewards, fringe benefits may be provided including:

The police force have adopted performance-related pay

* pension schemes

* subsidised meals or canteen services

* educational courses

* opportunities for foreign travel

* holiday entitlements

* crèches

* assistance with housing and relocation packages

* discount and company purchase plans (i.e. cheap purchases of company products)

* telephone costs

* discounts on insurance costs

* private healthcare, dental treatment, etc

* time off (sabbatical)

* sports, leisure and social facilities.

Theory into practice

The wages department of a large manufacturing organisation is deciding on the most appropriate payment systems in the following situations. What advice would you give them?

They want to provide a financial reward system for:

* sales people that rewards them according to the number of sales they make

* production line staff that encourages them to be careful in their work

* production line staff that discourages them from slacking off just before the Christmas period.

Non-financial incentives

Some of the fringe benefits listed above, e.g. a crèche on site or a company pension scheme, are non-financial incentives which may improve employee performance and help to create long-term commitment to the company.

Non-financial incentives can also include motivational factors such as goal setting, appraisals, work conditions and internal promotion.

Conditions of work

When you start work, an important motivational factor is the conditions in the workplace, for example the physical environment:

* are you working in a bright, clean and well-lit environment?

* is the temperature suitable for work (not too hot or too cold)?

* is the workplace safe?

The other important aspect is the 'culture' of the organisation. It is important to understand the term culture as it is applied in a business sense because it is such an important ingredient of motivation. We use the term culture to describe the typical way of working in an organisation – sometimes referred to as 'the way we do things around here'. A positive culture is one which encourages people to contribute and makes them feel valued. In contrast, a negative culture is one where people feel that they are not valued and often where they feel they are being criticised. The culture relates to the relationships and typical ways of interacting and doing things in the organisation. Different types of organisations have different cultures:

Favourable cultures	Unfavourable cultures
Warm and welcoming	Unfriendly
Encouraging	Discouraging and based on fear
Welcomes initiative	Have to do what you are told

Theory into practice

Identify one organisation which you have been a part of that had a favourable culture and another that had an unfavourable culture. Make a list of the key differences and discuss these with your class group.

Internal promotion

Promoting people within an organisation (internally) is another good motivating tool, because employees can see that they can develop themselves within the organisation.

Think it over…

Did you know that from the 1970s right through to the 1990s when Liverpool Football Club was so successful, many of its managers were former backroom staff. This encouraged the backroom staff to be loyal to the club with excellent results.

Goal setting

Establishing goals for employees to work towards can be an important motivational factor as the achievement of these goals then creates a sense of achievement and personal fulfilment. Goals can be established for an individual, team or for the whole organisation and achievement may be related to promotion at work.

Perks and status symbols

Perks and status symbols are useful motivational tools in a company. A perk is something extra that you get for doing a particular job. For example, employees of a railway company may get free rail travel for them and their families. A cinema employee may get free cinema tickets.

Status symbols are also important motivators. An obvious status symbol is having a bigger office, or having a sign outside your door with your name on. People often respond very favourably to status symbols because these mark them out as being special.

Appraisal

Most organisations today operate some form of staff appraisal or staff development scheme. Appraisals are a form of goal setting. Appraisals are usually conducted by a line manager or in some cases by someone at the same level in an organisation (peer appraisal). The individual being appraised (the appraisee) and the appraisor will sit down together to establish targets to work to in the coming period. These targets will normally be based on a review of performance in a previous period, and targets for the organisation or team as a whole. Appraisal interviews are carried out on a regular basis and provide an opportunity for the appraisee to communicate his or her needs and requirements. The line manager can also clarify the needs of the organisation.

An appraisal in progress

Appraisal is often related to performance-related pay. Appraisal also provides a good opportunity to establish training and development needs.

Key terms

Training refers to ways of improving the skills and knowledge of individuals so that they can help an organisation to meet its goals.

Development relates to the personal needs of an individual – e.g. to develop new skills, to do more fulfilling work, to take up opportunities for more education and training etc.

Performance appraisal

Key terms

Performance appraisal is a process of evaluating performance systematically and of providing feedback on which performance adjustments can be made. Performance appraisal works on the basis of the following equation:

Desired performance – Actual performance = Need for action.

The major purposes of performance appraisal are to:

* define the specific job criteria against which performance will be measured
* measure past job performance accurately
* justify the rewards given to individuals and/or groups, thereby discriminating between high and low performance
* define the experiences that an individual employee will need for his or her ongoing

development. These development experiences should improve job performance and prepare the employee for future responsibilities.

Stages of staff appraisal

Common stages of staff appraisal are as follows:

1   The line manager meets with the job-holder to discuss what is expected. The agreed expectations may be expressed in terms of targets, performance standards or required job behaviours – attributes, skills and attitudes.

2   The outcome of the meeting is recorded and usually signed by both parties.

3   The job-holder performs the job for a period of six months or a year.

4   At the end of the period, the job-holder and line manager or team leader meet again to review and discuss progress made. They draw up new action plans to deal with identified problems and agree targets and standards for the next period.

Think it over…

The process of 360° appraisal involves appraising an individual from above by a line manager, from the sides by work colleagues at the same level in an organisation and from below by people that the individual supervises or is in charge of.

Meeting training needs

Mentoring

Mentoring and coaching are seen by many organisations as essential ways of motivating employees so that they feel valued and cared for in their work.

Mentoring involves a trainee being 'paired' with a more experienced employee. The trainee carries out the job but uses the 'mentor' to discuss problems that may occur and how best to solve them.

This approach is used in many lines of work. For example, it is common practice for trainee teachers to work with a mentor who is responsible for their early training and development. The student teacher will watch the mentor teach before starting his or her own teaching. The mentor will then give ongoing guidance to the student teacher on how best to improve his or her performance. If the student teacher has any problems or difficulties he or she can talk to the mentor for advice.

Coaching

Coaching involves providing individuals with personal coaches in the workplace. The person who is going to take on the coaching role will need to develop coaching skills and will also need to have the time slots for the coaching to take place. The coach and the individual being coached will need to identify development opportunities that they can work on together – ways of tackling jobs, ways of improving performance, etc. The coach will provide continuous feedback on performance and how this is progressing.

Of course, coaching does not just benefit the person being coached; it also aids the coach's own personal development. It is particularly important in a coaching system that:

* the coach wants to coach the person and has the necessary coaching skills

* the person being coached wants to be coached and has the necessary listening and learning skills

* sufficient time is given to the coaching process

* the organisation places sufficient value on the coaching process.

Some of the best sports people in this country have improved their skills and abilities by working closely with a coach they respect.

A coach can be invaluable to a sports person

Having your training needs met in an organisation is also an important motivator. People who do not have their training needs met are not fully able to develop themselves and may be held back in seeking the promotion they would like. Intelligent organisations therefore carry out a **Training needs analysis** to find out the training needs of their employees so that these needs can be met.

Motivational theories

As we have seen, motivating people at work can be achieved through a combination of financial and non-financial rewards. Motivational theorists such as Maslow, Herzberg and McGregor show that true motivation can rarely be achieved through financial packages alone. They show that non-financial motivators are essential – such as creating an exciting work environment, and providing opportunities for individuals to develop themselves and to enjoy contributing to decision-making in the workplace.

Maslow

Maslow identified a hierarchy of needs split into five broad categories. He suggested that it is possible to develop a hierarchical picture of needs, split into the following:

Basic needs are for reasonable standards of food, shelter and clothing and those other items that are considered the norm to meet the needs of the body and for physical survival. This base level of need will be attained at work from receiving a basic wage packet that helps the employee to survive, for example by receiving the minimum wage.

Security needs are also concerned with physical survival. In the workplace, these needs could include safety, security of employment, adequate rest periods, pension, health schemes and protection from unfair treatment.

Group needs are concerned with an individual's need for love and affection (within a group). In groups there are always some people who are strong enough and happy to keep apart. However, the majority of people want to feel that they belong to a group. In small and medium-sized organisations (up to 200 people) it is relatively easy to give each member of the group a feeling of belonging. However, in large organisations individuals can lose their group identify, becoming just another number, a face in the crowd. Managers therefore need to think about how they can organise their people into teams so as to meet group needs.

Self-esteem needs are based on an individual's desire for self-respect and the respect of others. Employees have a need to be recognised as individuals of some importance, to receive praise for their work and to have their efforts noticed and rewarded.

Maslow placed *self-fulfilment* at the top of the hierarchy of needs. Self-fulfilment is concerned with full personal development and individual creativity. In order to meet this need, it is important for individuals to be able to use their talents and abilities fully.

Maslow argued that individuals firstly have to have their lower-level needs met, but if they are not to experience frustration it is also important for their higher-level needs to be met. Frustrated employees are likely either to develop a 'couldn't care less approach' or to become antagonistic to working life. If employees are to become committed to work these higher-level needs must be met.

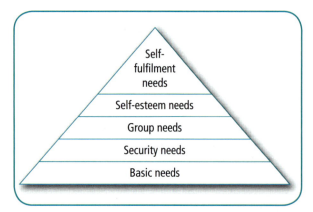

FIGURE 2.12 *Maslow's hierarchy of needs*

> **Think it over...**
>
> The Chinese philosopher Confucius said that 'The person that finds a job they like never does a day's work in their life.'

Which of Maslow's needs do you think the following scenarios are looking to satisfy at work? How might managers go about seeking to meet these needs?

1 Simon is working part time in a supermarket to save up enough money to go back to university with. He is prepared to work long hours, providing his total pay is good. He is not interested in taking on responsibilities, but wants to work in a safe environment.

2 Pritesh is a graphic designer who recently graduated from art college. Ideally he would like to do something which allows him to express his artistic talent. He feels that his current job working in an advertising agency does not allow him to express himself. He works in a junior role in the company copying work that has been created by senior designers.

3 Gillian has recently been promoted to the post of supervisor in the food processing plant where she works. This has meant a rise in salary enabling her to take out a mortgage to buy a house and put down a deposit on a new car. The supervisor post gives her the status she desires and she likes her working environment and the relationship she has with colleagues.

Herzberg

Herzberg carried out research on 200 engineers to find out what motivated them at work. He made a distinction between things that *move* people, which he referred to as KITA (kick in the ass), and factors that *motivate* people.

He argued that if he kicked his dog, this would get the dog to move (out of fear), but it would not motivate the animal. When we are motivated we do something because we want to do it. In other words it provides an intrinsic (internal) reward.

Herzberg identified nine factors which he referred to as 'dissatisfiers' and when these factors reached a certain level they would cause employee absenteeism, poor levels of output, resistance to change, obstruction, and other negative actions.

The '*dissatisfiers*' are:

* dominating or unpredictable company policy and administration
* low pay
* poor working conditions
* confrontational relationships between different levels in the organisation
* unfriendly relationships within the chain of command
* unfair management and supervision
* unfair treatment of employees
* feelings of inadequacy
* impossibility for development of the individual.

By reducing these dissatisfiers you can reduce negative feelings but they are not the real motivating drives.

In contrast, Herzberg identified five motivating factors which relate to the content of jobs. He called these '*satisfiers*'.

They are:

* recognition of effort and performance
* the nature of the job itself – does it provide the employees with appropriate challenges?
* sense of achievement
* assumption of responsibility
* opportunity for promotion.

Herzberg suggested that jobs could be given more meaning if they included elements of responsibility and a more creative use of individuals' ability, as well as opportunities to achieve.

From your own experience of working life, identify situations in which you felt highly motivated. How did these motivating factors relate to Herzberg's satisfiers?

Douglas McGregor

McGregor divided managers into two main types – theory X and theory Y.

Theory X managers tend to have the view that:

* the average person naturally dislikes work and so will avoid it when possible so management needs to encourage high levels of production by incentive schemes to encourage effort

* because people naturally dislike work, people need to be pushed, threatened and driven to get things done

* the average person likes to be told what to do and to avoid responsibility, they have little ambition, and therefore require 'managing'.

Theory Y managers have a contrasting view and believe in trusting employees to take on responsibilities. Theory Y managers have the view that:

* work is a natural activity which people can enjoy and it is up to the manager to create the right conditions in which work is enjoyable

* external control is not the only way to manage people as employees who identify with the organisation's objectives will be motivated to work hard

* the most significant reward that will motivate people is self-fulfilment (see Maslow) so managers need to identify opportunities for employees to fulfil themselves while working to meet company objectives

* the average human being learns, when given the opportunity, to accept and to seek responsibility

* many people can contribute to a business's objectives when given the chance

* people's potential is rarely achieved in the workplace.

McGregor saw the potential to make organisations far more effective by unleashing the people who work for them.

Rosabeth Moss Kanter

Moss Kanter

Rosabeth Moss Kanter argues that we can **empower** people by giving them greater responsibility in the organisation. Empowerment involves passing power and responsibility down in the organisation, so that good ideas can bubble up to the surface from below. Empowered individuals enable an organisation to be more successful by coming up with lots of good ideas. In turn, empowered people are motivated people.

Theory into practice

Study one organisation to find out about how it motivates its people. This can be done by:

1 Using your own work experience.

2 Interviewing a human resources manager.

3 Looking at the human resources section of a company website.

Think it over…

Employees at Rank Xerox are allowed to reward each other. Under a scheme called you deserve an X today any employee can give an X certificate to another employee. The X certificate is worth up to 50 dollars and is given for 'excellent support, excellent attendance, extra work or excellent co-operation'.

2.2.6 The legal dimension

There are a number of legal and ethical requirements which businesses must meet when obtaining employees to work for them. These laws seek to prevent **discrimination** in areas such as the recruitment and selection of staff. The European Union Equal Treatment Directive now makes it unlawful to discriminate on grounds of sexual orientation and religion or other belief. By 2006, age discrimination will also be unlawful.

The Sex Discrimination Act (1975 and 1986)

These acts were introduced to encourage equal treatment of people and respect for people in the workplace. The Sex Discrimination Act 1975 sets out rights for both men and women. This act was amended in 1986 to make it unlawful to discriminate on grounds of sex in employment, education, advertising or when providing goods, facilities, services and premises.

Unlawful discrimination means giving less favourable treatment to someone because of their sex or because they are married or single, and can be either direct or indirect. *Direct sex discrimination* means being treated less favourably than a person of the opposite sex would be treated in similar circumstances, for example, a policy to appoint only men to management levels. Direct marriage discrimination means being treated less favourably than an unmarried person of the same sex.

Indirect sex discrimination means being unable to comply with a requirement which, on the face of it, applies equally to both men and women, but which in practice can be met by a much smaller proportion of one sex. For example, an organisation may be indirectly discriminating against women if access to certain jobs is restricted to particular grades which in practice are held only by men.

Individuals have the right of access to civil courts and employment tribunals for legal remedies for unlawful discrimination under the Sex Discrimination Act.

Race Relations Act (1976 and 2000)

The Race Relations Act (1976 and 2000) makes it unlawful to discriminate against a person, directly or indirectly, in the field of employment, training and related matters on the basis of race, colour or national origin.

Direct discrimination means treating a person, on racial grounds, less favourably than other people are treated or would be treated in the same or similar circumstances. Segregating a person from others on racial grounds constitutes less favourable treatment.

Indirect discrimination consists of applying a provision, requirement or practice which, although applied equally to persons of all racial groups, is such that a considerably smaller proportion of a particular racial group can comply with it. Examples are:

* a rule about clothing or uniforms which disproportionately disadvantages a racial group and cannot be justified

* an employer who requires higher language standards than are needed for safe and effective performance of the job.

Disability Discrimination Act (1995 and 2004)

The Disability Discrimination Act (1995 and 2004) applies to people who are defined as disabled:

A disabled person is someone who has a physical or mental impairment, which has an effect on his or her ability to carry out normal day-to-day activities. That effect must be:

* *substantial (that is more than minor or trivial)*

* *long-term (that is, has lasted or is likely to last for at least 12 months or for the rest of the life of the person affected)*

* *adverse.*

Employers must cater for the needs of disabled employees by providing access to buildings as well as free movement around buildings and by providing training and development opportunities where appropriate. Employers

Theory into practice

Which of the following would be inappropriate questions for an interviewer to ask in an interview from an equal opportunities angle?

'Mrs Young, I see you are married. Do you intend to start a family soon?'

'What will happen when your children are ill or on school holidays? Who will look after them?'

'Your hair is very long, Mr Lang. If offered the job are you prepared to have it cut?'

'Mr Benjamin, as you are 55 do you think it's worth us employing you?'

'Miss Kiali, as a woman do you think you are capable of doing the job?

'Do you think your disability will affect your performance in the job?'

'How do you feel about working with people from a different ethnic background from yourself?'

'As a man, Mr Lazerus, you will be working in a department consisting mainly of women. Are you easily distracted?'

'Miss Gladstone, don't you think your skirt is rather short?'

must not discriminate against the disabled by limiting recruitment and selection opportunities in situations where disability does not impair an individual's ability to carry out work satisfactorily.

Ethics

In addition to the bare essentials of legal requirements outlined above, organisations need to consider the ethical side of their recruitment and selection policies. **Ethics** is about doing the right thing consistently rather than compromising sometimes. What this means in effect is that good employers will go beyond the letter of the law to provide excellent opportunities for all their employees.

2.2.7 Research

There are two main kinds of research: primary and secondary. You need to do both primary

and secondary research in order to produce an appropriate report for your unit assessment.

Primary research

Primary research involves finding out information by carrying out your own research rather than using someone else's existing research information.

The sorts of primary research that you will carry out will include the following:

* face-to-face discussions
* questionnaires
* interviews.

Face-to-face discussions

Face-to-face discussions are a direct way of finding out relevant information. For the purposes of your unit assessment, you should hold a discussion with a person from a human resource department. Discuss the following areas:

* a description of typical recruitment, selection, induction and motivation procedures
* typical paperwork which is used to support these processes (ask for examples)
* the importance of relevant legislation in determining how these processes should be carried out.

Discussing these processes first hand will give you a good insight into the running of this department. Important things to find out are:

* how is job analysis, specification and description carried out?
* what are the essential ingredients of a good job advertisement?
* what sort of criteria are used in the selection process?
* how can equal opportunities be assured in these processes?
* what sorts of characteristics is the company looking for in successful applicants?
* what are the key processes that you can learn from in order to inform your own work on recruitment and selection as well as induction and motivation?

Recruitment

How many new employees do you need to recruit each year?

Which of the following media do you use for advertising jobs?
- word of mouth
- job centres
- local newspapers
- national newspapers
- company websites
- specialist magazines and journals
- other (please state)

What are the main items that go into a job advertisement that you place in a newspaper e.g. title of job, location of job etc.?

Selection

Which of the following are most important in setting out criteria for selecting new employees?
- job description
- job analysis
- person specification
- job advertisement
- other (please state)

In the selection process are all candidates given the same set of questions to answer, or does this vary with the person being interviewed?

What other steps do you take to ensure equal opportunities in the selection process?

Induction

How long is the typical initial period / course for new employees?

What are the main ingredients of your initial induction course for new employees? Please list up to eight main ingredients.

What steps do you take to evaluate the effectiveness of your induction programmes?

Motivation

Does your company place more emphasis on financial or non-financial rewards to motivate employees? Please explain. Who is involved in the appraisal process for your employees? How often does appraisal take place?

FIGURE 2.13 *Example questions to ask a human resources department*

Questionnaires

Well-constructed questionnaires are an important way to find out information first hand. Working in a group, you may want to create a questionnaire to be used on a human resource department of one or more local companies:

* break down the questionnaire into relevant headings, e.g. recruitment, selection, induction and motivation

* create questions which are unambiguous and clear

* try to create questions that don't take too long to answer

* make sure that the answers to the questions are helpful to you in writing up your assignment report.

The table opposite gives examples of questions which could be included in your questionnaire.

The exemplar questions shown are only illustrative and you will probably be able to improve on them. You should note that some of the questions are closed while others are more open ended. For open-ended questions you should leave an appropriate amount of space for the person answering the questions.

The interview process

In carrying out the assignment for this piece of work, one of the most important pieces of primary research is the actual interview process. Your tutor will either allow you to choose a job role (manager, supervisor, IT specialist, customer-service worker or administrator) or will assign you one of these roles that you have to prepare documentation for a selection interview.

Preparing the paper work for the interview (job descriptions, advertisements, interview assessment checklists etc), and then conducting the interview will provide you with a lot of useful primary information and evidence to put in your report as follows:

* the paperwork that you created (e.g. job specifications, job descriptions, advertisements, application forms etc)

* A description of the process of recruitment, and selection. Set out in detail:
  * how the interviews were constructed
  * what happened in the interviews
  * what you were looking for in the successful candidate
  * why a particular candidate was chosen.
* A description of the induction and motivational activities that you have designed for the successful job applicant.

Secondary research

Carrying out secondary research involves using existing published sources. You can gather a lot of secondary research information that will be helpful in your assignment from the human resource departments of existing local companies. It always pays to have contacts, and perhaps your teacher can arrange for a group of students to interview someone from a local company (human resource manager) who will be willing to provide you with the relevant documentation.

Examples of material you might like to gather include:

Job advertisements used in the local business which are similar to those you are researching for your project e.g. manager, supervisor, IT specialist, administrator or customer-service employee.
A job analysis for one of these posts
A job specification
A job description
A job application form
A list of questions typically used at interviews
A set of criteria for selecting successful candidates
Any supplementary material setting out job selection procedures
Copies of induction materials used by the company
A programme for an induction activity
Details of financial rewards offered by the company
Details of non-financial rewards offered by the company

FIGURE 2.14 *Example documents and details worth collecting*

2.2.8 How to judge effectiveness

An important part of any report is an evaluation of the effectiveness of processes, procedures and actions that have been taken. You will therefore need to evaluate the effectiveness of the recruitment, selection, induction and motivational activities that you have prepared.

The assignment for this module asks you to assist in the recruitment and selection of an individual for a particular job role. You need to produce a report and supporting documentation of how you do this including a range of documents that you produce for the recruitment and selection process.

The tables in Figure 2.15 and Figure 2.16 will help you to evaluate the effectiveness of various documents that you produce for this purpose. By evaluating documents that are produced by organisations that you research during the module, and draft documents that you and classmates produce, you will be best placed to create effective documents to support your assignment work.

The issues that you need to consider include the following areas:

* Was the human-resource documentation fit for the purpose and likely to produce the desired end result?

* Did your procedures fit the legal framework within which human-resource activity is expected to take place?

* Was your research wide-ranging enough to inform the development and construction of your report? You were asked to carry out a range of both primary and secondary research to help you carry out your report. To what extent have you researched widely? Use the table in Figure 2.16 to record your results.

* Are there are any aspects of your chosen approaches that you would change if the activity were repeated or a different job role were chosen?

Was the job advertisement that you created attractive and informative? Perhaps you can create a short evaluation sheet to see what the people who applied for the job thought of the advertisement.	
Was the job description clear? Was it useful to job applicants in helping them to choose whether to apply for the job?	
Was the person specification clear? Did it cover the requirements of the job? How useful was it in enabling you to create a set of appropriate questions to ask at the interview?	
Was the job application form well structured? Was there enough room / space for the candidates to fill in the appropriate sections? Were there any important omissions that could have helped in choosing the best candidates to interview?	
Were there clear criteria for selecting the best candidates from the interview process?	
If you set tasks for the interviewees to do on the day, were they appropriate?	
How effectively was the interviewing carried out? Consider issues such as time given to each candidate, opportunity for candidates to ask questions, whether each candidate was given a fair opportunity to present their strengths and what they could offer the business etc.	
How effective were the materials provided for the induction activities for the selected candidate?	
How effective was the motivational package?	

FIGURE 2.15 *Evaluating the documents and activities you created*

Primary Research	
Have you carried out effective face-to-face discussions with a speaker from a human resources department? Did you make clear and relevant notes on these discussions?	
Have you constructed effective questionnaires for the human resources department of a local business? Have you used the results of the questionnaire to provide useful information for your report?	
Have you interviewed the group members who applied for the job role that was assigned to your group? Have you also found out what these group members thought about the quality of the paperwork provided, the interviewing process, and the equal opportunities aspects?	
Secondary Research	
Have you made good use of information available from an existing business such as human resource documentation?	

FIGURE 2.16 *Evaluating your research*

KNOWLEDGE CHECK

1 Explain how the responsibilities of a manager's role might differ from those of a supervisor. Give at least five examples to illustrate your answer.

2 Describe five major features that you would expect to find in a job description. What purposes are job descriptions likely to be used for?

3 How might a well-constructed person specification help with the recruitment process?

4 What suggestions would you make to someone filling in a job application which would help them to secure an interview for a post as a trainee market researcher?

5 What do you see as being the essential characteristics of a powerful CV (curriculum vitae)?

6 How does the creation of a shortlist help an organisation to select the best candidates for a particular interview?

7 Outline what you consider to be the most important aspects of positive body language that can be employed by an interviewer in the selection process.

8 What is a psychometric test? What is it used for?

9 Ramesh Pancholi is starting work in the Information Technology support department of a major retailing organisation. Describe five aspects of an induction programme for Ramesh which you regard to be essential. In each case describe the outcomes that you would expect Ramesh to achieve from that aspect of induction.

10 How might being attached to a coach help Ramesh to quickly build up appropriate skills required in the organisation? How will good coaching improve motivation?

11 Who or what is a mentor? What are the advantages to a) an employee, and b) an organisation from operating a mentoring scheme?

12 Describe a payment method that you think would motivate employees carrying out routine production work. Contrast this with a payment scheme that you feel would be a more effective motivator for a different type of worker.

13 How can payment schemes be complemented with non-financial incentives to increase motivation at work?

14 What do you understand by the term 'performance-related pay'? What do you see as being the benefits and drawbacks of operating such a scheme?

15 If you were going to introduce an appraisal scheme to a business or organisation that you are familiar with, what would be the key ingredients of the scheme? Justify your selection of different ingredients.

16 Give examples to show how individuals have basic needs, security needs, group needs, self-esteem needs, and self-fulfilment needs. Show how these needs could be met in a particular work setting.

17 Why do you think that Herzberg argued that what he termed 'dissatisfiers' could cause employee absenteeism, poor levels of output and other negative aspects of work behaviour? What did he see as the way of truly motivating employees?

18 How could you persuade candidates who are being interviewed for a particular post that your organisation will provide them with the sort of fulfilling work activities that will help to motivate them in the longer period?

19 Do you think that it is useful to distinguish between 'Theory X' and 'Theory Y' managers? How might an understanding of the differences help management training programmes?

20 Cite examples of legislation to combat discrimination which have benefited minority groups in the workforce. Explain how specific bits of legislation have benefited particular groups.

Resources

There is a wide range of textbooks aimed at Advanced Level Business candidates. The list below provides some useful examples which are appropriate for use at this level.

Textbooks

Arnold, J., *Managing Careers in the 21st century*, Pearson Books, London, 2003

Corfield, R., *Preparing Your Own CV*, The Times, London, 2003

Dransfield, R. et al *Business for the BTEC National Award*, Heinemann, Oxford, 2004

Dransfield, R., *Human Resource Management*, Heinemann, Oxford, 2002

Foot, M. and Hook, C., *Introducing Human Resource Management*, Longman, London, 2002

Jay, R., *The Successful Candidate: How to be the Person They Want to Employ*, Financial Times, London, 2004

Pettinger, R., *Mastering Employee Development*, Palgrave Master Series, Palgrave, Basingstoke, 2002

Yale, M., *The Ultimate CV Book*, Kogan Page, London, 2003

Websites

Some useful websites are listed below. These addresses are current at the time of writing. However, it needs to be recognised that new sites are being launched on the Internet on a regular basis and that older sites may change or disappear.

www.tt100.biz
www.bized.ac.uk
www.tutor2u.net
www.ft.com
www.aloa.co.uk

Journals and periodicals

Local and national newspapers, particularly the jobs advertisement pages and specialist pull-out sections on recruitment in particular sectors.

Videos

TV Choice provides a range of useful videos on recruitment, selection and motivation issues. For further details look at www.tvchoice.com

Other resources

If you or your tutor are able to undertake the following activities and collect the suggested resources, they will be helpful when following this unit:

* visits, work experience and part-time employment, providing opportunities for interviews and for collecting human resource documentation and data

* a talk by a human resource manager about the recruitment, selection, induction, and motivational programmes employed by his or her organisation

* briefings on current legislation produced by trades unions, employer organisations, and other interested parties

* case studies based on the recruitment and selection process

* role play activities, especially relating to recruitment, appraisal and induction for a particular job role.

UNIT 3

Understanding the business environment

This unit contains ten elements:

3.2.1   Business ownership

3.2.2   Sources of finance

3.2.3   Budgeting and budgetary control

3.2.4   Break-even analysis

3.2.5   Cash-flow forecasts and statements

3.2.6   Importance of accurate record-keeping and technology

3.2.7   Analysis of the current market position

3.2.8   Economic conditions and market conditions

3.2.9   Ethical, legal, social, political and environmental factors

3.2.10 Stakeholders

Introduction

Business decision-making is shaped by a range of factors that are internal to a business, such as the way that it is financed and the cash available to it, and external factors, such as changes in competition in the market place. This unit helps you to start to develop an understanding of these important internal and external factors.

The internal part of this unit involves examining factors which are inside a business that influence decision-making. As well as looking at financial

Well-known organisations are influenced by internal and external factors

factors you will also be expected to consider other internal factors such as the type of business ownership, internal stakeholders and the impact of technology on decision-making.

The external element requires an understanding of economic, social, legal, environmental, political and technological issues and external stakeholders who make up the broader business world in which any business operates. An important aspect of studying these external themes is that they need to be understood in theory and also in the context of the business within the case study pre-released before your examination.

How you will be assessed

This unit is assessed through a pre-released case study followed by an external assessment.

Throughout this unit there are a number of activities to reinforce your learning.

There are ten main aspects to consider:

* business ownership
* sources of finance
* budgeting and budgetary control
* break-even analysis
* cash-flow forecasts
* importance of accurate record-keeping and technology
* analysis of the current market position
* economic conditions and market conditions
* ethical, legal, social, political and environmental factors
* stakeholders.

3.2.1 Business ownership

Sole trader

The **sole trader** is the most common form of business ownership and is found in a wide range of activities, such as window cleaning, web page design, plumbing or electrical work. It is a business which is owned by one person although this business might employ several people.

No complicated paperwork is required to set up a sole trader business. Decisions can be made quickly, and close contact can be kept with customers and employees. All profits go to the sole trader, who also has the satisfaction of building up his or her own business.

However, there are disadvantages. As a sole trader you have to make all the decisions yourself, you may have to work long hours, you have to provide all the finance yourself and you do not have limited liability. This means that if the business does not do well and builds up a range of debts, the sole trader is personally liable for all of these debts which could mean selling personal assets in order to pay for them, such as a house, car and other personal possessions.

CASE STUDY
The creation of Pout cosmetics

Emily Cohen

When an afternoon of shopping for cosmetics in London failed to inspire her, Emily Cohen, the founder of Pout, started to think about setting up her own cosmetics business (although at the time she had no previous experience of running such an enterprise). Cohen felt that the existing make-up service offered by department stores was intimidating.

At the time (1999) Cohen had noticed a new trend for 'nail bars' was starting to develop in London after crossing over from the United States. It made her think that it would be possible to create a new non-intimidating make-up business in Britain. Her research at department stores showed that all the leading make-up brands such as Lancôme, Stila and Laura Mercier were international – she wanted to create a British brand.

Cohen wanted to create a new concept in which women of all ages would feel happy to play and experiment with lotions, tonics, creams and cosmetics. She saw potential in a beauty parlour where women could get make-up done, have eyebrows plucked or false eyelash extensions applied. Working with a friend and business partner, Chantal Laren, she developed a business plan and with a third partner, Anna Singh, they put in £50,000 each to set up the business. They remortgaged their homes to raise an additional £50,000, and an investor put £500,000 into the business.

This gave them £700,000 of capital to set up a flagship store. The following year they raised a further £1m of capital by selling 20% of Pout. The following year they raised an extra £1.5m from a small number of shareholders.

Pout's flagship store in Convent Garden was launched in June 2001. In the next three and a half years Pout opened up 95 outlets worldwide including boutiques in leading stores such as Harvey Nichols in Britain.

The concept of the brand is to make a woman feel sexy, whether she lives in America, Australia, Britain or Japan. In 2004, Pout's sales were £4.2m and are expected to reach £7.5m in 2005.

The Pout case study illustrates how a great business idea can be turned into a successful business. Of course, one of the most important decisions is to decide on the most appropriate type of business ownership.

1 **What was Emily's idea? Where did her idea come from and how did it evolve?**
2 **Discuss the challenges she faced in setting up the business and turning her idea into a reality.**

Key terms

Limited liability – if a business with limited liability goes **bankrupt** because it is unable to meet its debts, the owners will not be liable (responsible by law) to lose their possessions to pay the money that is owed. The maximum sum that they could lose is the sum that they have put into the business. Note that sole traders do not have limited liability.

Theory into practice

Looking at the case study of Pout cosmetics on this page, what would have been the advantages and disadvantages to Emily Cohen of setting up the business as a sole trader? Where does the balance of advantage / disadvantage lie?

	Initial capital	Area of expertise
Emily Cohen	£50,000	An expert in public relations
Chantal Laren	£50,000	12 years' experience in film production
Anna Singh	£50,000	A fashion retail background
Cohen + Laren remortgage their homes	£50,000	
Investor	£500,000	

Sources of capital for Pout

Partnership

An ordinary partnership can have between two and twenty partners. Professional partnerships may have more, for example, some modern accountancy partnerships are very large.

People in business partnerships can share skills and the workload, and it may be easier to raise the capital needed. For example, the partners that set up Pout had a range of expertise and were able to put up the initial capital using their own capital and by remortgaging their homes.

In a similar way, a group of vets is able to pool knowledge about different diseases and groups of animals, and two or three vets working together may be able to operate a 24-hour service. When one of the vets is ill or goes on holiday, the business can cope.

Partnerships are usually set up by writing out a deed of partnership which is witnessed by a solicitor. This sets out important details, such as how much each partner should put into the business, how the profits and losses will be shared, and the responsibilities of each partner.

Partnerships are particularly common in professional services, such as doctors, solicitors and accountants. A small business such as a corner shop may take the form of a husband and wife partnership.

The disadvantages of partnerships are that people may want to sever ties, ordinary partnerships do not have limited liability and partnerships can rarely borrow or raise large sums of capital. Business decisions may be more difficult to make (and slower) because of the need to consult all the partners, and there may be disagreements about how things should be

Theory into practice

Why might a partnership have been an appropriate format for Pout? What potential difficulties are there to running Pout as a partnership?

done. A further disadvantage is that profits will be shared.

Today, limited partnerships are allowed in large partnerships of accountants and solicitors so that individuals are protected against the liabilities of others in their business.

Companies

A **company** is set up to run a business. It has to be registered before it can start to operate, but once all the paperwork is completed and approved the company becomes recognised as a legal body.

The owners of a company are its shareholders. However, other individuals and businesses do not deal with the shareholders – they deal with the company. Shareholders put funds into the company by buying shares. New shares are often sold in face values of £1 per share but this is not always the case. Some shareholders will only have a few hundred pounds' worth of shares, whereas others may have thousands of pounds' worth. Directors are appointed to represent the interests of shareholders.

There are two types of company – private companies and public companies.

Private limited company

Private companies tend to be smaller than public ones and are often family businesses. There must be at least two shareholders but there is no maximum number. Shares in private companies cannot be traded on the Stock Exchange, and often shares can only be bought with the permission of the Board of Directors.

The **Board of Directors** is a committee set up to protect the interests of shareholders. The members of the board choose the managing director, who is responsible for the day-to-day running of the business. The rules of the business set out when shareholders' meetings will take place and the rights of shareholders.

Private companies may find it possible to raise more cash (by selling shares) than unlimited liability businesses. The shareholders can also have the protection of limited liability. The main disadvantages, compared with unlimited liability businesses, are that they have to share out profits among shareholders and they cannot make decisions quickly. They also cost more to set up, and accounting charges are likely to be higher. The real issue with private companies is that they cannot sell more shares to the general public by advertising them. This means that although they are limited companies they are not able to use the Stock Exchange to raise investment funds by selling stocks and shares, which is always likely to limit their size.

Public limited company

A public company has its shares bought and sold on the Stock Exchange. Companies can go to the expense of a 'full quotation' on the Stock Exchange.

The London Stock Exchange

The main advantage of selling shares through the Stock Exchange is that large amounts of capital can be raised very quickly. One disadvantage is that the original shareholders can lose control of a business if large quantities of shares are purchased as part of a 'takeover bid'. It is also costly to have shares quoted on the Stock Exchange.

In order to create a public company the directors must apply to the Stock Exchange Council, which will carefully check the accounts. A business wanting to 'go public' will then arrange for one of the merchant banks to handle the paperwork.

Being a public limited company gives a business access to huge sums of capital enabling it to expand and dominate its market. Examples of public limited companies are:

* top football clubs such as Tottenham Hotspur and Manchester United
* top retailers such as Tesco and Sainsbury's
* large high street banks such as Halifax.

Theory into practice

What would be the advantages and disadvantages to Pout of becoming a public limited company?

Co-operatives

Co-operatives are an alternative form of business organisation. The basic idea behind a co-operative is that people join together to make decisions, work and share profits. There are many different types of co-operative, the three most common are discussed below.

Producer co-operatives

Producer co-operatives are usually registered as companies 'limited by guarantee', which means that each member undertakes to fund any losses up to a certain amount. There are many types, for example a workers' co-operative is one that employs all or most of its members. In a workers' co-operative members:

CASE STUDY
Scenario

The growth of 'Exotic Fashions'

In 1986, Jenny Parsons set up her own dress shop selling her own designer dresses in a small shop in Nottingham. Over the years the shop gained in popularity and Jenny found that her dresses were being ordered by customers from all over the UK and even by other European customers.

As Jenny was designing the dresses and selling them herself this created a lot of work pressure. Of course, she was able to pay her own staff to make the dresses to her patterns which they did initially from a small workshop over the shop, but as orders built up Jenny hired a small factory unit on an industrial estate on the outskirts of Nottingham.

Jenny realised that she was overstretching herself but was fortunate in 1995 to meet Sylvia Burns who had just graduated from the London School of Fashion. Sylvia had recently come into an inheritance and was looking to branch out into business for herself. As part of a research project she had met Jenny, and she realised that they shared a common interest, had similar styles and a common flair for fashion. They decided to set up in partnership. With their combined capital they bought outright a new factory in Nottingham and

a large shop in central London. The London site was to become the focus for retailing operations.

Within months they had a backlog of orders from all over Europe and they realised that they would need to expand again. They decided to set up a private company in which they would be the major shareholders. However, they also needed extra share capital from a few wealthy individuals. They felt that the provision of limited liability would be a valuable protection. They were now dealing with some major buyers and if one failed to pay up they could end up with serious cash-flow problems. In addition, putting Ltd after the company name gave it extra status. They began trading as Exotic Fashions Ltd.

However, expansion seemed to demand further expansion. They had a chain of shops in ten major cities in the UK but there seemed to be a never-ending demand for their products. This time they decided to go public and sell shares on the Stock Exchange. They produced a prospectus for potential share buyers and on 15 August 2004 they went public. They sold £1 million of shares at £1 each. They could have sold over twice this number and on the day of issue share prices rocketed from £1.00 to £1.97.

1 Describe each of the forms of business ownership that Exotic Fashions has been through since 1986.
2 Why has it been necessary for Exotic Fashions to change its form of organisation?
3 What problems might Exotic Fashions have encountered when it changed from being a sole trader into a partnership?
4 What are the advantages of being a private company rather than a partnership?
5 What type of organisation is Exotic Fashions today? How would this be reflected in its name?
6 What are the disadvantages of having its current form of organisation?

* share responsibility for the success or failure of the business
* work together
* take decisions together
* share the profits.

Other examples of producer co-operatives are groups to grow tomatoes, to make furniture or to organise child-minding.

The main problem that co-operatives face is finance as they can find it difficult to raise the capital from banks and other bodies because they are not groups that primarily seek to make a profit. However, some co-operatives in recent years have raised finance by selling shares.

Marketing co-operatives

Marketing co-operatives are most frequently found in farming areas. The farmers set up a marketing board to be responsible for, among other things, grading, packing, distribution, advertising and selling their products.

Retail co-operatives

Retail co-operatives buy items for resale. A co-operative seeks to reward loyal customers and the community to which they belong rather than to make profit for a small group of shareholders.

The emphasis in a co-operative retailing society is on fair dealing. Co-ops in this country buy a greater percentage of products through fair trade than any other retailing organisation. For example, they pay a fair price to growers of cocoa (the raw material in chocolate manufacture) in countries of origin such as the Ivory Coast, in Africa. Co-ops also believe in paying fair wages to employees and getting involved in community activities such as giving money to local charities.

Theory into practice

Look at the following website: www.co-opunion.coop. Use the website address to make a list of the advantages of marketing co-operatives.

Not-for-profit or charity

The voluntary sector consists of organisations whose main aim is to provide a service rather than to make a profit. Many of these are charities, and they may use the services of volunteer staff, but most of their staff are employed on a professional basis.

In recent times new government legislation has been introduced to tighten up the rules about charities. The main aim of a charity should be to serve the wider community. Under new legislation, the objects of a charity which are recognised as being lawful are:

* the prevention and relief of poverty
* the advancement of education
* the advancement of religion
* the advancement of health
* social and community advancement
* the advancement of culture, arts and heritage
* the advancement of amateur sport
* the promotion of human rights, conflict resolution and reconciliation
* the advancement of environmental protection and improvement
* other purposes beneficial to the community.

An example of a charity is Childline, the free 24-hour helpline for children and young people in the UK. Children and young people can call the helpline on 0800 1111 about any problem, at any time – day or night.

Theory into practice

Find out about a charity. You may use literature delivered at home to help you or investigate using the World Wide Web. Identify the objectives for the charity and describe briefly how it operates.

Franchise

In the USA, about one half of all retail sales are made through firms operating under the franchise system. It is a form of business organisation that has become increasingly popular in the UK.

Franchising is the 'hiring out' or licensing of the use of 'good ideas and business systems to other companies'. A franchise grants permission to sell a product and trade under a certain name in a particular area. If I have a good idea, I can sell you a licence to trade and carry out a business using my idea in your area. The person taking out the franchise puts down a sum of money as capital and is issued with equipment by the franchising company. The firm selling the franchise is called the franchisor and a person paying for the franchise is called the franchisee. The franchisee usually has the sole right of operating in a particular area.

Examples of this type of trading include Pizza Hut, Dyno-Rod (in the plumbing business), Body Shop and Prontaprint. Recent franchises include Energie Fitness Clubs, Wiltshire Farm Foods, Green Clean and Contours Express. There are now numerous franchise opportunities in the health and fitness sector.

Where materials are an important part of the business, such as hamburgers or confectionery,

Think it over...

McDonald's makes a large percentage of its sales through franchise outlets particularly in the USA. McDonald's has its own training scheme for employees in the USA, and some of its training takes place at McDonald's University where one of the courses available for graduate study is a degree in 'hamburgerology'.

A well-known franchise opportunity

the franchisee must buy an agreed percentage of supplies from the franchisor, who makes a profit on these supplies as well as ensuring the quality of the final product. The franchisor also takes a percentage of the profits of the business, without having to risk capital or become involved in the day-to-day management.

CASE STUDY

The Countrywide Estate Agents Group

The Countrywide Estate Agents Group that includes Bairstow Eves and Mann & Co is in the process of setting up estate agency franchises. The Group feels that franchising will help it to increase its share of the estate agency market and franchising will also help it to distribute its products and services through a larger number of agency outlets.

The Group is offering franchises of its own brands, either to established businesses or on a start-up basis, to infill the existing owned network and extend network coverage. The lead brand being franchised in this way is Bairstow Eves as this is the Group's biggest brand with over 300 outlets across the UK.

The Bairstow Eves brand will provide the franchisee with the advantages of:

* the strength of a national network of agents
* independent ownership
* franchisees being able to run and operate their own business within the franchise package
* other benefits such as centralised work referrals, purchasing and supply systems, marketing materials, training and other activities.

1 Why do The Countrywide Estate Agents Group want to use franchises to expand their business?
2 What are the benefits for the franchisee?

The franchisee benefits from trading under a well-known name and enjoys a local monopoly. Training is usually arranged by the franchisor. The franchisee is his or her own boss and takes most of the profits.

Business decisions and objectives

The type of decisions a business makes is shaped by the objectives of the business. For example, there are substantial differences between the decisions made by 'not-for-profit' organisations like charities and voluntary organisations and those made by 'for-profit' organisations such as sole traders, partnerships and companies.

Decisions made by 'not-for-profit' organisations involve seeking to achieve wider social objectives such as to provide famine relief (Oxfam) or confidential support for children (Childline). Decisions prioritise the needy and socially disadvantaged.

By contrast, in 'for-profit' organisations, decisions favour the interests of shareholders – although customers and other groups are also highly important. Because of the relatively small scale of sole trader organisations and partnerships their objectives and decisions may also be relatively limited, e.g. focusing on decisions to provide products in relatively local areas. In contrast, the objectives and decisions made by a company (particularly a public company) can be far more ambitious because, with access to more funds, they are able to set their sights on 'being the market leader' or 'developing a major presence in international markets'.

Decisions that co-operatives make will be influenced by their members who may balance not-for-profit with profit-based objectives. As we shall see in the next section, for whatever type of organisations we study, the accessibility and amount of finance available will constrain objectives and thus the decisions that the organisation is able to make.

3.2.2 Sources of finance

Another important managerial responsibility is obtaining finance for a business or part of a business. Each year, individual managers will need to bid for funds. This involves putting

Theory into practice

Think of three examples of managers bidding for funds in an organisation.

forward a case for levels of funding that are appropriate to the activities that need to be carried out. For example:

* a course manager in a school or college will need funds to manage a course

* a production manager in a factory will need to bid for funds to buy new machinery, equipment, and to purchase stocks of raw materials.

Internal sources of finance

It is usual to think of finance coming from outside the business organisation, but it is possible to raise money from within the business. For example, one of the most frequent sources of finance is from retained profits. Most organisations only allocate a portion of their profits each year to their shareholders, and hold back some profits either to form reserves or to reinvest in the business. Initially, profits are subject to corporation tax, payable to the Inland Revenue. Corporation tax is a tax upon the profits of a business, taxed as a percentage of the final or net profits of a business. Then a proportion of what is left is distributed to shareholders as **dividends**. Finally, profits can be ploughed back into expansion.

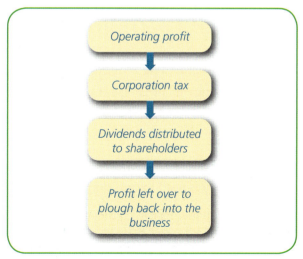

FIGURE 3.1 *Retained profits are a source of internal finance*

Another way of raising finance within the business organisation is to take money from working capital. **Working capital** is the 'liquid' capital required to run the business, comprising the short-term funds such as the money in the bank, money owed to the business by debtors and stocks less short-term debts such as money owed to suppliers or **creditors**. If the business reduces its stocks and calls in money owed to it from its **debtors**, it can, by having more liquid cash around, use such liquidity for investment, possibly in fixed assets such as machinery. Many organisations try to manage their short-term finances in a way that enables them to use these finances to benefit the business.

It is possible to raise finance within the business by selling off some of the fixed assets of the business. For example, it may be possible to sell off some property in order to raise finance. In recent years some organisations have injected finance into their activities, by selling off their property and then leasing it back. Sale and lease-back involves a firm selling its freehold property to an investment company and then leasing it back over a long period of time. This releases funds for other purposes.

At an organisation-wide level financial managers will have responsibility for securing funds for the business to enable it to operate well.

External sources of finance

Organisations have available to them a number of sources of external finance such as:

* individuals
* organisations providing venture capital
* banks and other financial institutions
* suppliers
* government.

In deciding what types of finance to draw on, financial managers need to consider:

* the length of time for which they need the finance
* the cost of raising the finance in one way rather than another.

Owner's capital

Owner's capital is raised from individual owners of a business such as partners or shareholders. This type of capital is raised when starting up a new business venture or when expanding a business.

When issuing shares, careful consideration needs to be given to the need to pay a dividend (share of the profit) to shareholders. The amount of dividend paid is decided on by the Board of Directors of the organisation. One advantage of raising finance from shareholders is that the organisation is not legally obliged to pay a set return each year (as for example, it has to do with loans). However, if the company keeps asking shareholders for more funds they will lose confidence in the company.

Venture capital

Venture capital companies such as 3i provide finance in return for an equity (ordinary) shareholding in the company and an element of control. This is a quick and relatively cheap way for a new business to raise capital but it may not want to lose some control to the venture capitalist.

Borrowing

The charge made for borrowing money from the bank and other financial institutions is termed interest.

Bank loans

Bank loans are taken out for a fixed period, and repayments are made either in instalments or in full at the end of the term. Banks generally provide funds on a short-to-medium term basis, with relatively few loans over more than ten years' duration. As well as the interest payment there may be an arrangement fee.

Debentures

Debentures are certificates issued by companies acknowledging their debt. The debt is paid at a fixed rate of interest and the certificate sets out the terms of repayment at the end of the period of debt. Debentures can usually be traded on the Stock Exchange.

Bank overdrafts

Bank overdrafts are the most frequently used form of short-term bank finance and they are used to ease

The charges for exceeding your arranged overdraft limit are very high. Not only will you pay a much higher rate of interest but you will also be charged for the bank writing to you. Don't get into this position.

cash-flow problems. Arrangements are made between the customer and the bank to include an agreed limit on an account beyond which the customer will not draw. Interest is calculated on the level of the overdraft on a daily basis. Often a bank will make a special charge for arranging an overdraft. A bank can take away the customer's right to use an overdraft if they think the position is being abused.

Hire purchase

Hire purchase (HP) allows a business to use an asset, for example, a photocopier or computer, without having to find the money immediately. A finance house buys the asset from the supplier and retains ownership of it during the period of the hire-purchase agreement. The business pays a deposit and then further payments to the finance house, as set out in the agreement. At the end of the HP agreement, ownership of the asset is passed to the business. The repayments made by the business are in excess of the cash price of the item. The difference is the finance charge to the finance house.

Leasing

Leasing an asset provides similar benefits to hire purchase, in that a leasing agreement with a finance house (lessor) allows the business (lessee) to use an asset without having to buy it outright. However, leasing does not give an automatic right to eventual ownership of the asset. It is a very popular form of finance for company vehicles, office equipment and factory machinery.

The lessee benefits from not having to put up large sums of capital to be able to use the asset and they can exchange the asset for a more modern version when technology changes. The lessor is also usually responsible for the maintenance of the item.

Mortgages

A commercial mortgage is a loan secured on land and buildings and can either be used to finance

the purchase of the property or to provide security for a loan applied to some other purpose. It is a long-term financing arrangement typically from 10 to 30 years. Repayments are made including a considerable interest rate.

Suppliers

Suppliers are a valuable source of finance for many businesses. Many businesses buy raw materials and finished goods from suppliers. Typically they will buy these goods on credit and only pay for them later (for example 30 days later). The business is thus effectively receiving finance for the period they are given credit for. Just as the business may give credit to its own customers, the firm may be able to negotiate credit terms with its suppliers. Credit terms are typically 30 days from date of supply or the end of the month following a delivery, i.e. 30 to 60 days. This essentially means that for a period of time a business has the use of goods and services 'free', which is essentially a form of short-term borrowing until they are paid for.

Factoring

A debtor is an individual or business that owes you money – for example, because you have supplied them with goods which they have not paid for yet.

When a business is owed money by its debtors but has to wait for them to pay and requires cash urgently it can sell off part or all of this debt for collection by a third party – a factoring company. The factoring company will buy the debts of the business and provide immediate cash for their urgent needs.

Government loans

Businesses can acquire loans and grants from the government for various purposes depending on circumstances. These grants and loans may come from European Union sources, UK national government or from local government. National Lottery funds can be obtained in some circumstances. Typical purposes might be funds for helping with government schemes such as Modern Apprenticeships and job creation schemes. Other grants may be for building development, and machinery purchase particularly in areas of economic decline.

CASE STUDY

The Countryside Stewardship Scheme

The ancient craft of dry stone walling is thriving in 21st-century England, thanks in part to the Countryside Stewardship Scheme. The Countryside Stewardship Scheme offers payments to farmers and land managers to improve the natural beauty and diversity of the countryside under ten-year agreements. Payments range from £20 to £555 per hectare depending on the type of land management agreed.

The scheme has helped to protect an important countryside feature and provide a better habitat for valuable wildlife as well as a better habitat for plants. Areas under Stewardship have seen a marked increase in previously declining bird species, including the stone curlew, cirl bunting, bittern and lapwing. Around 13,500 miles of grass margins have been established, almost 9,000 miles of hedgerows have been restored or planted and over 800 miles of permissive footpaths have been provided for the enjoyment of the public. At the same time it has helped to maintain and promote a valuable countryside skill.

1 What was the purpose of the Countryside Stewardship Scheme?
2 How has it influenced the actions of farmers?

Theory into practice

You are the financial manager of an organisation that is opening a petrol station on a new city by-pass. Match the organisation's financial needs with the possible sources of finance available:

Needs:

* Land and buildings: £500,000
* Shopfittings: £50,000
* Petrol pumps: £100,000
* Stocks of petrol and retail items: £75,000
* Computer terminal: £6,000
* First few weeks wages: £8,000

Possible sources of finance:

* Hire purchase or leasing
* Bank loan for two years
* Commercial mortgage
* Bank overdraft
* Trade credit
* Owners capital: £100,000

Theory into practice

Imagine you are a financial manager in the following organisations. What type of finance would you use in each case?

1 A school wishes to replace its existing photocopier with a more elaborate version which they want to pay for over a period of time.

2 The Queen's Medical Centre in Nottingham wishes to build a new hospital wing on vacant land close to its existing site.

3 Prakesh Patel needs a new computer system costing £7,500 for his business. Identify two ways of financing the purchase and state the circumstances in which either would be most appropriate.

4 A medium-sized company wants to expand its factory building. The cost will be £1m. Identify two ways of financing the expansion and state the circumstance in which either would be more appropriate.

5 A small firm is temporarily having problems with its cash flow. Identify two ways of financing any shortfall it might currently have in its cash requirements and state the circumstances in which either would be more appropriate.

Short-term vs long-term sources of finance

Organisations may need long-term, medium-term or short-term finance for the following reasons:

* Long-term finance   e.g. to purchase other businesses, or buildings

* Medium-term finance e.g. to update machinery, equipment and fittings, motor vehicles

* Short-term finance   e.g. to buy new stocks, to pay wages etc

An organisation needs to match the sort of finance they require to the time period they require it for. For example, in the short term they may simply want to pay wages or buy new stocks. In order to do this they will probably raise money within the organisation, perhaps from their debtors, so as to have more cash to pay outstanding debts, pay wages and make other pressing payments.

Alternatively, they may consider some form of factoring.

An organisation might need medium-term finance to buy machinery. A suitable form of finance for this might be a loan of some description. Finally, for longer-term finance such as buying a building they may seek to take out a mortgage or possibly increase their shareholding. It would be inappropriate and possibly damaging for a business to use the wrong source of finance for the wrong purpose. For example, taking out a long-term loan to meet debts in the short-term would simply push up the costs of the business because they would have to make interest payments on the borrowing), even if it did provide them with cash in the short period.

Type of ownership and business decisions

Different forms of finance are used by different types of organisations, and some businesses may find it difficult to raise finance, whereas for others,

Long-term finance is required for property ownership

it might be much more straightforward. Sole traders, for example, cannot issue shares and are likely to have more difficulty raising finance than long-established large companies, with untarnished reputations and a good market position.

Whereas a large public limited business may simply issue more shares, a sole trader, as a much smaller business, has fewer options. They may want to change their ownership structure by becoming a partnership, but that might not be a good option for them, and so they would have to think carefully about whether they approach a bank, attempt to factor some of their debts or go and discuss their situation with an enterprise agency.

3.2.3 Budgeting and budgetary control

Budgets help businesses to plan, set targets and control expenditure. To understand how budgets are used you need to know what they are, how they work and their particular purposes. You will need to be able to identify and interpret variance and explain the benefits of budgeting to businesses.

Financial planning involves defining objectives and then developing ways to achieve them. To be able to do this, a financial manager must have a realistic understanding of what is happening and what is likely to happen within the organisation, for example, when is money going to come in, what is it needed for and would it be possible to use some of it for expansion and development? In the 'money-go-round' (see Figure 3.2), capital and sales revenue come into a business, but is there enough left over, after paying all the costs, for expansion and development?

Looking into their future helps all organisations to plan their activities so that what they anticipate and want to happen can actually happen. This process of financial planning is known as budgeting. It is considered to be a system of **responsibility accounting** because it puts a duty on budgeted areas to perform in a way that has been outlined for them, and its success will depend upon the quality of information provided. Businesses that do not budget may not be pleased when they view their

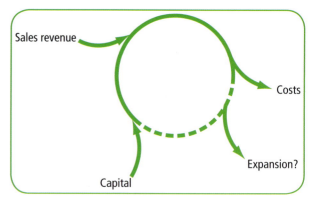

FIGURE 3.2 *The money-go-round*

final accounts. Budgeting helps the financial manager to develop an understanding of how the business is likely to perform in the future.

We all budget to a greater or lesser extent. Our short-term budget may relate to how we are going to get through the coming week and do all the things we want to do. Our slightly longer-term budget may involve being able to afford Christmas presents in two months' time. Our longest-term budget could involve the planning necessary to afford the car tax, MOT and motor insurance, which all fall due in ten months from now, or planning when we can afford in the longer term to replace the car.

CASE STUDY
Managing student finances
One of the big problems for most students today is how to manage their finances effectively. The need to spread their income and student loan across all of their financial responsibilities calls upon students to be both sensible and resourceful. Students have many different financial commitments and yet for many of them, it is the first time away from home, in a different environment and in a situation where they have to manage money for the first time. Some of the consequences of not managing their money can be quite serious.

1 Why is it important for students to budget?
2 What practical steps could they take to budget?

Theory into practice

Identify a range of activities in which you participate that you think could be helped by some form of budgeting. For example, these may include your personal finances or a club responsibility. Explain how in each instance.

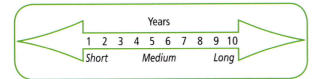

FIGURE 3.3 *Budgetary periods*

A budget is a financial plan developed for the future. Many businesses appoint a budget controller whose sole task is to co-ordinate budgetary activities. A short-term budget would be for up to one year, a medium-term budget would be for anything from one year to five years, and a budget for a longer period than this would be a long-term budget (see Figure 3.3).

Wherever budgeting takes place, it is important to draw upon the collective experience of people throughout the business. A budgeting team might consist of representatives from various areas of activity. The team will consider the objectives of the budgeting process, obtain and provide relevant information, make decisions, prepare budgets and then use these budgets to help to control the business.

Budgeting provides a valuable benchmark against which to measure and judge the actual performance of key areas of business activity. There are many benefits of budgeting:

* It helps to predict what the organisation thinks will happen. Given the experience within the organisation, budgets help to show what is likely to take place in the future.

* Budgets create opportunities to appraise alternative courses of action. Information created for budgeting purposes forms the basis of decisions that have to be taken. The research necessary for budgeting will look at alternative ways of achieving the organisation's objectives.

* Budgets set targets. If communicated to people throughout the organisation, the budgets will help them to work towards the targets that have been set.

* They help to monitor and control performance. This can be done by studying actual results, comparing these to budgeted results and then finding out why differences (known as **variances***) may have occurred. Sometimes variances are bad, while at other times they may be good. Whatever the causes of the variances, they are a useful starting point for dealing with issues within the business.

* Budgets are fundamental to the process of **business planning**. They provide a series of quantitative guidelines that can be used for co-ordination and then followed in order to achieve the organisation's business objectives.

* They can be used as a source of **motivation**. As part of the consultation process, budgets help to keep people involved. They also help to ensure that the aims and objectives of the individual are the same as those of the organisation.

* Budgets are a form of communication. They enable employees from across the organisation to be aware of performance expectations with regard to their individual work area.

Budgeting may also have some useful spin-offs. Every year the business is reviewed and this gives members of the various departments a better understanding of the working of the organisation as a whole. In fact, by participating in the budgetary process they feel their experience is contributing to policy decisions.

It also increases co-operation between departments and lowers departmental barriers. In this way, members of one department can become aware of the difficulties facing another department.

By being involved in the budgetary process, non-accountants also appreciate the importance of costs.

In reality, budgeting may take place in almost all parts of an organisation. Budgeting should also be viewed as something that is going on all the time and as a source of useful information and guidance for managers.

The process of budget setting

The process of setting budgets has to be seen within the context of the longer-term objectives and strategies at the highest level of management of any organisation. The administration of the budgeting process will usually be the responsibility of the accounts department. Many organisations set up a budget committee to oversee the process.

The budgetary process is usually governed by a formal budget timetable. This helps to link the budget in with all other aspects of business planning (see Figure 3.4).

Spreadsheets are an effective 'what-if' tool that are often used to help within the budgeting process.

Setting up a system of 'responsibility accounting' such as budgeting involves breaking down an organisation into a series of 'control centres'. Each individual manager then has the responsibility for managing the budget relating to his or her particular control centre.

Budgetary reports, therefore, reflect the assigned responsibility at each level of the organisation. As all organisations have a structure of control, it is important the budgetary system fits around this. The reports should be designed to reflect the different levels within the organisation and the responsibilities of each of the managers concerned.

If the budgeting process reflects the different levels of control, managers will be kept informed not just of their own performance but also of that of other budget holders for whom they are responsible. They will also know that managers above them will be assessing their performance. This system can be reviewed regularly at meetings attended by all the individual managers concerned.

Budget timetable for year 1 April 2004 to 31 March 2005

Date	Narrative	Responsibility
1 Sept	Board of directors to review long-term objectives and strategies and specify short-term goals for the year	Directors
22 Sept	Budget guidelines and standard forms issued to line managers	Accounts
6 Oct	Actual results for year are issued to line management so that comparisons can be made with current budget and last year's actual results	Accounts
20 Oct	Budget submissions are made to the management accountant	Line management
27 Oct	First draft of the master budget is issued	Accounts
3 Nov	First draft of the budget is reviewed for results and consistency – line managers to justify their submissions	MD and individual directors
8 Nov	New assumptions and guidelines issued to line management	Accounts
12 Nov	Budgets revised and resubmitted	Line management
22 Nov	Second draft of master budget issued	Accounts
29 Nov	Final review of the draft budget	MD and Financial director
1 Dec	Final amendments	Accounts
10 Dec	Submission to the board for their approval	Financial director

FIGURE 3.4 *A budget timetable*

Theory into practice

Find out more about the budgeting process within your school or college. For example, how are budgets set, what processes take place and who are the budget holders? What happens if budget holders overspend?

Budget plan

Working from one year to another assumes that changes can be predicted and that the business is working in a linear way, which does not always realistically reflect business activity. Parts of the business may expand more quickly than others and this can be limited by the system of historic budgeting (see page 119). The result is that historic budgeting can carry over mistakes from one year to another. However, even though it does mechanise the budgeting process, it is quickly applied and does not require extensive consultation with budget heads.

Zero budgeting (see page 119) needs to be justified and this helps to minimise expenditure. It allows the person supervising the budgetary system to spring clean the budgets every year and start from scratch so that budget heads have to justify all new items of expenditure. This provides everybody with a good understanding of changes within the business but can be time consuming and difficult for those who find some of these justifications complex.

The overall budget, as a plan, will have real value only if the performance levels set through the budget are realistic. Budgets based upon ideal conditions are unlikely to be met and will result in departments failing to meet their targets. For example, the sales department may fail to achieve their sales budget, which may result in goods remaining unsold. Budgets can be motivating only if they are pitched at a realistic level.

There are two approaches to budget setting. The top-down approach involves senior managers specifying what the best performance indicators are for the business across all departments and budgeted areas. The bottom-up approach builds up the organisational budget on the basis of the submissions of individual line managers and supervisors, based upon their own views of their requirements. In practice most organisations use a mixture of both methods (see Figure 3.5).

Budget setting should be based upon realistic predictions of future sales and costs. Many organisations base future predictions solely on past figures, with adjustments for forecast growth

and inflation rates. Although the main advantage of this approach is that budgets are based upon actual data, future conditions may not mirror past ones.

One of the dangers of budgeting is that, if actual results are dramatically different from the budgeting ones, the process could lose its credibility as a means of control. Following a budget too rigidly may also restrict a business's activities. For example, if the budget for entertainment has been exceeded and subsequent visiting customers are not treated with the usual hospitality, orders may be lost. On the other hand, if managers realise that towards the end of the year a department has underspent, they may decide to go on a spending spree.

Budgeting is a routine annual event for many different types of organisations. The process may start in the middle of the financial year, with a revision of the current year's budget and with first drafts of the budget for the coming year. Some organisations plan further ahead with an outline plan for three to five years.

Variance analysis

An essential feature of the budgetary control system is the feedback of actual results. The process of measuring the difference between budgeted (intended) and actual outcomes is known as variance analysis. Wherever actual differs from budgeted performance a variance takes place. Variance analysis makes it possible to detect problems. Reasons can be sought for variances and speedy action can be taken to improve performance.

Variances are recorded as being either adverse (A) or favourable (F), depending upon whether actual expenditure is more or less than budget. For example, if actual expenditure is less than budgeted expenditure, the variance would be favourable; i.e. actual expenditure

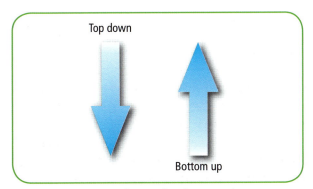

FIGURE 3.5 *Approaches to budget setting*

Theory into practice

If the wages of a business over a half year are £15,000 and the budgeted amount for wages was £12,000, is this an adverse or favourable situation? What decisions might managers take based upon this situation?

could be £10,000 and if this is less than budgeted expenditure of £12,000, then there is a favourable variance. On the other hand, if actual expenditure is more than budgeted expenditure, the variance is adverse; i.e. if actual expenditure was £25,000 and budgeted was £15,000, then there would be a £10,000 adverse variance.

Variances may arise for a number of reasons. These include:

* *Random deviations* which are uncontrollable. As we saw above, these are outside the control of individual managers.

* *An incorrectly-set budget.* This may require further research and management action.

* *Failure to meet an agreed budget.* This would be because a manager has failed to meet the appropriate figures and deadlines.

CASE STUDY

Scenario

Wayne's Workout Warehouse produces high quality sportswear and equipment. The shop has recently expanded and has introduced two new lines: trampolines and compact multi-gyms. Look at the sales budget below.

	Nov	Dec	Jan	Feb	Mar	Apr
Trampoline	£1,140	£2,185	£1,615	£760	£1,045	£1,235
Compact multi-gym	£1,575	£3,500	£2,625	£875	£1,750	£2,100
Total	£2,715	£5,685	£4,240	£1,635	£2,795	£3,335

1 Where could the sales manager get information on which to base these expected sales revenues?

2 Trampolines are sold at a price of £95 each. How many does the firm plan to sell in December and January? Would reducing the price of the trampoline automatically cut the firm's sales revenue?

3 Compact multi-gyms are £175 each. What would the firm's planned revenue be in April if they sell all their Compact multi-gyms at £185 each?

4 Assume the cost of producing each trampoline is £70. How many trampolines would Wayne need to sell in a month to earn a profit of £500 on this product?

Theory into practice

Calculate the variances and complete your own table stating in the 'comment' column whether the variance is favourable or adverse.

January budget

	Budget	Actual	Variance	Comment
Sales revenue	150	180		
Less material costs	(75)	(90)		
Less labour	(15)	(21)		
Gross profit	60	69		
Less overheads	(20)	(22)		
Net profit	40	47		

CASE STUDY

Scenario

Tupps Curtains is a business based in the East Midlands. They manufacture curtains and blinds for domestic use. Their main fabric supplier is a small, local, family-run firm which they have been dealing with for many years. This supplier has decided to retire and sell the premises. The management team has reviewed their budget for December and has held a management meeting to discuss any variances in the budget. Their findings were that:

- sales have dropped by 15 per cent compared to what was predicted in the budget
- labour costs have increased by 5 per cent
- material costs have fallen by 20 per cent.

You are hired as a consultant to analyse the findings at a budget meeting.

1 **Explain why the variances have occurred.**
2 **What suggestions would you make to avoid further adverse variances?**
3 **Explain the importance of variance analysis.**

Historic budgeting

Historic budgeting occurs where the year's targets for costs and revenues are based upon last year's budget. For example, it should be possible to forecast next year's costs and revenues by looking backwards at previous costs and revenues and analysing how they have changed from year to year.

Zero budgeting

Zero budgeting is where the budget is initially set at zero and then each department has to justify their spending and negotiate funds for the oncoming year. This is an important way for departments to calculate and then negotiate their spending based upon where they expect to be over the next accounting period. It helps managers to plan ahead and gives them the freedom not to base their spending upon previous years, but to seek and then justify other avenues in which their areas are developing.

Budgeting contexts

There are many different forms of budget ranging from those for sales and production, through to raw materials budgets, labour budgets, overhead budgets, capital budgets and cash budgets. The reason for this is that almost every activity within a business organisation can be budgeted for. Budgets are simple to prepare using appropriate information. They do not involve extensive analysis, but they do involve logically putting the right information in an appropriate format.

Sales budget

The purpose of the sales budget is to forecast sales and sales **turnover** for a forecast period. An example of a sales budget is shown below in Figure 3.6, where an organisation intends to sell 1,000 units per month for the next six months (January–June) at a selling price of £50.

Theory into practice

Construct a sales budget for a six-month period. For January to March sales are likely to be 1,000 units per month and for April to June 1,500 units. The selling price is to be £85 per unit.

	Jan	Feb	Mar	Apr	May	Jun	Total
Forecast sales	1,000	1,000	1,000	1,000	1,000	1,000	6,000
Selling price	£50	£50	£50	£50	£50	£50	£50
Sales turnover	£50,000	£50,000	£50,000	£50,000	£50,000	£50,000	£300,000

FIGURE 3.6 *Example of a sales budget*

Direct labour budget

A direct labour budget might be as follows:

An organisation intends to make 9,000 cabinets over a year. It takes 3 labour hours to make a cabinet and the wage rate per hour is £10. The direct labour budget would be:

Forecast production units	9,000
Direct labour hours per cabinet	3
Total direct labour hours	27,000
Wage rate per hour	£10
Total wages	£270,000

The direct labour budget would, therefore, have forecast the cost of labour over the period of a year.

Capital budget

A capital budget might be as follows:

A forecast for a business shows that over six months £50,000 is needed for a CNC machine, £20,000 for two motor vans, £5,500 for a new building extension, £40,000 for improving the production line and £9,500 for installing a new air-conditioning system.

The capital budget (see Figure 3.7) quickly provides an indication that £125,000 is needed for capital purchases for the six months and then itemises the amounts required month by month.

Potential problems with the budgetary process

Budgetary and control systems vary from one organisation to another. They are found both in the private sector and the public sector, and in all sorts of organisations from the very small to the very large. Given the different aims of organisations, budgetary systems reflect the context in which they are put to use. There are, however, certain problems associated with budgeting processes that have to be recognised.

First, reliance upon budgeting and its processes is no substitute for good management. Budgeting should simply be viewed as one tool among many for managers to use. If forecasting is poor or inadequate allowances are made, the process may create unnecessary pressure upon managers to perform in a particular way. This may be stressful and cause antagonism and resentment within the organisation.

The creation of rigid financial plans that are 'cast in stone' may cause inertia in certain parts of a business and reduce its ability to adapt to change. Budgets may also not reflect the realities of the business environment and act simply as a straitjacket upon the performance of managers and decision-makers. It has also been argued that delays and time lags can make it difficult to compare budgeted and actual results.

3.2.4 Break-even analysis

Before looking at **break-even analysis** we need a basic understanding of costs. One method of classifying costs is according to changes in output. This identifies costs as either fixed or variable.

Fixed costs

Fixed costs are costs that do not increase as total output increases. For example, if an organisation

	Jan	Feb	Mar	Apr	May	Jun	Total
CNC machine				£50,000			£50,000
Motor vans	£20,000						£20,000
Building extension			£5,500				£5,500
Production line			£40,000				£40,000
Air-conditioning						£9,500	£9,500
Total	£20,000	–	£45,500	£50,000	–	£9,500	£125,000

FIGURE 3.7 *Example of a capital budget*

has the capacity needed it might increase its production from 25,000 units to 30,000 units. However, its fixed costs such as rent, rates, heating and lighting will be the same, since they also had to be paid when the organisation was producting 25,000 units.

Variable costs

In contrast, **variable costs** are those costs that increase as total output increases because more inputs need to be employed in order to increase outputs. For example, if you produce more items you need more raw materials.

Marginal costing

Marginal costing is a commonly employed technique that uses costs to forecast profits from the production and sales levels expected in future periods. The benefit of marginal costing over other costing methods is that it overcomes the problem of allocating fixed costs – only variable costs are allocated as we shall see.

> **Key point**
>
> **Contribution** = Selling price per unit less variable costs per unit.

Marginal costing is particularly useful for making short-term decisions – for example, helping to set the selling price of a product, or deciding whether or not to accept an order. It might also help an organisation to decide whether to buy in a component or whether to produce it themselves.

The difference between an item's selling price and the variable costs needed to produce that item is known as **contribution**. By producing and selling enough units to produce a total contribution that is in excess of fixed costs, an organisation will make a profit.

For example, Penzance Toys Ltd manufactures plastic train sets for young children. They anticipate that next year they will sell 8,000 units at £12 per unit. Their variable costs are £5 per unit and their fixed costs are £9,000. From the above formula we can deduce that the contribution is £12 minus £5, which is £7 per unit. Therefore, for each unit made, £7 will go towards paying the fixed costs as shown in the figures and the table below.

	(£)
Sales revenue (8,000 × £12)	96,000
Less: Marginal costs (8,000 × £5)	40,000
Total contribution	56,000
Less: Fixed costs	9,000
Net profit	47,000

Units of production	Fixed costs (£)	Variable costs (£)	Total costs (£)	Revenue (£)	Profit / loss (£)
1,000	9,000	5,000	14,000	12,000	(2,000)
2,000	9,000	10,000	19,000	24,000	5,000
3,000	9,000	15,000	24,000	36,000	12,000
4,000	9,000	20,000	29,000	48,000	19,000
5,000	9,000	25,000	34,000	60,000	26,000
6,000	9,000	30,000	39,000	72,000	33,000
7,000	9,000	35,000	44,000	84,000	40,000
8,000	9,000	40,000	49,000	96,000	47,000
9,000	9,000	45,000	54,000	108,000	54,000
10,000	9,000	50,000	59,000	120,000	61,000

Theory into practice

Rovers Medallions Ltd produce a standard size trophy for sports shops and clubs. They hope to sell 2,000 trophies next year at £9 per unit. Their variable costs are £5 per unit and their fixed costs are £4,000.

Draw up a profit statement to show how much profit they will make in the year. Also, construct a table to show how much profit they will make at each 500 units of production up to 3,000 units.

Break-even point

The concept of break-even is a development from the principles of marginal costing. **Breaking even** is the unique point at which an organisation neither makes profit or loss. If sales go beyond the break-even point, profits are made, and if they are below the break-even point, losses are made. In marginal costing terms, it is the point at which the contribution equals the fixed costs.

Key point

The **break-even point** is the point at which sales levels are high enough not to make a loss, but not high enough to make a profit.

To calculate the break-even point there are two stages:

1 Calculate the unit contribution (selling price less variable cost per unit)

2 Divide the fixed costs by the unit contribution:

$$\text{Break-even point} = \frac{\text{Fixed costs}}{\text{Unit contribution}}$$

For example, in Penzance Toys Ltd the contribution per unit is £7 and the fixed costs are £9,000. The break-even point would therefore be:

$$\frac{9,000}{7} = 1,286 \text{ units (to nearest unit)}$$

Sales value at break-even point

The **sales value** at the break-even point can be calculated by multiplying the number of units by the selling price per unit. For Penzance Toys this would be:

$$1,286 \times £12 = £15,432$$

Penzance Toys has covered their costs (fixed and variable) and broken even with a sales value of £15,432. Anything sold in excess of this will provide them with profits.

Profit target

If an organisation has a profit target or selected operating point to aim at, break-even analysis can be used to calculate the number of units that need to be sold and the value of sales required to achieve that target.

For example, if Penzance Toys wanted to achieve a target of £15,000 profit. By adding this £15,000 to the fixed costs and dividing by the contribution, the number of units can be found that need to be sold to meet this target:

$$\frac{£9,000 + £15,000}{7} = 3,429 \text{ units (to nearest unit)}$$

Margin of safety

The difference between the break-even point and the selected level of activity designed to achieve the profit target is known as the **margin of safety**.

Theory into practice

B Hive Beehives Ltd is a small business selling hives to local keepers. Each hive is sold for £25. Fixed costs are £18,000 and variable costs are £13 per unit. The company wishes to achieve a profit of £18,000. Calculate the break-even point in both units and sales value. Calculate both the units and sales value necessary to achieve the selected operating profit.

Break-even charts

A break-even chart can be used to show changes in the relationship between costs, production volumes and various levels of sales activity. The following procedure should be followed to construct a break-even chart:

* label the horizontal axis for units of production and sales

* label the vertical axis to represent the values of sales and costs

* plot fixed costs – fixed costs will remain the same over all levels of production, so plot this as a straight line parallel to the horizontal axis

* plot the total costs (variable and fixed costs) – this will be a line rising from where the fixed cost line touches the vertical axis and is plotted by calculating the total costs at two or three random levels of production

* sales are then plotted by taking two or three random levels of turnover – the line will rise from the intersection of the two axes.

The break-even point will be where the total cost line and the sales line intersect. The area to the left of the break-even point between the sales and total cost lines will represent losses and the area to the right of the break-even point between these lines will represent profit.

For example, Eddie Bowen plans to set up a small restaurant. In doing so he knows he will immediately incur annual fixed costs of £10,000. He is concerned about how many meals he will have to sell to break even. Extensive market research indicates a typical customer will pay £8 for a meal, and Eddie knows that variable costs (such as cooking ingredients and the costs of serving customers) will amount to about £3. Eddie has set himself a profit target of £14,000 for the first year of operation. Eddie needs to work out the number of meals he has to sell and find out his margin of safety.

Eddie's *unit contribution* is:

£8 – £3 (selling price – variable cost)

= £5 per meal

His *break-even* point in units will be:

£10,000 (Fixed costs) divided by £5 unit contribution = 2,000 meals

The *sales value* of the meals will be:

2,000 meals × £8 (Selling price) = £16,000

His *profit target* will be achieved by:

$$\frac{£10,000 \text{ (Fixed costs)} + £14,000 \text{ (Profit Target)}}{£5 \text{ (Unit contribution)}} = 4,800 \text{ meals}$$

The *margin of safety* will be the difference between the selected level of activity and the break-even point. It will be between 4,800 meals with a turnover of £38,400 and 2,000 meals with a turnover of £16,000.

The three random levels of variable costs and sales chosen for the purpose of plotting the break-even chart are at 1,000 meals, 3,000 meals and 5,000 meals. They are:

	1,000 meals	3,000 meals	5,000 meals
Variable costs (£3 per meal)	£3,000	£9,000	£15,000
Fixed costs	£10,000	£10,000	£10,000
Total costs	£13,000	£19,000	£25,000
Sales	£8,000	£24,000	£40,000

We can now plot the break-even chart (see Figure 3.8) which shows graphically the break-even point of 2,000 meals with a sales revenue of £16,000. The margin of safety can be seen on the chart if we identify the selected level of profit (at 4,800 meals) and the targeted turnover (of £38,400), and compare this point with the break-even point.

The break-even chart is a simple visual tool enabling managers to anticipate the effects of changes in production and sales upon the profitability of an organisation's activities. It emphasises the importance of earning revenue and is particularly helpful for those who are unused to interpreting accounting information.

The break-even chart can be used to explore changes in a number of key variables. These may include:

* *Sales volume and value.* By looking at the chart it is possible to predict the effects of changes in sales trends. For example, a sudden fall in sales may lead to a loss and a sudden increase may improve profitability.

* *Profits or losses at a given level of production.* The break-even chart enables a business to monitor levels of production. By doing this, important decisions can be made if changes take place.

* *Prices.* It is possible to use the break-even chart to analyse different business scenarios. For example, given market research information, what would happen if the price was reduced by £2?

* *Costs.* The effects of any sudden change in costs can be plotted on the break-even chart.

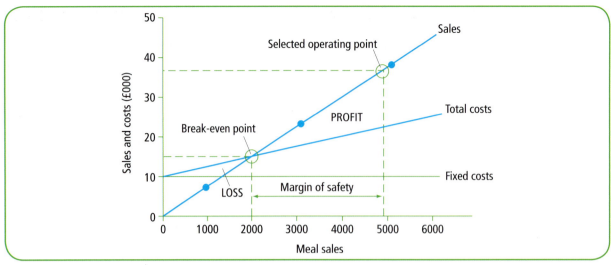

FIGURE 3.8 *Eddie Bowen's break-even chart*

CASE STUDY

Scenario

Saul Brinestone had a visit from an aged relative who wanted advice. For many years she has run a small hotel in a market town in the Thames Valley. After careful consideration she has decided to 'call it a day' and retire, but she is keen to see the business continue and wishes to retain her ownership in it.

Saul is interested in a proposition she has put forward, which involves running the hotel on her behalf. The hotel has been allowed to deteriorate over the years and, in Saul's opinion, it is obvious that extensive refurbishment is necessary before he could realistically consider her proposal. The hotel is, however, in a prime spot, was extensively used little more than ten years ago, and Saul feels that, with hard work, it has the potential to become successful again.

He has arranged a number of quotations to be made for the building work. The most favourable received is for £180,000, which involves extensive interior redecoration and refurbishment as well as completely reorganising the reception and kitchen areas.

Saul's intention is that the finance for the building work should come from a five-year bank loan with a fixed annual interest rate of 10%, payable each calendar month and based upon the original sum. The loan principal would be paid back in five equal annual

instalments. He has estimated the following fixed and variable costs:

Fixed	– Annual loan repayment	£36,000
	– Annual interest on loan	£18,000
	– Business rate and water rates	£7,000 per annum
	– Insurance	£4,500 per annum
	– Electricity	£1,300 per quarter
	– Staff salaries	£37,000 per annum.

Variable

These include direct labour (such as cleaners and bar staff), as well as the cost of food, bar stocks, etc. After careful research Saul has estimated these to be £2,000 for each 100 customers who visit the hotel.

Saul has organised for a local agency to conduct an extensive market research survey and feels confident that the hotel will attract about 100 customers per week, who will each spend on average (including accommodation, food and drinks) about £70 in the hotel.

1 Work out the break-even point for the hotel in both numbers of customers and value.
2 Work out the numbers of customers required to make a gross profit of £35,000.
3 Draw a break-even chart showing the break-even point, the profit target and the margin of safety.
4 What other information might Saul require before deciding to go ahead with the project?

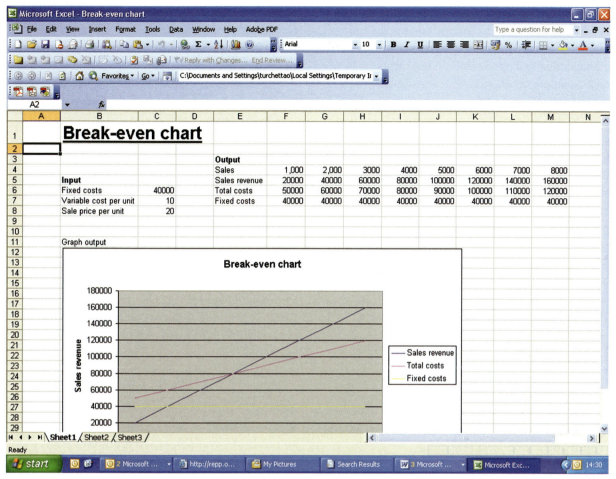

FIGURE 3.9 *An example of a break-even chart using a spreadsheet package*

The spreadsheet shown contains the following data:

Break-even chart

Input:
- Fixed costs: 40000
- Variable cost per unit: 10
- Sale price per unit: 20

Output								
Sales	1,000	2,000	3000	4000	5000	6000	7000	8000
Sales revenue	20000	40000	60000	80000	100000	120000	140000	160000
Total costs	50000	60000	70000	80000	90000	100000	110000	120000
Fixed costs	40000	40000	40000	40000	40000	40000	40000	40000

CASE STUDY

Scenario

Theme Holidays Ltd are a private company that specialise in overseas theme park holidays for adults and children. Half the packages are based upon Disneyland Parks, while the other half are based upon theme park destinations in the USA.

Theme Holidays are currently reviewing their profitability for 2005. They anticipate fixed overheads will be £450,000 for the year. With the Disneyland Paris packages, a quarter of the variable costs will go on travel costs, at an average of £30 per package. They anticipate selling packages at an average of £160 per holiday in 2005.

The American holidays are sold at an average price of £650 per holiday. Travel costs of £200 for the American holidays comprise half the variable costs of the holiday.

Market research has revealed that, during 2005, Theme Holidays expects to sell 400 holidays.

1 **Work out the contribution for both the European and American holidays.**

2 **Calculate the company's profit for the year before tax and interest.**

3 **Market research also revealed that, if Theme Holidays reduced their prices by 10%, they could sell 300 more holidays per year. Calculate how this would affect profitability and advise accordingly.**

4 **Theme Holidays are aware of the size of their fixed overheads. How would a 10% reduction in fixed overheads through cost-cutting measures affect both of the above?**

Any of these changes may affect an organisation's ability to achieve its selected operating point and margin of safety. The break-even chart is a useful management tool upon which to base action that enables an organisation to achieve its plans.

Entering figures into a spreadsheet can also be used for break-even analysis. The great benefit of doing this is that spreadsheets such as Excel are linked to charting tools and the spreadsheet can be used as a basis for producing a break-even chart shown in Figure 3.9. In the example the fixed costs are £40,000, variable cost per unit £10 and sales price per unit £20. Output is then calculated at various levels from 1,000 units to 8,000 units. These are then highlighted and an appropriate line chart is chosen, such as the one on page 125.

Break-even analysis limitations

Break-even analysis does have the following limitations:

* it can be argued that, in real situations, fixed costs actually vary with different levels of activity, and so a stepped fixed-cost line would provide a more accurate guide

* many organisations fail to break even because of a limiting factor restricting their ability to do so (e.g. a shortage of space, labour or orders)

* the variable cost and sales lines are unlikely to be linear (i.e. straight) as discounts, special contracts and overtime payments mean the cost curve is more likely to be curved

* break-even charts depict short-term relationships, and forecasts are therefore unrealistic when the proposals cover a number of years

* break-even analysis is (like all other methods) dependent upon the accuracy of forecasts made about costs and revenues – changes in the market and in the cost of raw materials could affect the success of this technique.

3.2.5 Cash-flow forecasts and statements

Whereas profit is a surplus from trading activities, cash is a liquid asset that enables an organisation to buy the goods and services it requires in order to add value to them, trade and make profits. It is therefore possible for an organisation to be profitable while, at the same time, creditors have not been paid and liquid resources have not been properly accounted for.

On the other hand, an organisation must look carefully to see that its use of cash is to its best advantage. For example, if it holds too much cash in the bank, it might be sacrificing the potential to earn greater income.

An organisation must therefore ensure it has sufficient cash to carry out its plans and that the cash coming in is sufficient to cover the cash going out. At the same time it must take into account any cash surpluses it might have in the bank.

Looking carefully at the availability of liquid funds is essential to the smooth running of any organisation. With cash planning or budgeting it is possible to forecast the flows into and out of an organisation's bank account so that any surpluses or deficits can be highlighted and any necessary action can be taken promptly. For example, overdraft facilities may be arranged in good time so funds are available when required.

The **cash-flow forecast** is an extremely important tool within an organisation and has a number of clear purposes as follows:

* The forecast can be used to highlight the timing consequences of different expenditures, ensuring that facilities, such as an overdraft, can be set up to pay bills.

* It is is an essential document for the compilation of the business plan. It will help to show whether the organisation is capable of achieving the objectives it sets. This is very important if the business applies for finance, where the lender will almost certainly want to know about the ability of the applicant to keep on top of the cash flow and meet the proposed payment schedules.

* It will help to boost the lender's confidence and the owner's confidence. By looking into the future it will provide them with the reassurance they require that their plans are going according to schedule.

* It will also help with the monitoring of performance. The cash-flow forecast sets benchmarks against which the business is expected to perform. If the organisation actually performs differently from these benchmarks, the cash-flow forecast may have highlighted an area for investigation. As we have seen, investigating differences between forecast figures and actual figures is known as variance analysis.

To prepare a cash-flow forecast you need to know what receipts and payments are likely to take place in the future and exactly when they will occur. It is important to know the length of the lead-time between incurring an expense and paying for it, as well as the time lag between making a sale and collecting the money from debtors. The art of successful forecasting is being able to calculate receipts and expenditures accurately.

When working though a cash-flow forecast, it is important to look carefully at the timing of every entry.

Theory into practice

Prepare the cash-flow forecast of S. Huang Ltd. The business has £250 in the bank and the owner anticipates his receipts over the next six months are likely to be as follows:

Jan	Feb	March	April	May	June
£1,400	£1,600	£1,500	£1,000	£900	£700

He has also worked out his payments and expects these to be:

Jan	Feb	March	April	May	June
£1,100	£700	£900	£1,400	£1,000	£900

Prepare S. Huang Ltd's cash-flow forecast for the six months.

Most business transactions take place on credit and most payments are made weeks or months after the documentation has been sent (see Figure 3.10). For example, goods are often paid for three months afer a sale. This means that in April the cash for sales in January will be received.

Example 1

C. Moon Ltd has £500 in the bank on 1 January. The owner, Christine Moon, anticipates that her receipts over the next six months are likely to be:

Jan	Feb	March	April	May	June
£2,300	£1,400	£5,300	£6,100	£4,700	£1,400

She has also worked out what her payments are likely to be over the next six months:

Jan	Feb	March	April	May	June
£1,400	£4,100	£5,600	£5,000	£3,100	£900

Christine Moon is concerned about whether she needs an overdraft facility and, if so, when she is likely to use it. She constructs the following cash-flow forecast:

	Jan	Feb	Mar	Apr	May	Jun
Balance	£500	£1,400	(£1,300)	(£1,600)	(£500)	£1,100
Receipts	£2,300	£1,400	£5,300	£6,100	4,700	£1,400
	£2,800	£2,800	£4,000	£4,500	4,200	£2,500
Payments	£1,400	£4,100	£5,600	£5,000	3,100	£900
	£1,400	(£1,300)	(£1,600)	(£500)	1,100	£1,600

The forecast shows that C. Moon Ltd needs to set up an overdraft facility between the months of February and April.

Example 2

A cash-flow forecast for the six months ended 31 December 2005 can be drafted from the following information:

1 Cash balance 1 July 2005: £4,500

2 Sales are £15 per unit and cash is received three months after the sale. For the period in question, the sale of units is:

2005

Mar	April	May	June	Jul	Aug	Sept	Oct
60	60	75	90	55	140	130	150

		2006					
Nov	Dec	Jan	Feb
150	160	170	150

3 Production in units

2005

Mar	Apr	May	June	Jul	Aug	Sept	Oct
40	50	80	70	80	130	130	150

		2006					
Nov	Dec	Jan	Feb
145	160	170	160

4 Raw materials cost £4 per unit and these are paid for two months *before* being used in production.

5 Wages are £5 per unit and this is paid for in the same month as the unit is produced.

6 Running costs are £4 per unit. 50% of the cost is paid for in the month of production, while the other 50% is paid for in the month after production.

7 Sundry expenses of £50 are paid monthly.

Receipts from sales			£
July	60	(April) x 15 =	900
August	75	(May) x 15 =	1,125
September	90	(June) x 15 =	1,350
October	55	(July) x 15 =	825
November	140	(Aug) x 15 =	2,100
December	130	(Sept) x 15 =	1,950

Payments per month
July

Raw materials	130	(Sept) x 4 =	520
Wages	80	(July) x 5 =	400
Running costs	80	(July) x 2 =	160
	70	(June) x 2 =	140
Sundry expenses		=	50
			£1,270

August

Raw materials	150	(Oct) x 4 =	600
Wages	130	(Aug) x 5 =	650
Running costs	130	(Aug) x 2 =	260
	80	(July) x 2 =	160
Sundry expenses		=	50
			£1,720

September

Raw materials	145	(Nov) x 4 =		580
Wages	130	(Sept) x 5 =		650
Running costs	130	(Sept) x 2 =		260
	130	(Aug) x 2 =		260
Sundry expenses		=		50
				£1,800

October

Raw materials	160	(Dec) x 4 =		640
Wages	150	(Oct) x 5 =		750
Running costs	150	(Oct) x 2 =		300
	130	(Sept) x 2 =		260
Sundry expenses		=		50
				£2,000

November

Raw materials	170	(Jan) x 4 =		680
Wages	145	(Nov) x 5 =		725
Running costs	145	(Nov) x 2 =		290
	150	(Oct) x 2 =		300
Sundry expenses		=		50
				£2,045

December

Raw materials	160	(Feb) x 4 =		640
Wages	160	(Dec) x 5 =		800
Running costs	160	(Dec) x 2 =		320
	145	(Nov) x 2 =		290
Sundry expenses		=		50
				£2,100

These can now be transposed into a cash-flow chart as shown below:

	July	Aug	Sept	Oct	Nov	Dec
Receipts						
Sales	900	1,125	1,350	825	2,100	1,950
Total receipts	900	1,125	1,350	825	2,100	1,950
Payments						
Raw materials	520	600	580	640	680	640
Direct labour	400	650	650	750	725	800
Variable expenses	300	420	520	560	590	610
Fixed expenses	50	50	50	50	50	50
Total payments	1,270	1,720	1,800	2,000	2,045	2,100
Receipts – payments	(370)	(595)	(450)	(1,175)	55	(150)
Balance b/f	4,500	4,130	3,535	3,085	1,910	1,965
Balance c/f	4,130	3,535	3,085	1,910	1,965	1,815

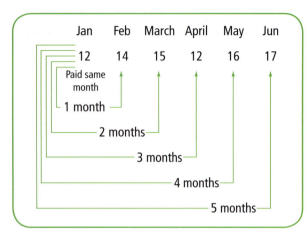

FIGURE 3.10 *Payments made on credit*

3.2.6 Importance of accurate record keeping and technology

Look at the financial pages of any newspaper and you will see the extent to which external confidence in the management of a large business is determined by its financial performance. Shareholders and other external stakeholders keenly await information on financial performance in the business. If you are working for the business, your work will contribute to this financial performance and you may have a role in recording the financial transactions of the business. Even the smallest transaction will be audited so that the final accounts accurately represent what the business has been doing during the year. Public confidence in a business and the confidence of all employees will rely upon good accounts.

Monitoring business performance

Accounting is concerned with identifying, measuring, recording and reporting information relating to the activities of an organisation. Accounting information may be used both within and outside an organisation. It involves providing important data that may form the basis for decisions.

We can break each of the accounting activities down into the following:

* *Identifying.* This involves capturing all the financial data within a business related to how it is performing. For example, this would include all information about the sales of goods to customers, data about the payment of expenses (such as wages and rent) and also information about the purchase of any stock, as well as data about the purchase of new vehicles and machinery.

* *Measuring.* Money, in the form of pounds and pence, is used as the form of measurement of economic transactions. In the future, the form of measurement might change to become euros. For accounting purposes, instead of saying a business sold 10 cars in a week which can be meaningless if you do not know the value of the cars, it may be useful to specify the value of the cars. For example, 10 cars valued at £15,000 would mean a turnover during the week of £150,000.

* *Recording.* Accounting data and information must be recorded into either handwritten accounting books or into a suitable computer package, such as a specialised accounting package or a spreadsheet.

* *Communicating.* The reporting of financial information may take a variety of different forms. For example, although some financial information may be required and extracted from the accounts weekly, such as sales totals, there are standard financial statements (such as profit and loss accounts and **balance sheets**) that have a set format for reporting the activities of organisations.

It is important that, throughout this accounting process, the accounting information is:

* reliable – free from errors and bias

* comparable – accounting information should be comparable with information from other organisations

* relevant – accounting information should relate to many of the decisions that have to be made about the business

* understandable – information should be capable of being understood by those at whom it is targeted.

Decision-making

In a fast changing business environment both managers and employees need information that will help them with decision-making. Accounting information provides help with knowing what to order and the requirements within the business for the next few months. At a more senior level, managers may be concerned with profitability and some of the wider decisions that need to be taken within the business organisation.

Credit control

As we have seen most products or services transacted by business organisations are done on credit. Credit control involves managing the credit transactions within a business organisation. Financial information will help a credit controller to understand who the business owes money to and the period over which it has been owed. Depending upon that and what is considered to be a reasonable credit period, bills will be settled. Similarly, it helps the organisation to know who owes them money and over what period so that phone calls or some other form of contact can be made in order to bring some money in.

Financial position

Every business has to meet internal and external reporting requirements to show its financial health and to meet legal and other requirements. The following stakeholders of a business need financial information about the performance of the business:

* internal users – groups within the organisation, such as managers
* external users – groups outside the organisation, such as shareholders and creditors.

Every business environment is competitive and some will inevitably perform better than others. Where a business does well, there are many rewards and benefits for individuals and organisations affected by its actions. However, if a business has a bad year or does not do well, there can be a range of consequences for individuals and organisations that may be affected by its poor performance.

CASE STUDY

Not all businesses are profitable

There are around 460 loss-making companies listed on the London Stock Exchange and some of these are fairly well-known companies. So, is it advisable to buy shares in organisations that make losses? Many new businesses are loss-makers from the moment they start and never seem to make money. Some organisations make losses because a sudden change in their business environment causes them to make losses. For example, the events of 11 September 2001 suddenly hit the aviation industry. For companies like Sabena this was the final nail in their coffin.

Some businesses make losses over a considerable time as it is difficult to generate revenues to cover expenses. For example, with new high-tech companies or drug companies it may take years to generate revenues.

Despite their lack of profits, many investors like loss-makers, mainly because there is always a chance of a turnaround, and the shares may be cheap.

1 Why do we assume that all businesses will be profitable?
2 Is it possible to identify a sector in which few businesses are profitable?
3 Why might an investor wish to buy shares in unprofitable companies?

Meeting legal requirements

Businesses also need to keep accounts in order to meet a range of legal requirements from Companies Acts and other legislation. In addtion, they also need to provide information for the tax authorities such as the Inland Revenue and Customs & Excise.

Financial and management accounting

The process of accounting can be divided into two broad areas:

* financial accounting
* management accounting.

Financial accounting

Financial accounting is concerned with the recording of financial transactions and the preparation of financial reports to communicate past financial performance.

Subject to accounting regulations, financial accounting:

* provides reports/statements that follow a standard approach
* provides a broad overview of the whole business using totals
* provides information to a particular date
* produces general statements and reports
* quantifies information in monetary terms and values.

Management accounting

Management accounting involves looking to the future using a knowledge of past performance where relevant, to aid the management of the business.

In management accounting, reports are only for internal use so no restrictions are necessary. This sector of accounting:

* provides extracted information which relates to parts of the organisation where it is used to help with a particular decision

* will look at future performance as well as at past perfomance
* produces reports with a specific decision in mind
* may include non-financial information such as stocks.

Theory into practice

Which of the following are forms of financial accounting and which are forms of management accounting?

* recording transactions from source documentation
* calculating what the profit is likely to be over a range of outputs for the launch of a new product
* producing financial statements to show what has happened to the business during the past year
* advising a business on its tax liability
* creating a budgetary system to improve control over the costs within a business
* setting the prices of products or services.

Think it over...

The UK insurance industry is the largest in Europe and the third largest in the world.

Profitability and liquidity (solvency)

Managing a business organisation requires those within it to keep accurate and up-to-date records, so that decisions can be made about a range of issues that involve profitability and liquidity. The records help the organisation to pay bills upon time and meet the requirements of their creditors; they are also used to assess their tax liabilities. Such records are then used to assess whether a business is profitable, so that managers can make key decisions that help it to make the most of opportunities that arise.

Profitability

Following the financial reports in any newspaper will reveal that one of the key newsworthy areas constantly emphasised by the press is that of profits. For example, 'Eurostar' might be 'rocked by profit warnings' or 'Somerfield to retreat to the high street'. Profits are a key indicator when judging business performance. It is the first point of reference for many organisational stakeholders.

It is all very well saying that sales have risen, productivity is soaring and the organisation is growing. However, shareholders and providers of capital will always ask the question: 'But, have you been making a profit?'

> ### Think it over...
>
> In 2004, the net rate of return upon the capital invested for UK private businesses was 13.6 per cent. For manufacturing companies it was at 7.6 per cent, but for service companies it was 17 per cent.

Liquidity / solvency

The words '**liquidity**' or '**solvency**' mean 'to be able to meet financial obligations'. A business becomes 'technically **insolvent**' when it has sufficient assets to meet all its financial obligations, but insufficient time to convert these assets into cash. It is 'legally insolvent' if it is in a situation of permanent cash shortage.

A number of users of accounting information will want to check regularly on the solvency of business organisations. For example, owners and shareholders will want to know their money is 'safe'. In this respect they will want to look at the distribution of assets and liabilities a company has. In other words, they will want to know what a business owns and what a business owes. For example, the company may have money coming in at 'some time in the future'. However, unless it has money coming in now, tomorrow and the next day, it may face cash-flow problems that make it 'technically insolvent'.

Lenders of money to organisations want to know their loans will be repaid and that interest will be paid at regular intervals. Employees and other stakeholders in organisations will want the security of knowing the organisation is solvent.

Managers will want to know the extent of solvency so that they can restructure assets and liabilities into an appropriate form. For example, they will want to manage their assets in a way that enables them to pay bills as and when they arrive in the organisation, without being too liquid and having too much cash not doing anything. Solvency is a base-line for ongoing business operations.

When auditors carry out a periodic audit of an organisation's accounts, one of the key areas they need to emphasise is how solvent the organisation is.

Use of modern technology

The success of business organisations depends on the efficient and accurate production of goods or services and on the rapid and accurate processing and distribution of information. In today's business environment this process is almost totally dependent upon new technology. This is because:

* the scale of many large organisations makes it impossible for every meeting to be conducted face-to-face

* many organisations are geographically spread out and require communication links between interrelated plants and offices

* modern business decision-making frequently requires up-to-date information from a variety of sources

* competition between business organisations is more fierce

* the pace of industrial development has increased so organisations must be quicker in responding to factors such as technological change, market forces and competition from rivals.

Technology is now an ongoing issue for many organisations. Technology has been associated with having the knowledge and competence necessary to ensure that organisations compete successfully within their chosen market sectors.

Advantages of using ICT

Technology provides a range of benefits such as:

* increased productivity – with new machinery and equipment producing goods or providing services at lower cost

* although introducing technology can be expensive, over a longer period the costs of technology can be recovered through improved efficiency

* the ability to compete more efficiently – technology provides a range of updated and more efficient processes, for example, technology may help a production line to run more quickly

* speed and accuracy of operations – technology not only enables things to work more quickly but may improve the way in which customer needs are met with better accuracy and few problems and mistakes

* the need for fewer staff and reductions in operational costs – in many circumstances technology takes staff away from mundane and boring jobs, and reduces costs, where the technology takes over the tasks

* technology allows staff to do more and increases the variety of tasks they undertake, enabling both the staff and the organisation to become more flexible

* better presentation of materials – the finish of materials as well as the quality can be improved through technology

* improved forms of communication – information and communication technologies have transformed the way in which people share thoughts and ideas

* a more modern feel about an organisation – technology and its uses often say a lot about an organisation and have the potential to improve how others perceive it.

Technology can have a huge influence upon staff performance and productivity and dramatically increase the efficiency of different members of staff. Although it may push up costs it can dramatically improve quality and provide a

A typical modern office

different feel about perceptions of an organisation and its brands.

Disadvantages of ICT

The disadvantages of using modern technology in an organisation are as follows:

* the need to constantly invest in new technologies in order to retain their market position

* staff have to adapt and gain experience of different technologies and this means that they need to be trained and the costs of such training can be high

* if technology improves efficiency, this could lead to redundancies as organisations are able to operate with fewer staff

* staff must work in a way that maximises the investment in such technologies

* over-dependence upon a system may lead to a range of serious issues if the system fails

* there is a constant security risk – somebody could enter the system and manage to obtain access to data.

Theory into practice

List the different ways you communicate with friends in a typical day. How many of these different forms of communication such as MSN Messenger and the telephone are dependent upon technologies? Describe how such technologies are transforming the ways in which individuals communicate.

Replacement of technology takes place all of the time as does the need to update and redevelop software. In response to this staff have to be constantly trained to meet new technological requirements.

Software applications

Over the last ten years the modern office workplace has changed dramatically. Paper may still be around in many of these offices, but it is usual for almost every employee to have access to a computer terminal and the expectation is that, where employees use computers, they have the capability to use the many different software applications relevant for their particular jobs. For example, when using computers individuals may be required to use a range of applications such as databases, spreadsheets, word-processing packages, the use of the Internet, e-mail, and so on.

Spreadsheets

A **spreadsheet** is a table of numbers which can be organised and altered on a computer according to preset formulae. Spreadsheets are particularly useful for forecasting and financial modelling as they show the effects of financial decisions without the need to repeat the calculations manually. An organisation can make a forecast of all the money coming in and going out over a twelve-month period, and a spreadsheet is able to alter the inputs to calculate the effect, for example, of lowering a heating bill by a certain amount each month. The computer will automatically recalculate the columns to change the heating figures, total cost figures and cash flows for each month. In this way a manager, accountant or other user of a spreadsheet can quickly carry out business calculations such as introducing and finding out the effect of minor changes of variables.

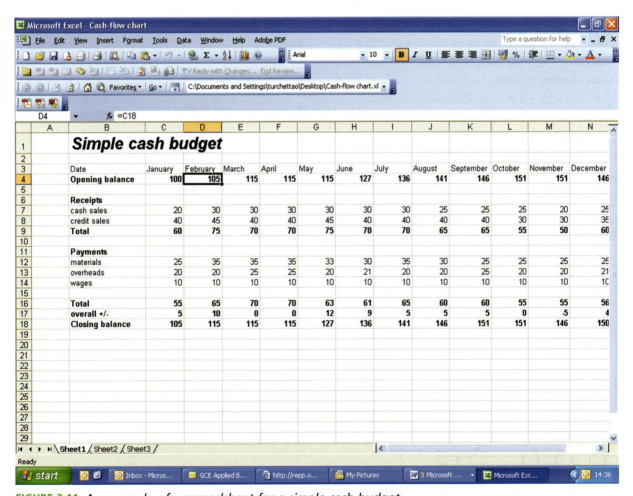

FIGURE 3.11 *An example of a spreadsheet for a simple cash budget*

One of the benefits of using a spreadsheet is that, having developed and entered the formulas, it is possible to change figures and predict different outcomes.

The example shown on page 135 is of a spreadsheet. The receipts simply involved totalling two boxes to produce total receipts which in this instance involved the sum of C7+C8. The total for payments involved totalling materials, **overheads** and wages which came out at C12+C13+C14. Overall +/– was C9-C16 and the closing balance was C4+C9–C16. The closing balance has to become the opening balance for the next period and so C18, the closing balance on the first column, is the same as D4, now shown to =C18. Calculations can be extended across the page.

Spreadsheets that forecast either cash or profits are relatively simple to construct and easy to change. By simply changing the opening balance at the beginning of the spreadsheet all of the other calculations instantly change. The widespread use of computers by all types of organisations has seen many organisations opt to computerise their book-keeping systems.

Accounts packages

There are a number of advantages of using computerised accounting packages:

* computers help to improve the control of funds coming into and going out of an organisation and make this control more effective

* they improve accuracy, particularly where large amounts of data are entering into accounts (i.e. they take away much of the tedium of data entry into double-entry accounts)

* accounting data is, by its very nature, arithmetical, which is well suited to being recorded and maintained by computer

* computerised book-keeping systems can supply reports and account balances much more quickly (such as trial balance, stock valuation, payroll analysis, VAT return, etc.)

* many reports can be produced quickly and easily in a way that would not be possible in a manual system because of time and cost, for example, it would be easy to go through the sales ledger to find out all the customers who have not paid their debts and send them reminders to do so

* they help to provide managers with a readily accessible view of how the business organisation is functioning.

Computer programs for financial accounts usually follow the same system of ledger division into general and personal. In doing so the system provides an element of continuity with past practices. Commercially available accounting software is usually described as an '**integrated accounts package**', covering a range of accounting activities. For example, an accounting package would:

* update customer accounts in the sales ledger

* update supplier accounts in the purchases ledger

* record bank receipts and payments

* print out invoices

* make payments to suppliers and for expenses

* adjust records automatically.

Many packages offer more than just the control of each of the ledgers. Some may also provide for payroll, stock control production planning, electronic data interchange (EDI) and financial planning. These can be integrated with the rest of the accounting system.

An integrated accounting system means that, when a business transaction takes place and is input into the computer, it is recorded into a range of accounting records at the same time. For example, if a sales invoice is generated for a customer:

* the customer's account will be adjusted with the invoice total

* the sales account will increase and VAT will be applied

* stock records will change.

Databases

A **database** is an organised collection of information and data. By having data organised in such a way, it is possible to have easy access to huge volumes of information. Databases enable:

* an organisation to store information only once and access information from several files

* files to be linked together so that it is possible to update a whole range of files at the same time

* rapid access to information

* files to be accessed and manipulated quickly with little likelihood of data becoming lost.

The main problem with databases is that if a computer breaks down, it may be difficult to access information. Another problem might be unauthorised access to records, although data can be protected with passwords. Training in the use of databases can be costly.

Theory into practice

Use a range of tabulated information which you collect from a range of sources. It might simply be market research information, or information about the hobbies of members of your class. Put the data into a spreadsheet and then graphically present it in at least two forms together with appropriate labels.

3.2.7 Analysis of the current market position

Businesses operate in competitive markets. In making decisions about their position in the market, businesses need to be aware of the actions of competitors.

SWOT analysis

Organisations keep a very close eye on each other by carrying out a SWOT analysis (see page 32) which involves assessing:

* the internal strengths of the company (S)

* the internal weaknesses of the company (W)

* the external opportunities (O)

* the external threats. (T)

The SWOT analysis is also sometimes referred to as a WOTS-up analysis. We use the term WOTS-up because it is a way of finding out any problems that an organisation might be having which can be put right. It is easy to remember because people often say 'What's Up?' – meaning 'What is the problem?' In this book however, we will use the expression SWOT because you will need to carry out a SWOT as part of your assessment. It is a very useful tool in helping the business to achieve its marketing objectives.

Marketing objectives are the end purposes which the business hopes to achieve through marketing activities. Examples of marketing objectives might be:

* to become the market leader in a particular market

* to increase market share

* to become more customer focused.

Carrying out a SWOT analysis helps the business to focus its activities on these marketing objectives. For example, to become the market leader it helps to be able to:

* identify strengths relative to competitors, and then to build on these strengths

* identify internal weaknesses and to seek to reduce and eliminate these weaknesses. For example, an internal weakness might be that the company is not market focused enough. Addressing this weakness might involve employing more people who understand about marketing and market research.

* identify opportunities – such as new products and new markets that are developing

* identify threats – such as the development of a new product coming onto the market produced by a rival – helps a business to respond appropriately.

CASE STUDY
Shell and BP

In February 2005, Shell and BP both announced record profits for British companies. They operate in the same sector – oil and gas exploration, refining and sale and have similar but slightly different approaches.

BP's strategy has been to invest heavily in oil and gas exploration, seeking new fields to exploit. They have been very successful, but the problem is that oil and gas are finite resources – the discovery of new fields is limited. Increasingly, to exploit new fields exploration has had to take place in remote areas of the globe and pipelines have to cross politically sensitive areas.

Shell has pursued a strategy of exploration but not to the same extent as BP. Instead, Shell has focused a lot of investment in the development of so called 'future fuels' which are seen as the ones that will replace hydrocarbons. For example, future fuels include the development of a hydrogen fuel for the hydrogen car (service stations for hydrogen fuel have already opened up in Iceland and Japan). Other future fuels are based on bio-fuels, such as burning plant matter, and wind farming.

These two companies keep a very close eye on each other by carrying out SWOT analyses. We can set out a simple SWOT analysis for BP to compare its position with Shell in the following way:

Strengths – a very profitable company with exploration taking place across the world. Oil and gas drilling, refining and distribution taking place on a global scale. One of the best-known names in oil and gas in the world.	**Weaknesses** – oil and gas are finite resources. The company may be over relying on the future of hydrocarbons.
Opportunities – possibilities to develop new pipelines in areas of the world that are opening up such as China and Eastern Europe. As oil and gas become increasingly scarce their prices will rise.	**Threats** – global warming may lead to government actions to ban hydrocarbon fuels. Threats of wars and military action may threaten BP facilities across the globe. Competitors may develop future fuels.

Set out a SWOT analysis for Shell to compare its position with BP.

Theory into practice

Carry out a SWOT analysis for an organisation that you are familiar with, e.g. one where you are carrying out work experience, one that you have researched on the Internet or in the newspaper, or even your local college or school. Show what needs to be done about the internal strengths and weaknesses of the organisation. Explain how the organisation should respond to market opportunities and threats in order to achieve its marketing objectives.

CASE STUDY

Tesco supermarket

The supermarket industry in this country is very competitive – but one store stands head and shoulders above the rest in terms of its success in recent years. In January 2005 the market share of the main firms in the industry stood as follows:

Food retailer	% share of the market
Tesco	29
ASDA	17
Sainsbury's	16
Morrisons and Safeway	13

Source: Euromonitor International

Tesco takes almost one in three pounds spent in Britain's grocery stores. It has almost 2,000 stores across the UK and stocks a range of items from music downloads to household mortgages. Tesco has been very successful in clothing lines (such as Florence and Fred) and its cut-price electrical stores have been very successful.

There are some indications of unrest with the success of Tesco, particularly coming from environmental pressure groups and local residents who fear the effect that the arrival of Tesco will have on local shopping choice. As Tesco is making record profits, many people feel that we are becoming too dependent on the store and that it is limiting our choice.

Set out a SWOT analysis for Tesco using the information provided in this case study and the Internet (try www.tesco.com to start).

Of course, because Tesco operates in a highly competitive market environment the nature of this environment may have changed – for example, with the development of increased competition from rivals like Sainsbury's and ASDA.

CASE STUDY

Time for a change for Smarties

The maker of Smarties announced in February 2005 that it was replacing the sweet's tube-shape packet after almost 70 years. Nestlé Rowntree will be replacing the cylindrical design known to generations of children with a long, hexagonal pack. The plastic disc on the top of the tube will also be replaced in favour of a cardboard flip-top lid.

The confectionery giant said the revamp was needed to ensure the brand remained 'fresh and interesting' to youngsters. The so-called Hexatube packet will be sold in stores from the summer of 2005.

Nestlé Rowntree carried out extensive market research which showed that young people have so many different influences that they want to keep the products that they buy contemporary. Nestlé Rowntree realised the importance of keeping the packaging and the brand fresh and interesting for consumers.

1 How would a SWOT analysis have helped Nestlé Rowntree to decide to make the change?
2 What was the significance of market research in driving the change?
3 What marketing tools has Nestlé Rowntree used in making the change?

PEST and SLEPT analysis

Another type of analysis that most businesses carry out in order to analyse their market position is the PEST or **SLEPT analysis**.

These analyses are used to examine the environment in which the business operates. They are employed because modern businesses operate in very turbulent environments in which it is essential to understand the changes that are taking place.

Theory into practice

Set out a SLEPT analysis to outline ways in which a particular product or group of products can be made more sensitive to market conditions as a result of a SLEPT analysis. For your table, use the same headings shown in the case study on page 141.

PEST analysis	
P – Political factors	Political factors include such things as a change in government. For example, the election of a Conservative government might lead to the lowering of some business taxes.
E – Economic factors	These are changes in the wider economy such as changes in general economic activity. For example, is the economy growing leading to lots of spending in the shops which would encourage businesses to invest more? Other important economic factors include changes in the interest rates (the price of borrowing money), the price of the £ in exchange with other currencies, the level of unemployment etc.
S – Social factors	Changes in social trends are very important for business. They include such things as changes in the age structure of the population, for example, there are more elderly people than in the past. Other factors include changes in tastes and buying patterns, for example, as people live busier lives they purchase more ready-made meals rather than cooking their own.
T – Changes in technology	New technologies regularly come on stream, making old ways of doing things old-fashioned. Successful businesses are ones that adapt and apply new technologies.

FIGURE 3.12 *PEST analysis*

SLEPT analysis	
S – Social	Changes in social trends.
L – Legal	Changes in the law – businesses must keep abreast of changes in the law e.g. changes in environmental legislation requiring tougher pollution controls, changes in equal opportunities laws requiring better facilities for disabled workers etc.
E – Economic	Changes in economic variables.
P – Political	Political changes.
T – Technology	Changes in technology.

FIGURE 3.13 *SLEPT analysis*

CASE STUDY

Carrying out a SLEPT analysis

The following SLEPT analysis was carried out for a well-known chocolate bar which had been marketed as being 'supersize'.

1 What would be the purpose of this SLEPT analysis?

2 Use an example from below to show how the SLEPT might have influenced some management decisions.

SLEPT factor	Description	Implication for company
S – Social	Increasingly consumers are becoming aware of the importance of healthy eating. Some are turning away from products with lots of calories – although many are still eating highly-calorific chocolate bars.	Company may need to produce smaller size products – although perhaps it should continue to cater for those seeking a supersize bar. The company should seek ways of reducing fat and sugar content in chocolate bars.
L – Legal	Government legislation requires food manufacturers to specify the content of food products including calorific content. Government is also looking at how food products are advertised – particularly to children.	Essential to comply with legal requirements.
E – Economic	Rising living standards mean that increasing numbers of people are able to afford treats such as chocolate products.	Economic trends indicate that people across the globe are increasingly able to afford to buy chocolate products.
P – Political	The UK (Labour) government has placed a strong emphasis on healthy eating, bringing the attention of the public to the importance of a healthy diet. The government has created a Healthy Schools programme encouraging teachers to make pupils aware of the importance of diet and exercise, and making sure that schools focus on providing healthy products for pupils.	It is important for companies to comply with government requirements. There is a danger that companies that produce unhealthy products and promote unhealthy practices will be 'named and shamed'. Therefore an important requirement for companies to focus on is producing 'healthier' chocolate bars e.g. with less sugar and fat content.
T – Technology	New technologies provide sophisticated ways of mixing and making existing products as well as producing appropriate packaging.	Food technology can be combined with an understanding of healthy eating issues to change the make-up of chocolate bars to make them 'healthier'. Packaging can be altered to alert consumers to the need for a balanced diet.

Linking SWOT and SLEPT analysis

You should be able to see that the SWOT and the SLEPT analyses are closely related.

The SLEPT analysis examines changes in the external environment. It therefore primarily relates to the opportunities and threats facing a business.

Whereas these SLEPT factors primarily relate to opportunities and threats (i.e. external factors in

	Opportunity	Threat
S – Social factors	e.g. changes in tastes and hence demand in favour of our product.	Changes in the population structure that have an adverse effect on demand for our product.
L – Legal factors	A change in the law that our company is already prepared for e.g. we have in place all the necessary environmental controls.	A new law that our company is not ready for.
E – Economic factors	Rising living standards, falls in interest rates etc.	e.g. a downturn in the economy.
P – Political factors	e.g. government policies that favour business.	e.g. a government that taxes businesses more heavily.
T – Technological factors	e.g. new technologies that our business can adapt quicker than competitors.	e.g. new technologies which our rivals have adapted more quickly than us.

How a SLEPT analysis helps us to understand our business's environment

a SWOT analysis) we also need to look at internal strengths and weaknesses.

Strengths primarily relate to having the right type of resources to do well in the market. These resources include:

* having managers who can make change happen and who understand the market.

* having good human resources – people who are flexible and are equipped to satisfy the market, for example, through interacting well with customers (customer service).

* having a good financial resource base, for example, from making healthy profits.

* having an excellent marketing department that understands what customers require.

In addition, organisations which have adopted the most suitable technologies will flourish.

Weaknesses stem from having inappropriate resources to satisfy customers and from being weak compared with rivals.

When you are analysing the current market position of a business you should make links between external and internal issues. For example, any economic data such as high interest rates (an external issue) needs to be linked to the effect on loan capital of the business (an internal issue). A firm with a lot of borrowing will be adversely hit by a rise in interest rates. The threat (rising interest rates) combines with the weakness (too

much borrowing) to create a double problem for the business.

In a similar way, changes in social trends (an external issue) e.g. consumers wanting to spend more money on lifestyle goods will combine with the success of a firm having excellent market research and marketing (an internal issue).

Theory into practice

Give examples of the way in which:

1 A change in technology (external issue) will combine favourably with a company being a technology leader (an internal strength).

2 A change in the law (external issue) will combine with a firm having strong management (an internal strength).

3 A change in the actions of competitors (an external issue) will combine with a firm having excellent and highly motivated employees (an internal strength).

3.2.8 Economic conditions and market conditions

There are a number of external influences that affect businesses and these factors can have a real impact on day-to-day business decision-making.

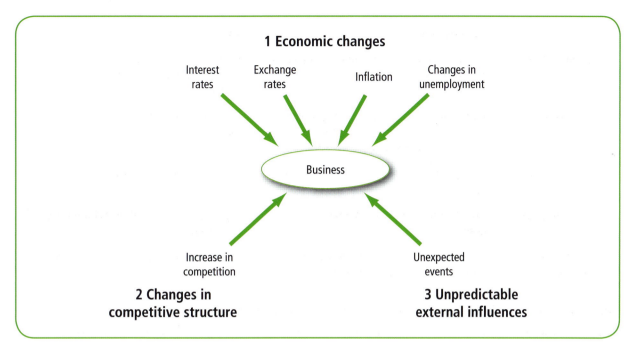

FIGURE 3.14 *External influences on organisations*

These influences relate to:

* changes in economic indicators such as interest rates (the price of borrowing money)

* changes in the competitive structure of the market the organisation operates in, for example, the arrival of new competitors make the market more competitive

* unpredictable changes such as the influence of 11 September 2001 when a terrorist attack on the heart of New York's central business district led to a sudden loss of confidence in the world economic system.

Changes in economic indicators

Organisations are affected by conditions in the local and wider economy:

* when the economy is booming this leads to a general increase in demand for products and also an increase in business costs

* when the economy is depressed this leads to a general slump in demand for products and costs fall.

Important economic changes that affect organisations are shown above.

Inflation

Inflation is a sustained increase in the general price level which leads to a fall in the value of money.

The rate of inflation is measured by the annual percentage change in the level of consumer prices. The British government tries to keep inflation within a target level of 2 per cent. The average increase in prices is measured using a measuring tool known as the Consumer Price Index (CPI). The Consumer Price Index is a monthly indication of the average price changes to a particular 'basket' of consumer goods and is used as a general indicator of price inflation. The CPI therefore shows how average prices are changing over time. This is an important measure. For example, it shows how prices are changing in comparison with incomes (a measure of how well-off households are).

Inflation is a problem for business because it adds to business costs. One of the most common reasons for inflation is increases in the price of essential raw materials and goods. For example, oil prices are much higher than they were 20 years ago and are likely to rise in the future as oil reserves run out. As oil is an essential fuel that goes into producing so many goods this is

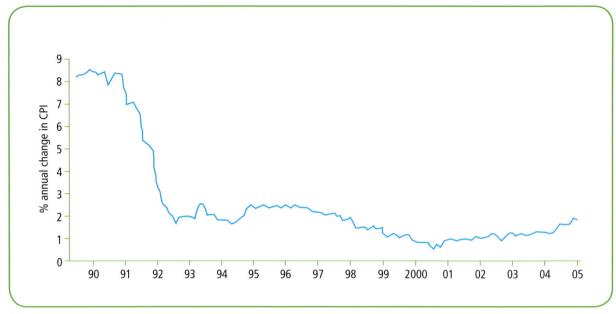

Source: Central Statistical Office Monthly Report

FIGURE 3.15 *Consumer price inflation in the UK*

likely to have an inflationary impact. There are also some other factors that have brought prices down such as the widespread use of computer-based technology in so many different goods and services. As computers have become more efficient prices have fallen.

The chart in Figure 3.15 shows that consumer price inflation in the UK has been at quite a low level over the last 10 years.

Theory into practice

Explain how inflation might affect:

* a motor car manufacturer

* a taxi firm

* a large insurance company.

Think it over...

In the chronic German inflation of 1926 the value of money fell so quickly that when one day a man took a wheelbarrow full of money to buy food at his local shops, a thief tipped out the money in the street and stole the wheelbarrow.

Interest rates

Interest rates are closely related to inflation. In this country interest rates are set by the Bank of England's Monetary Policy Committee. When inflation starts to rise the Monetary Policy Committee (MPC) may raise interest rates to discourage people from borrowing money. This is to dampen down the demand for goods and services in the economy. If there is too much demand this pushes up prices (leading to inflation) which can be harmful to business.

However, when the MPC raises interest rates this can have an adverse effect on businesses that have borrowed money. This is because they have to pay more in interest on the sums they borrowed than before. If they have borrowed a lot of money this can raise their costs substantially and lower their profits.

The Monetary Policy Committee seeks to set interest rates that help the government to achieve its target of keeping inflation at the 2 per cent target level.

Exchange rates

The exchange rate measures the external value of a currency, for example, the pound sterling in terms of how much of another currency it can buy – such as how many euros you can buy with £1.

Raise interest rates.	Raises business costs. Helps to lower demand inflation.	Can lead to a reduction in business profits (some businesses go bust).
Lower interest rates.	Lowers business costs. Helps to raise demand inflation.	Can help to raise business profits.

FIGURE 3.16 *Effect of a change in interest rates*

The daily value of the pound is determined in the foreign exchange markets (FOREX) where billions of pounds of currencies are traded every hour. The value is determined by the demand and supply. If lots of people want to buy pounds, for example, to be able to buy British goods, then this will raise the value of the pound.

The problem is that the pound is used in a fairly small market place – the UK is a market of only 60 million people. It is a nuisance for businesses to have to buy foreign currency to buy goods from overseas, or vice versa because often there is a charge for making the transaction. This is why many large British businesses would like to join the euro zone. The euro zone is made up of all those countries that use the common currency of the euro including the Netherlands, Germany, France, Italy and Spain.

In recent times the pound has fallen in value against the euro. This means that when we want to buy goods from the euro zone we have to give increasing numbers of pounds to purchase the same quantities of goods and services than we did before the fall of the pound.

When the sterling exchange rate is high, it is cheaper to import raw materials, components and machinery and equipment. Of course, this is good news for businesses that rely on imported components or who are willing to purchase high-tech machinery and equipment from abroad.

A strong exchange rate, however, has the beneficial effect of keeping inflation down because British suppliers now face more intense competition from cheaper imports and will look to cut their costs accordingly.

Theory into practice

What do you think are the advantages and disadvantages of having a weak (falling value) pound? Set out your findings in a table.

Unemployment

The level of unemployment in a local area is important for an organisation as they may need to compete for the scarce resource of labour.

The official way to count the numbers unemployed is to record those who are registered as able, available and willing to work but who cannot find work despite actively searching for a job.

In recent years there has been a fall in those measured as being unemployed.

There are two main ways of counting the unemployed:

1 The Claimant Count covers those people who are eligible to claim the Job Seeker's Allowance.

2 The Labour Force Survey covers those who have looked for work in the past month and are able to start work in the next two weeks. Typically the Labour Force Survey measure is higher than the claimant count method by about 400,000.

Theory into practice

In recent years there has been a fall in those measured as being unemployed as shown by the following table.

Year	Labour Force Survey %	Claimant Count %
1995	8.8	7.6
2000	5.6	3.6
2003	5.2	3.1
2004		

Find out the unemployment figures for 2004 and enter them into the above table.

The level of unemployment is very important to business particularly in:

* *Determining costs.* The lower the level of unemployment, the higher the level of wages is likely to be. This is because labour is scarce relative to demand and employers are likely to have to compete for labour by offering higher wages and better opportunities.

* *Determining the investment required in the labour force.* When unemployment is low employers will need to invest more in training, developing and motivating their existing employees in order to keep them.

Theory into practice

Interview a local employer to find out how the level of unemployment affects their wage costs and the sorts of actions that they take to retain labour.

Changes in the competitive structure of the market

Businesses are continually aware of the competitiveness of the markets in which they operate. For example, if we look at supermarkets in this country, there is a clear competitive structure:

Tesco	The market leader with £1 out of every £3 of grocery sales.
Sainsbury's and ASDA	Are some way behind Tesco but are continually seeking to gain a bigger market share.
Morrisons	In fourth position and has recently taken over Safeway.
Other smaller supermarket chains	Each fighting for remaining sales – often taking a different position in the market, e.g. low-cost / limited range of items such as ALDI and NETTO.

In banking, the main competition is between:

* HSBC
* Halifax
* Barclays
* Lloyds TSB
* NatWest.

In markets like banking and supermarket retailing there are considerable advantages to being large. For example, a giant bank like Halifax is well placed to compete with smaller banks by offering better rates of interest to new customers. Supermarket chains like Tesco are able to buy millions of units from suppliers in any one order and therefore drive down costs.

Most markets where there are considerable **economies of scale** to be had are dominated by a small number of firms.

Key terms

Economies of scale refers to the advantages which large firms have from their scale enabling them to produce or sell larger quantities at low unit costs.

Large firms are able to:

* invest in the best assets
* spend more than their rivals on advertising and marketing
* get the best terms from suppliers
* invest heavily in market research to find out what customers want.

Theory into practice

Examples of firms that in recent years have dominated their markets include:

Supermarkets	Tesco
Football	Manchester United, Arsenal and Chelsea
Rugby union	Leicester Tigers
Soft drinks	Coca-Cola, PepsiCo
Food	Nestlé, Kraft, Heinz, Unilever
Computer systems	Microsoft
Web search engines	Google

Can you think of other examples of firms that have dominated the competitive structure of their industry in recent years?

Of course, the competitive position is always changing – new firms enter the market, and new technologies and other opportunities present themselves for the development of competition.

For example, the development of the Internet as a way of buying goods online has threatened businesses such as:

* wine merchants
* book sellers
* travel agents.

However, in some ways the development of new technologies and other cost cutting developments can also reduce competition:

* although there is now intense competition between the major supermarket chains, they face reduced competition from small grocers and retail shops many of which have had to close down because they can't compete on costs
* many door-to-door milk rounds have closed down because small sellers can't compete with supermarket prices.

Theory into practice

Identify examples of situations where:

* competition has increased in an industry
* competition has been reduced in an industry.

Explain how these changes impact on the decisions that businesses make about their own future development in these industries.

Theory into practice

Your old TV is doomed which is great news for electrical retailers. By 2012 we will all need digital TV equipment because the analogue signal will have been switched off. Explain how this is likely to affect competition in the market for TV equipment. What objectives might firms have in order to win a leading position in this market?

Unpredictable external influences

Although businesses can think ahead and anticipate many changes in the market such as possible changes in interest rates and the arrival of new competitors, there are some occurrences which are too unpredictable to be anticipated.

One such occurrence was when terrorists attacked the heart of New York's business district

11 September 2001 – the terrorist attack led to a collapse of business confidence worldwide

CASE STUDY

Marks & Spencer

In March 2005, Marks & Spencer decided to take on its high street rivals by slashing the price of key items in its springwear collection. The high street giant confirmed that it had begun introducing new cheaper products in line with a strategy outlined by the company. M&S saw the price cutting as part of a way of creating lower entry price points into the market.

M&S embarked on the strategy in February, bringing down the prices of basic items such as T-shirts, jeans and trousers, and this was seen as part of a plan to refocus on the customer – giving the customer greater quality and value.

Overall, the costs cut M&S prices by 24% with clear implications for profit margins. At Christmas 2004 M&S was forced to make deep cuts to get rid of excess stock.

1 To what extent do you think the cuts at M&S were dictated by changing market conditions?
2 What will be the knock-on effect of M&S's strategy on rivals?
3 What do you think will be the likely outcome of M&S's strategy of moving to lower entry price points?

in September 2001. When this event happened there was panic in the world's stock markets and the value of many investments plummeted overnight, leading to a loss of confidence. For example, there was a dramatic fall in airline traffic and tourism during the ensuing year. This had a knock-on effect as other businesses also suffered leading to rising unemployment and a lot of businesses went bankrupt.

A similar catastrophe was the South East Asian crisis in the 1990s when there was a sudden loss of confidence in banking systems in countries like South Korea. This had a massive impact on business confidence across the globe.

Coping with changing economic and market conditions

Businesses need to create plans to deal with changes in the economic and market conditions. Important areas of planning include:

* *Managing finance.* Businesses shouldn't borrow too much externally because if market conditions take a downturn, then they may not be able to pay the high interest rates on borrowed money.

* *Keeping costs under control.* Businesses that allow their costs to rise too much when things are going well will struggle when profit margins fall. For example, Manchester United always keep their wage costs at under 50 per cent of their turnover.

* *Investing in market research and marketing activities.* Businesses that find out what customers want today and tomorrow will stay ahead of the competition.

* *Trying to become the market leader.* The market leader produces on a larger scale than rivals and therefore has lower costs.

* *Always being aware of current interest rates and exchange rates* means that businesses can make plans for any unfavourable changes.

* *Finding out what your competitors are doing.* Businesses should anticipate their strategies to keep one step ahead.

* *Always being prepared for unforeseen events.* Businesses must have a contingency plan to fall back upon.

* *Keeping employees informed* about what is going on in the business, in the economy and in the market will enable employees to help the business to be successful.

3.2.9 Ethical, legal, social, political and environmental factors

To stay competitive, modern businesses cannot solely focus their plans and activities on making a profit. They have to take on board what is referred to as a Triple bottom line. This term refers to the profit that appears on the bottom of a profit and loss account. The Triple bottom line refers to not only being successful in the economic (profit based) bottom line, but also in looking after society (a social bottom line) and the environment (an environmental bottom line).

Think it over…

Sir Terry Leahy, Chief Executive of Tesco, believes that each of the three parts of the bottom line are mutually supportive. He describes this as a win-win situation. In his 2004 statement in the Tesco Corporate Social Responsibility report he said that: 'Corporate responsibility is a win-win for Tesco and for the communities we serve. Because we have served more customers over the past year, we have grown as a business and have created 16,000 new jobs in the UK, many in deprived areas. Our regeneration and award-winning training schemes have created rewarding and fulfilling careers in retail for many people including staff who were previously long-term unemployed. We have given £8m in computer equipment for schools, and have raised £2.5m for Barnardo's, our charity of the year.'

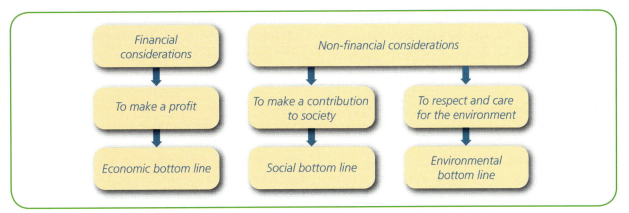

FIGURE 3.17 *The Triple bottom line*

Laws and ethics

Laws

Many of the activities that businesses carry out are constrained by laws. Laws are created in two main ways:

1 By Act of Parliament. New laws have to be passed by Parliament and then they become legally enforceable. In addition to UK national laws, many activities are controlled by European Union created laws. Some laws that affect business are created by local councils.

2 Other laws have been created by custom and practice over long periods of time. These are referred to as common law.

The sorts of laws that businesses are constrained by include:

* employment law governing issues such as contracts of employment, minimum wage legislation (the minimum wage is now set at over £5 an hour), rights to maternity leave, paternity leave, sick leave and other benefits

* Health and Safety at Work legislation governing an employer's and employees' responsibilities for health and safety practices

* equal opportunities and discrimination at work legislation

* laws governing the way in which businesses offer credit terms, control interest rate payments and the conditions of loans

* laws about company formation, limited liability, and the running of companies

* data protection legislation governing the sorts of information which companies must make publicly available and the types of information that data holders cannot put into the public domain

* laws about contracts that businesses can make with others etc.

* laws about the limitation of wastes that businesses create and the control of pollution.

* many other laws that affect business dealings with external parties and dealings that take place within a business.

Businesses must comply with legislation. Failure to comply with legislation can lead to penalties such as warnings, fines and even prison sentences for directors and others that break the law.

> **CASE STUDY**
> **Smoking bans**
> In March 2005, it was widely reported that more than 30 cities and town in England were considering local bans on smoking in public places following the government's refusal to implement national rules. Some were expected to follow the example of Liverpool and the Greater London Authority which started preliminary steps to enable them to implement a ban in 2006.

Ethics

Ethics are moral principles or rules of conduct generally accepted by most members of society. Most organisations today believe it is necessary to take a stance that shows the public they operate in an ethical manner. Emphasis on the interest of the consumer is a key aspect of many organisations. Some ethics are reinforced through the legal system and provide a compulsory constraint on business activities, while others are the result of social pressure to conform to a particular standard.

Potential areas of concern for organisations include product ethics, where issues such as genetically modified foodstuffs or contaminated food may seriously and quickly affect short-term demand. For example, complaints about the marketing of various baby milk products in developing countries in the 1980s resulted in widespread criticism and boycotts of powdered milk manufacturers. The fact these practices ended 20 years ago is not fully appreciated by many members of the public and shows that bad business practice takes a long time to forget.

Another area of concern relates to business practice, where restrictive practices and poor treatment of employees have been highlighted in the media, and businesses have faced criticism from the public. The trading policies of companies who buy cheap imports from overseas organisations involved in 'sweat-shop labour', or who trade with businesses employing young children in unacceptable conditions, have also faced critical scrutiny from both the media and the public. For example, in the early 1990s Nike was found to be using some factories in South East Asia to produce Nike products, where child labour was being employed, for example, to stitch footballs. Since this time Nike has been able to put this right, and makes sure that as far as possible child labour is not employed in the factories where it gives contracts to produce Nike branded products.

Differences between legal and ethical responsibility

The law provides the baseline for sound business decision-making. Good businesses comply with every aspect of the law. However, 'better' businesses go further than just complying with the law. They also seek to do the right thing because they believe that this is the way to conduct business. In other words they take a moral/ethical stance.

CASE STUDY

Bad business practice

In 2004 the respected charity Christian Aid produced a report 'Behind the mask: the real face of corporate social responsibility'. The report focused on case studies of British American Tobacco and Coca-Cola highlighting some of the bad practices of these companies. The report argued that legislation is required to control the activities of business, because business on its own does not effectively regulate itself.

British American Tobacco stresses the importance of upholding high standards of health and safety among those working for them and claims to provide local farmers with the necessary training and protective clothing. However, contract farmers in Kenya and Brazil claim this does not happen and report chronic ill health related to tobacco cultivation.

Coca-Cola emphasises 'using natural resources responsibly'. Yet a wholly owned subsidiary in India is accused of depleting village wells in an area where water is notoriously scarce and has been told by an Indian court to stop drawing ground water.

1 Should we allow businesses to regulate their own activities or do we need laws to keep businesses doing the right things?
2 What other pressures can be put on business to do the right thing?
3 How might a business benefit from taking an ethical approach?
4 What other recent examples can you think of which reflect bad business practice? What have been the financial implications for the businesses concerned?

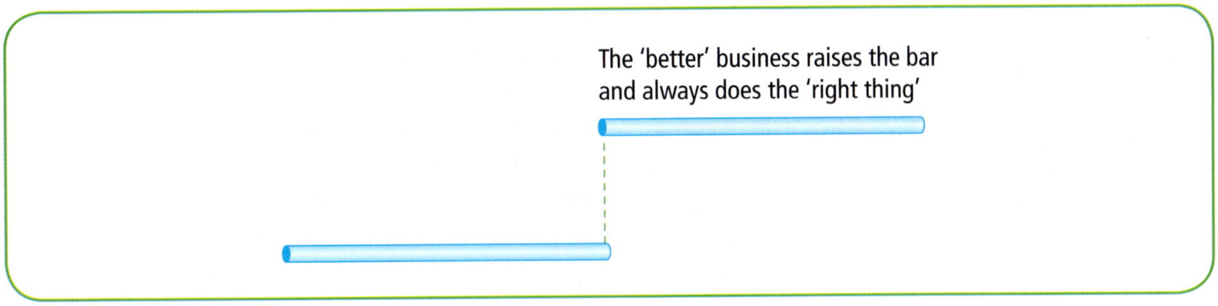

> The 'better' business raises the bar and always does the 'right thing'

FIGURE 3.18 *A 'good' business complies with every aspect of the law*

CASE STUDY

Tesco's business ethics policy

Here is an extract from Tesco's business ethics policy:

> Tesco is committed to conducting business in an ethical and socially responsible manner. This relates to all aspects of our business, treating employees, customers, suppliers and shareholders in a fair and honest manner and ensuring that there are constant and open channels of communication.
>
> Tesco has a Code of Ethics for its staff, which includes a policy on the receipt of gifts and a grievance procedure that covers employment issues. In 2003, Tesco launched a confidential telephone help line, Protector Line, for any employee who wishes to raise concerns relating to alleged criminal offences, failure to comply with legal obligations, miscarriages of justice, health and safety, damage to the environment and concealment of any of these issues.

1 Why has Tesco got an ethics policy?
2 Provide an example of who benefits from such a policy. Describe why they might benefit.

CASE STUDY

Banks cheating customers

A report produced by savings account provider ING Direct in March 2005 showed that many banks are taking advantage of loyal customers. Existing customers are losing out to new customers because banks are failing to offer them the best rates.

Savers and borrowers who stick with their bank are likely to suffer huge financial penalties because they are not offered the competitive deals designed to attract new customers. The big banks make a good part of their profits by penalising those customers they consider 'captive'.

The ING Direct survey found that 60 per cent of customers wanted financial services companies to stop short-term, headline-grabbing deals – commonly found on credit cards, mortgages and savings accounts – and instead offer products with competitive rates available to all.

The ING survey showed that 40 per cent of individual customers who had left a financial institution in the past year did so because of the way the bank treated its loyal customers.

1 What do you think of banks' policies of rewarding new customers at the expense of existing ones?
2 Do you think that this is good or bad business practice?
3 Is it legal? Is it ethical?
4 Why might it be bad business practice in the longer term?
5 How should banks treat new and existing customers if they want to act in an ethical way?

Changing social trends

Over time many changes take place in society which are relevant to business including changes in population, in tastes and buying patterns and in employment patterns. An example of a change in employment patterns includes the growing numbers of women in the workplace which has led to an increased demand for convenience food. Other important social changes are shifts in values and culture, education and health, and distribution of income.

Social trends typically relate to such factors as:

* changes in values and attitudes over time which influence buying patterns, for example, people becoming more environmentally aware or health conscious

* changes in population structures which affect demand patterns, for example, the growth in the number of elderly people and those living in cities rather than rural areas.

Theory into practice

The following newspaper headlines outline examples of changes in social trends that affect business:

> **Worries about obesity create new crash diet fads and drive more people to the gym**
>
> **Busy working women have less time for preparing family meals**
>
> **Worries about food additives and hyperactivity among children**

For each headline suggest which types of businesses will be most affected and the sorts of decisions that they might take as a result of these social trends.

The importance of environmental responsibility

In recent years, environmental issues have been highlighted by accidents at chemicals plants or at sea with oil tankers. These accidents can damage the image of the organisation concerned as well as wildlife and the environment.

With many companies' environmental performance becoming central to their competitiveness and survival, a range of new tools for environmental management have been developed. These include environmental impact assessments, which assess the likely impact of major projects and environmental audits or eco-audits, which involve carrying out an audit of current activities to measure their environmental impact. Alternatively, by looking at the environmental impact of a product through its life-cycle, from the sourcing of raw materials to the final disposal of waste products, a product life-cycle analysis can be established.

Taking a cost-benefit approach

A cost-benefit approach is often used by businesses in weighing up the advantages of particular actions.

* Costs include all the financial, social and environmental costs of taking a particular action. These costs will be measured in money terms.

* Benefits include all the financial, social and environmental benefits of taking a particular action. These benefits are measured in money terms.

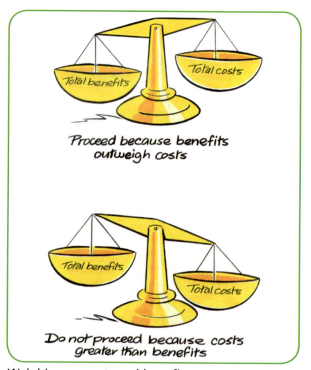

Weighing up costs and benefits

Total benefits − Total costs = Net benefit

In taking a particular action, organisations need to see that the total benefits outweigh the total costs. For example, if a supermarket decides to replace some of its non-organic fruit and vegetables with organic ones then the benefits and costs would include:

* *Economic benefits*. More customers for the shop who spend more on other goods which leads to greater profits.

* *Social benefits*. Leads to healthier society, better incomes for organic farmers and a better reputation in society for the supermarket.

* *Environmental benefits*. Less pollution as pesticides and chemicals are not used which can damage land, water and air systems.

* *Economic costs*. Might lose some customers who prefer non-organic produce. Organic products are more expensive to buy from farmers and therefore prices charged have to be higher.

* *Social costs*. Some non-organic farmers may suffer and have to close down their farms.

* *Environmental costs*. Few.

More and more businesses are realising the importance of corporate social responsibility because it helps a company to project a strong image. People trust some companies more than others. Companies with a good triple bottom line such as Tesco and Boots are much more highly thought of than companies who don't place much emphasis on corporate social responsibility.

Theory into practice

Can you think of examples of situations in which a businesses reputation has been threatened by the following:

* mis-selling products to the wider public

* failure to maintain appropriate standards of product safety.

* a business causing harm to the environment.

Theory into practice

Identify recent actions taken by companies that you are familiar with or are in the news which involve a corporate social responsibility dimension. For each action identify what you perceive to be the benefits and the costs. Estimate whether the benefits will outweigh the costs.

Think it over…

The term corporate social responsibility has been defined as an organisation taking responsibility for society which goes beyond the legal minimum requirement.

3.2.10 Stakeholders

Stakeholders are a number of different groups of individuals who have a stake in the decision-making process of a business:

* owners
* employees
* suppliers
* pressure groups
* creditors
* government
* society
* local community.

In the past businesses typically placed most emphasis on meeting the needs of its owners (shareholders). The emphasis was therefore on creating profit, and so decisions involving profit maximisation where given priority. However, today businesses are more aware of the need to create a successful triple bottom line. Businesses will create policies and plans covering a wide range of corporate social responsibility areas. For example, Boots have policies about:

* looking after disabled employees and customers

* Animal Rights – not testing new products on animals

* giving fair deals to suppliers
* making sure that all their supplies are created in ethical conditions e.g. no exploitation of child labour
* the environment, waste minimisation and pollution control.

Meeting the needs of all stakeholders

Business leaders at Shell coined the phrase 'earning a licence to operate' from stakeholders. It is all very well complying with the law to keep on the right side of government. However, the 'better' business recognises the needs of all of its stakeholder groupings and sets out to serve them. Businesses need to balance the needs of the various stakeholder groupings.

Meeting the needs of customers	Finding out what they want through market and customer satisfaction research, and then serving the needs of customers.
Creditors	Paying up on time and in a friendly spirit.
Employees	Paying them good wages, offering opportunities for promotion and personal development. Giving them a company to work for that they can be proud of.
Government	Paying the right amount of taxes on time and backing government initiatives such as those in relation to the environment.
Communities	Creating attractive jobs, providing clean and attractive premises, getting involved in community activities, giving money, time and skilled personnel to help with community projects.
Other stakeholder groups	Meeting the needs and requirements of these groups

Meeting stakeholder requirements

Theory into practice

Today we talk about businesses earning a licence to operate. This is a recognition that if businesses are going to be able to continue to operate in the long term they need to earn the approval of the full range of their stakeholder groups. Business decision-making is closely tied up with keeping the various stakeholders happy.

Examine a local case study that is published in a local newspaper which shows that a local business is having to respond to pressures from a range of stakeholder groups in order to earn a licence to operate.

Shareholders

The **shareholders** have invested funds in a business. They receive two benefits from the firm doing well: the shares may rise in value if the firm is successful and also dividends that they receive will increase if profits improve. Conversely, they could lose all of the value of their investment should the business fail. Shareholders will vote at the AGM in support of or against decisions taken by directors. Shareholders can therefore have a direct impact on business decision making:

* they can vote to elect directors with ideas similar to their own
* the can vote off directors they disapprove of
* the can vote not to accept a company report
* they can threaten to sell their shares if they are not happy with company policy and direction.

No Board of Directors can ignore the wishes of major shareholders and shareholder groupings.

Directors

Directors are chosen by the shareholders to represent their interests. Their jobs will depend upon the success of the firm, as may the level of their remuneration. This may vary according to bonuses related to the financial success of the firm. Directors often hold positions of authority and make senior decisions across the whole of an organisation.

Directors therefore are key decision makers. They shape the policies and plans of the organisation. They create guidelines for managers to implement in making day-to-day decisions.

Employees

Employees' jobs also depend on the success of the firm, but the nature of the work that they are required to do may change according to its success. A firm in a competitive environment may experience regular change and the nature of work and the levels of responsibility that workers may be required to undertake may change. Firms that are struggling may 'release' some staff which would mean remaining staff may then have to take on more responsibility than they would choose. A solid firm, however, provides the employees with job security which lends security to their personal lives.

Employees are important stakeholders with a range of potential sanctions such as industrial action. They are also, of course, internal customers. Such power might influence senior managers who might be cautious about making decisions that would affect morale and influence the actions of the workforce. Most modern organisations involve a considerable amount of empowerment. Empowerment means passing the responsibility for decision making to lower levels within the organisation. This means that ground-level employees have considerable decision-making powers – e.g. how to deal with a consumer complaint, what to do if faults are occurring in production etc.

In large decentralised organisations many important decisions will be taken a long way away from the Head Office, or from the central directors of the organisation.

Customers

If a company works in a competitive market, customers may benefit through lower prices, but too much competition could leave them looking for a new company to buy from. If customers are unhappy with a business organisation, they may not buy its products. Customers therefore should be seen as key decision makers in determining what a company produces, where it sells those products, and how it presents those products.

We can see the power that consumers have in decision making by taking the example of modern university courses. Students decide what they want to study by choosing from different degree programmes – those that are unpopular may have to close down. They decide how they want to study e.g. at a university campus or by distance learning. They decide whether the course is good enough for them – by staying on the course or leaving if they are not satisfied. They also voice their opinions about the quality of the teaching and the resources they are provided with – even about the times of their lectures.

Suppliers

Companies that supply goods or services to a firm will want the firm to do well so that they have regular customers. Such suppliers may take sanctions against late payments by the organisation.

Suppliers provide terms of payment for the organisation. If the organisation does not work in their interests, they may change the terms. The Rover Group had to stop trading when suppliers started to refuse to offer them credit in April 2005. Where suppliers are very large compared to the buyer, suppliers are in a much better position to dictate terms. For example, a company like Coca-Cola which supplies in huge quantities can often dictate how its goods will be displayed, how they will be promoted, and other aspects of the marketing mix. However, when buyers are also very large – e.g. massive supermarket chains such as Tesco and ASDA there is greater equality in decision making.

Creditors

Creditors are people or organisations that are owed money by a business, for example, bankers who have lent the business money. They would like to see the firm succeed so that they get their money back and make a profit from the deal. If the company fails, the bank could be left with a bad debt, but if it is successful the relationship could be mutually profitable.

Creditors have considerable influence within the workplace. If a creditor suffers from late payment, they have a variety of sanctions at their disposal that might influence business decisions. For example, creditors may go to the courts to demand repayment, or request that the business that owes them money be placed into receivership. (An official receiver is then appointed to sell off the goods, machinery and equipment of that firm.)

Creditors are in good position to influence decisions made by a business. For example, when a bank lends a business money it may insist that it carries out certain actions or behaves in certain ways.

Government

Every firm pays corporation tax from profits and most raise VAT through sales, so all firms are of some interest to the government. Some firms are more significant, however. The government would not like to see a company that is a major employer in a town struggling. If it should fail that would leave the government with a substantial problem in terms of the number of newly-unemployed people.

Government also influences business through creating laws which a business must comply with. Decisions made by government (e.g. to create tighter environmental regulations) directly affect a business. Businesses spend a lot of time and money seeking to make sure that they comply with government rules and regulations.

Pressure groups

Pressure groups are collections of individuals who are organised into a group to create pressure on organisations to make a specific change in policy, plans or activities or a general change in the way in which organisations operate. Examples include Friends of the Earth or specific organisations such as a rail users protest group. Many pressure groups are highly organised to influence decision-making processes in an organisation. Actions of pressure groups range from buying shares in a company (so that they can have a voice at the AGM – **Annual General Meeting**) to direct action protests, such as unfurling a banner at the top of Nelson's Column in Trafalgar Square.

Pressure group activities

Pressure groups are designed specifically to influence decision making. Some of them are highly organised to campaign on specific issues such as the environment. They will identify businesses with a poor record on environmental issues and then concentrate on forcing businesses to change the way they operate e.g. through high profile campaigns in the press etc.

Society

Society would like to see businesses trading in a responsible manner so that danger to the public is minimised along with damage to the environment. If the firm is struggling, cost cutting may compromise these objectives. Pressure groups may be formed to put pressure on the firm to conform. In the 21st century most firms have become aware of the need to make sure that they have policies for Corporate Social Responsibility (CSR) which is all about building good relationships with society at large.

Local community

There are many local businesses that will depend on the success of another business. A number of businesses will spring up to service the needs of a large local company and to provide for the needs of the people who work there. Newsagents, public houses, restaurants and sandwich shops will all rely on the business continuing to succeed. If it fails, they may go down with it.

CASE STUDY

Healthy eating

Statistics show increasing levels of obesity in this country, largely caused by lack of exercise and poor diet. A number of food companies have come under public scrutiny, because of the amounts of fat, sugar, and salt contained in items such as chocolate bars and processed meals. Well-known food companies have therefore been forced to rethink their strategies and to seek to become providers of healthier foods.

Explain how each of the following stakeholder groups might have influenced the decision of these companies to become more closely associated with providing healthier foods:

* owners (shareholders)
* local community
* suppliers
* pressure groups
* customers.

UNIT ASSESSMENT

Expanding a business

Julie set up a sandwich making business called Healthy Appetites two years ago, in partnership with her brother Simon. The initial finance for the business came from a loan from their parents, and a bank loan. This enabled them to buy the equipment, and to take out a rolling lease on a High Street premise.

In addition to offering sandwiches, cakes, tea, coffee and other refreshments to customers six days a week, they also launched a van delivery service to local firms. Key issues in setting up and running the business have been those of complying with Health and Safety, and Food Safety laws. These are 'hot' issues for any business involved in providing food to the general public, and it is a costly business to create the systems and maintain them to guarantee the required standards of safety.

Healthy Appetites focuses on providing 'healthy' options eating, for example, by using wholemeal bread, salad fillings and minimising the use of fats, sugar and salt in food products offered. Julie and Simon both enjoy a healthy lifestyle and are passionate about providing good quality food. Their approach has found favour with customers. Two gyms and a health club have recently set up in town, and many of their customers are healthy livers who like to keep fit.

They were able to borrow money from the banks in 2002 when interest rates were very low (the UK base rate was under 4%).

The business has been very successful and has built up a regular clientele, both for the High Street premises and for the delivery service. The business is situated in the small market town (population 30,000) of Littleham. In recent years the town has been growing as more businesses have been setting up there.

However, Simon is due to go to University in September, and so will be pulling out of the business. This leaves Julie with some difficult decisions to make. One option would be to bring in another partner, a friend called Helen who she went to school with. Helen has no experience of working in the food business, but has good Information Technology skills and is currently studying for a book-keeping and accountancy qualification. Another alternative would be to set up a private limited company. She could then convert the loan she has had from her parents into shares in the business, and perhaps bring in one or two family friends as shareholders. A third option might be to go it alone as a sole trader, taking a further bank loan. The business is in need of a fresh injection of cash, because the existing delivery van is now unreliable. Making reliable deliveries to factories and offices in the town is very important, because failure to deliver could lead to a loss of orders. A new van will cost £20,000.

The business has only just started to break even. It took Simon and Julie longer than they expected to break even because the initial costs of setting up were higher than expected. Now that the break-even point has been reached it is important to start making profits in order to repay some of the start-up loans.

A number of factors are likely to influence the potential to make profits in the future. One of these is that unemployment has been falling steadily in Littleham and the surrounding villages.

The following figures for unemployment have been calculated using the Labour Force Survey method of calculation:

Unemployment in Littleham (LFS method of calculation)

Year	Numbers
1995	2,470
2000	1,633
2005	1,200

Another issue that Julie is concerned about is the development of competition. Since she started up, some of the major retailers in the town, including Boots, have also added a sandwich service to their existing services. There is also talk of a well-known 'coffee shop' multiple setting up on the High Street in a vacant premise not far from Healthy Appetites.

In order to make her decision Julie has set out a cash-flow forecast to cover the 12 months starting from January 2006. (assuming she purchases the van)

	Jan	Feb	Mar	Apr	May	Jun	Jul	Aug	Sep	Oct	Nov	Dec
Income												
Sales	9500	10000	10000	11000	11000	12000	12000	12000	12000	12000	12000	12000
Loan	20000											
Total income	29500	10000	10000	11000	11000	12000	12000	12000	12000	12000	12000	12000
Expenditure												
Materials	2200	3300	3800	3800	3800	3800	3800	3800	3800	3800	3800	3800
Labour	2000	2800	3200	3200	3200	3200	3200	3200	3200	3200	3200	3200
Fixtures and fittings	5000						5000					
Rent	2000	2000	2000	2000	2000	2000	2000	2000	2000	2000	2000	2000
Insurance	50	50	50	50	50	50	50	50	50	50	50	50
Electricity	30	30	30	30	30	30	30	30	30	30	30	30
Water	25	25	25	25	25	25	25	25	25	25	25	25
Advertising	100	100	100	100	100	100	100	100	100	100	100	100
Bank Loan Repayments	500	500	500	500	500	500	500	500	500	500	500	500

	Jan	Feb	Mar	Apr	May	Jun	Jul	Aug	Sep	Oct	Nov	Dec
Total expenditure	11905	8805	9705	9705	9705	9705	9705	9705	9705	9705	9705	9705
Net cash flow	17595	1195	295	1295	1295	2295	2295	2295	2295	2295	2295	2295
Opening balance	2000	19595	20790	21085	22380	23675	25970	28265	30560	32855	35150	37445
Closing balance	19595	20790	21085	22380	23675	25970	28265	30560	32855	35150	37445	39740

Here is some additional information that was available to Julie about changing economic circumstances in early 2005 when Julie was making her decision.

Monetary Policy Committee decisions on interest rates

Month	Change in interest rate	New interest rate
Feb 2005	0	4.75%
Jan 2005	0	4.75%
Dec 2004	0	4.75%
November 2004	0	4.75%
October 2004	0	4.75%
September 2004	0	4.75%
August 2004	+0.25%	4.75%
July 2004	+0.25%	4.5%
June 2004	+0.25%	4.25%
May 2004	+02.5%	4.0%

Labour market statistics showed that in February 2005 employment continued at record levels but the number of unemployed was also growing. 28.52 million people were in work in October to December (2004) according to the Labour Force Survey. This was up by 90,000 over the last three months and up by 296,000 over 2004.

At the same time there was clear evidence of earnings growth in the economy.

Banks offering better deals for new customers

Many High Street banks are offering exciting packages to new account holders. What this means is that if you are an existing business, with good growth prospects it is possible to switch from your existing bank to a new bank and gain a number of perks which are there to attract you. Such perks include deferral of interest repayments on loans for up to six months and a special low rate of interest on certain types of loans. Banks also are offering free business advice to new business customers.

In the questions, figures in brackets show available marks.

1   Identify and describe two advantages to Julie of setting up her business, Healthy Appetites, as a private limited company.

Advantage 1 _____

_____ (1)

Description _____

_____ (1)

Advantage 2 _____

_____ (1)

Description _____

_____ (1)

2 What would be the potential problems of setting up as a partnership with her old
   school friend?

_____

_____

_____

_____ (2)

3 Julie's bank manager has said that he would be prepared to give her a loan to buy the
   vehicle she requires.
   a Explain what is meant by a loan   (2)
   b What might be the dangers to the business if Julie takes out a loan?   (2)
   c Explain one other method of financing the vehicle that would involve less risk to the business.
      Evaluate why it would be less risky.   (3)

4 Complete the SWOT Grid for Healthy Eating at the time Julie took over control of the business
   after the partnership with Simon terminated.

SWOT analysis for Healthy Appetites

Strengths	Weaknesses
1	1
2.	2
Opportunities	**Threats**
1	1
2	2

(10)

5 Complete the SLEPT grid for Healthy Appetites

Social	
1	2
Legal	
1	2
Economic	
1	2
Political	
1	2
Technological	
1	2

(10)

6 In setting up Healthy Appetites, Julie and Simon were very concerned to make sure that they provide people with Health Foods. They are very aware of new government concern and legislation to make sure that food producers put less salt and fat into foodstuffs and take the issue of obesity seriously. Julie is very aware of nutritional issues and has studied all the legal requirements about what goes into food produce. She believes strongly that the business should operate in an ethical way.

   a Explain what is meant by the term business ethics. (2)

   b What is the difference between ethical and legal requirements. (2)

   c Analyse why the issue of ethical responsibility is important to Julie and her business. (2)

   d Evaluate one of the costs to Healthy Appetites if the business failed to adopt an ethical approach. (2)

   e Assess the implications of the government passing stricter laws on food safety and food contents for the food manufacturing industry as a whole. (8)

7 Quality of written communication is assessed in this question.

A major constraint on the future success of Healthy Appetites is the level of competition in the sector of the ready-made food market that Julie is operating in. New competitors are entering the market.

Advise Julie on whether she should continue to grow her business by purchasing a new van and by expanding the range of food and drinks that she offers in her store:

You should make reference to the following factors:

✱ the nature of the competition and market conditions

✱ economic trends (12)

8 When Julie and Simon first set up they identified the following information that was relevant to their business.

> Average selling price per item sold by Healthy Appetites £1.40
>
> Average variable cost per item 60p
>
> Fixed Costs £54,100

a Define the term 'break-even point' (3)
b Explain the formula for working out the break-even point using contribution. (2)
c Calculate the break-even point for Healthy Appetites using the information above.

> Show your working
>
> Break-even point =

(2)

d Explain the impact on the break-even point if the cost of materials used by Healthy Appetites proved to be lower than expected. (2)
e Evaluate the likely impact on the break-even point of a fall in interest rates (2)
f What is meant by the term 'margin of safety'? Why might Simon and Julie want to calculate the margin of safety for a given level of sales? (3)

9 In planning out the first year of the business Julie and Simon created a budget.

a Explain what is meant by a budget (2)

b Who are budgets typically produced for? Give three examples. (3)

c Critically analyse one way in which creating the budget would have given Simon and Julie greater control of their business. (4)

10 Examine the following figures for Healthy Appetites at the end of year one. Calculate the variances between the actual figures and the budgeted figures.

	Budget	Actual	Variance
Income			
Sales	135500	140000	
Loan	20000	20000	
Total income	155500	160000	
Expenditure			
Materials	43500	41000	
Labour	36800	37000	

	Budget	Actual	Variance
Fixtures and fittings	10000	10000	
Rent	24000	26500	
Insurance	600	700	
Electricity	360	370	
Water	300	320	
Advertising	12000	15000	
Bank loan repayments	6000	6000	
Total expenditure	133560	136890	

(7)

11 Identify one variance which you think would cause concern to Healthy Appetites and explain one management action that could be taken to try and correct this variance. (4)

12 Discuss how using computer accounting packages would help Simon and Julie to manage the budgetary control of their business effectively. Explain the costs and benefits of using this type of technology. (5)

Total available marks: (100)

Resources

There is a wide range of textbooks aimed at Advanced Level Business candidates. Some good up-to-date sources include:

Dransfield, R. et al., *BTEC National Business*, Heinemann, Oxford, 2004

Marcouse et al., *Business Studies*, Hodder and Stoughton, Tonbridge, 2004

Dransfield, R. and Dransfield, D., *Economics Made Easy*, Nelson Thornes, Cheltenham, 2003

For the more financial elements of this unit:

Dransfield, R. and Coles, M. *Accounts Made Easy*, Nelson, Thornes, Cheltenham, 2002

Dransfield, R., *Financial Information Made Easy*, Nelson Thornes, Cheltenham, 2002

Websites

Some useful websites are listed below. These addresses are current at the time of writing. However, it needs to be recognised that new sites are being launched on the Internet on a regular basis and that older sites may change or disappear.

www.tt100.biz
www.tutor2u.net
www.ft.com
www.uk.finance.yahoo.com
www.aloa.co.uk

BIZ / ed – business education on the Internet

This is a free information service on the Internet which provides a range of notes and worksheets. This includes:

* key economic statistics

* company information

* case studies

* outline assignments and study skills

* curriculum updates.

Its address is www.bized.ac.uk

Videos

TV choice (www.tv.choice.com) produces a range of useful business videos including *The Balance Sheet*, and *The Profit and Loss Account*.

Glossary

Annual General Meeting under company law, the directors of a company must present a report to shareholders each year at an annual general meeting; at this time shareholders have the right to ask questions and in some cases can vote to replace directors.

Applicant a person applying for a job.

Appraisal interview between a manager and employee to agree targets for the future.

Arithmetic mean total of values divided by the number of values.

Balance sheet a snapshot of a firm's assets, liabilities and sources of capital at a moment in time.

Bankruptcy where a business or person is taken to court to prevent further trading.

Board of Directors Senior directors of a company who have been appointed to direct company activities.

Body language communication involving sending signals by the ways in which we position and use our bodies e.g. through hand signals, gestures, facial expressions, crossing of the arms etc.

Brand symbol, image or sign associated with a particular product or service.

Break-even analysis comparison of a firm's revenue and its fixed and variable costs, to identify the minimum sales level needed to break even; it can be shown on a break-even chart.

Break-even point the level of output at which total revenue equals total costs.

Breaking even making sure costs are covered.

Budget plan set out in numbers for the future.

Business plan an organised document that enables a business to prepare for the future and forecast all of the events and actions it takes within the context of a range of forecasts.

Candidate individual who has applied for a job and will continue with the recruitment process.

Cash-flow forecast a technique for estimating the future bank balance of a company and anticipating overdraft requirements.

Closed questions questions that limit the range of responses and often obtain a yes or no answer or a number.

Company any type of business that has a legal separate identity from its members; most companies are limited and most are registered under the Companies Act.

Consumers people who use / consume a product.

Contribution the money contribution that each unit of an item sold makes towards paying off the fixed costs of a business; for example, if the variable cost of producing a chocolate bar is 10p and the chocolate bar is sold for 40p, each bar is contributing 30p (revenue variable cost; 40–10 = 30).

Creditor a business or person that the firm owes money to.

Current assets items that a business owns that can be turned into cash in the short term, such as stock or debtors.

Current liabilities things that the business owes in the short term, such as goods bought and not paid for, or loans borrowed that must be paid back.

Curriculum Vitae (usually called a CV) is a summary of your career to date.

Customers people who buy a product.

Database a computer programme for storing data records.

Debtors people who owe money to a business.

Development	the process of identifying and then finding opportunities to meet the needs of individuals within an organisation.
Discrimination	treating individuals less favourably than others on account of factors such as gender and disability.
Dividend	payment to shareholders out of company profits.
Economies of scale	the financial advantages that a larger firm has over a smaller one, enabling them to produce and supply larger quantities at lower unit costs.
Empowerment	giving responsibility to staff lower down the organisation so that individuals are given power to make decisions, rather than being told what to do.
Encoding	putting an advertising or promotional message into a form that provides meaning for customers and consumers.
Ethics	moral principles or rules of conduct generally accepted by most members of a society.
External constraints	influences outside the control of an organisation.
Fixed cost	a business cost that does not vary with the level of output or sales.
Focus groups	small groups of customers who are able to discuss their needs in some depth.
Human resources department	department dealing with the management of policies and procedures relating to the people who work for an organisation; it covers areas such as payroll, sickness monitoring, grievance and disciplinary procedures.
Indirect discrimination	setting out a requirement which on the face of it may appear to be non-discriminatory but which is in fact more difficult for some groups of people to meet than others.
Induction	sessions introducing new staff to the work and work environment in an organisation.
Insolvent	not having enough funds to meet pressing liabilities (debts).
Integrated accounts 'package'	accounting system running across a business organisation taking into account budgeted areas and departments that use the system.
Intention-to-buy	expressing a likelihood of purchase.
Internal constraints	controllable influences within an organisation.
Interviewing	the process of asking questions and giving tests to candidates in order to select the most suitable person to fill a job role.
Intranet	network within an organisation providing an internet-like framework with limited and exclusive access.
Investment	two principal meanings in business. 1. Sums of money invested in a business for which investors expect to receive a return. 2. Purchase by the business of an item that contributes to further production, e.g. a machine or tool.
Job analysis	a study of the tasks that are required to do a particular job.
Job application	details supplied to an employer typically in a job application form by someone seeking a post with an employing organisation.
Job description	the list of working conditions for a job e.g. pay, hours and duties.
Learning	is generally defined as 'a relatively permanent change in behaviour that occurs as a result of practice or experience'.
Liquidity	how quickly a business can turn its assets (anything it owns that is valuable into cash).
Manager	is someone with responsibility, usually for others, for making decisions and for managing resources.
Margin of safety	the difference between a selected level of output and the break-even point.
Market research	'the systematic gathering, recording and analysis of data about problems related to the marketing of goods and services'.

Market segment	The result of dividing up large heterogeneous markets with similar needs into smaller markets (segments) according to shared characteristics.
Market share	the sales of a product by a company expressed as a percentage of total sales in a market; if a company sells 20,000 products and the total number of those product sold overall is 200,000, the company has a market share of 10%. Often market share is measured in sales revenue i.e. in £'s rather than the physical number of units sold.
Marketing	'the management process responsible for identifying, anticipating and satisfying customer requirements profitably'.
Marketing mix	a series of variable factors such as the four Ps (product/price/place/promotion) used by an organisation to meet its customers' needs.
Marketing objectives	the targets that the organisation seeks to meet through its marketing activities.
Marketing plan	a plan that uses the marketing mix to identify and then meet consumers' requirements
Mass marketing	marketing to all potential customers within a whole of a market in a way that fails to take into account parts of a market.
Median	middle number in an array of figures.
Mode	a value that occurs more frequently than others.
Motivation	the personal drive to achieve targets and get things done.
Open questions	questions that provide the respondent with the freedom to answer in a variety of ways.
Overheads	costs that do not change when the firm sells more, and are not incurred by a specific department of the company, e.g. rent.
Percentages	figures expressed as an amount of one hundred.
Performance appraisal	a process of systematically evaluating performance and providing feedback on adjustments that can be made.
Person specification	list of attributes needed by a person to perform a job, such as personality type or experience.
PEST analysis	analysis examining political, economic, social and technological factors.
Positioning	placing a product within the overall market e.g. at the 'no frills' end or at the 'luxury' end of the market.
Price-maker	organisation that has the freedom to set prices within the market.
Price-taker	organisation that sets prices at the market price dictated by market forces.
Primary information	information an organisation compiles by its own efforts perhaps commissioning a specialist market research agency.
Primary research	original research to find out information e.g. by asking questions and interviewing people.
Probability	likelihood or chance of achieving predicted outcomes.
Product life-cycle	key stages in the life of a product e.g. launch, introduction, growth, maturity, decline.
Profit	the difference between revenue and cost.
Psychometric or aptitude testing	tests designed to check that a candidate has the right sorts of personality characteristics (psychometric) or the right sort of approach or is suited (aptitude) to fit a particular job role.
Questionnaire	systematic list of questions designed to obtain information from people about specific events, their attitudes, their values and their beliefs.
Rank order scale	questions that ask respondents to express preferences.
Recruitment	the process of attracting, and finding employees to apply for posts being offered by an organisation.
Resources	the means of supplying what is needed.

Responsibility accounting	providing departmental areas with the responsibility and freedom to act within the confines of a budget.
Revenue	the value of sales (in money terms) that the product is likely to have achieved or has achieved.
Sales value	total sales value in pounds.
Secondary information	published data collected by another organisation and not specific to the project in hand.
Secondary research	research using work already carried out by someone else for some other purpose.
Selection	the process of choosing suitable candidates to fill a post being offered by an organisation.
Selection criteria	requirements that must be met when choosing the best individual to fill a post.
Semantic differential scales	market research technique with words describing opposites.
Shareholders	part owners of a company who own shares in it.
Shortlisting	involves drawing up a list of the most suitable applicants from those that have applied for a post with an organisation.
SLEPT analysis	Social, Legal, Economic, Political and Technological changes in the business environment that influence decision-making.
Sole trader	single owner of a business.
Solvency	ability to pay wages, supplier's bills and other obligations as they fall due.
Spreadsheet	a computer program that allows the user to manipulate figures and perform both simple and complex mathematical tasks.
Stakeholder	someone with an interest in the running of a business.
Strategy	the long-term plans of an organisation, large plans involving substantial quantities of resources.
Supervisors	have responsibility for supervising a particular task or group of people.
SWOT analysis	analysis of an organisation and its external environment to assess its internal strengths and weaknesses, and the opportunities and threats that exist in the operating environment.
Tangible	physical item that you can touch and see.
Targeting	developing strategies for particular segments.
Trade association	organisation set up to represent a range of businesses within an industry.
Training needs analysis	a study to find out what training an individual needs to become a more knowledgeable and skilled worker in order to help the organisation to meet its goals.
Turnover	the money value of sales made by a company, also referred to as sales revenue.
Undifferentiated marketing	mass marketing to a whole market, without distinguishing between the parts.
Variable cost	a cost that increases with the level of output or sales, e.g. the cost of ingredients in producing chocolate bars.
Variance	the difference between a budgeted (planned) figure and what actually materialises. For example, if actual costs are higher than budgeted costs this would be described as a negative variance.
Wholesalers	organisation that links manufacturers and retailers within the chain of distribution.
Working capital	current assets less current liabilities.

Index

Page numbers in italics refer to illustrations and diagrams.

absenteeism 83
accounting
  see also budgets; finance
  financial 130–3
  management 132
  software 136
achievements, of job applicant
  61–2
administration 12, 58
advertising 7, 40–3, 41–2, *41*
annual general meeting (AGM)
  154
application forms 59, *70*, 71
application letters 68, *69*, 71
appraisals 86, 88–9
aptitude tests 74, 76
arithmetic mean 29
assets, fixed 110

balance sheets 130
body language 77–8, *78*
borrowing 110–12, 124, 126, 127,
  144
brands 8, 33–4
break-even analysis 120–6, *124,
  125*
budgets 10, 11
  see also accounting; finance
  benefits 115
  capital 120, *120*
  historic 116, 119
  labour 83, 120
  performance levels 117
  periods 114–15, *115*
  plans 116–7
  reports 116
  sales 119, *119*
  setting 116, *116*, 117
  variance analysis 115, 117–18
business
  decision-making 109, 113–4,
    131, 142, 153–7
  funding 109–14
  growth 60
  objectives 60, 80–1, 109, 126
  ownership 102–9
  performance 130–1, 133
  planning 115, 116, 126

risks 17
  taxes 109, 156
buyer-readiness 40, *40*
buyers 13, 16

capital 104, 105, 110, 114, 120
cash-flow forecasts 126–30,
  128–9
charities 44, 46, 107
communication 7, 39–40, *40*
companies 85, 104–5, 109
competence, of job applicants
  63, *63*
competition 4–5, 6, 38–9, *39*, 137,
  143, 146, 147, 155
constraints, marketing 8–10
consumers 15–16, 19, 20
Consumer Price Index (CPI)
  143, *144*
contribution 121, 122
co-operatives 105–7
corporate social responsibility
  148, 150, 153, 154, 156
cost-benefit analysis 152–3
cost-plus pricing 38, *38*
credit control 131
creditors 126, 155–6
culture, of organisations 87
curriculum vitae (CV) 71–2, *73*
customer needs 3–4, 10, 11, 14,
  51, 134
customer service 11, 17, *58*, 58–9
customers, as stakeholders 155

databases 25, 57, 137
debtors 110, 111
decision-making, business 109,
  113–4, 131, 142, 153–7
departments, of organisations
  10–13, 51
directors, company 104, 154–5
disabled employees, needs of
  93–4
discrimination 93–4, 149
distribution 46–7, 48, *48*
diversification 35
dividends 86, 109, 110
duties, of job holder 65

e-commerce 12, 49, 60
economic conditions, changes in
  31–2, 140, 142–8
economies of scale 35, 38, 146
employees
  experience of 59
  motivating 12, 84–92
  payment schemes 84, 86
  position in organisation 65
  qualities needed in 59, 61–2
  stakeholders 155
  working conditions 87
employment
  ethical issues 93, 94
  health and safety 82–3
  legislation 93–4, 149
empowerment 92, 155
encoding 39
environmental responsibility
  140, 152
equal opportunities 74, 93–4,
  140, 149
ethical issues 93, 94, 148–51
euro zone 145
evaluation
  interviews 79
  marketing proposal 51–2
  workplace recruitment 96–7,
    97–8
exchange rates 143, 144–5, 148
experience, of job applicants 59,
  62–3, 68
experiments, market research
  20–1
external data, market research
  26–8

face-to-face discussions 94
factoring 111, 113
feedback, from interviews 76,
  80
finance 11
  see also accounting; budgets
  legislation 132
  management of 114–15, 148
  reports 131
  sources of 109–14
fixed costs 120–1, 122, 123

focus groups 19, 24–5
forecasting 17, 30–1, 116, 135–6
formal acceptance 79
franchises 108–9
fringe benefits 86–7

goals, employee 88
government 111, 140
    as business stakeholder 156
    statistics 19, 26–7

health and safety 82–3, 149
Herzberg, Frederick 91
hierarchy of needs, motivational
    theory 90
historic budgeting 116, 119
human resources (HR) 12, 61,
    83, *95*

ICT 12–13
    e-commerce 12, 49, 60
    IT operatives 57–8
    software 135–7
    technology 133–5
ideas 5–6
induction process 80–4
inflation 143–4
information 19
    accounting 130, 131
    market research 17
    sources of 19, 25–8
intention-to-buy scale 23, *23*
interest payments 110, 113
interest rates 111, 142, 143, 144,
    145, 148
intermediaries 47–8
internal data, market research
    25–6
Internet 15, 27, 48, 60, 147
interviews *75*
    see also appraisals; market
        research
    applicant selection 79–80
    assignment 95–6
    body language 76, 77–8
    evaluation 79
    feedback 76, 80
    preparation for 74, 76–7, *77*
    questions 75–6, 78
    techniques 77–9, *79*

job advertisements *59*, 65–7, *65*,
    66
job analysis 60–1

job applications 67–73
job descriptions 28, 57, 59, 60,
    63, *64*
job roles 56–8
job selection *67*, 73–80
job titles 63–5, *64*

Kanter, Rosabeth 92

labour budgets 83, 120
legislation 9, 107, 140
    accounting 132
    discrimination 93–4
    employment 93–4, 149
    equal opportunities 140, 149
    health and safety 82–3, 149
letters, job application 68
Likert scales 22, *22*
limited liability 102, 103, 104,
    105
liquidity (solvency) 132–3
loans 110, 111, 113
loyalty incentives 26, *26*, 45, 46

management accounting 132
managers 56, 58, 86, 92
margin of safety 122, 123, 126
marginal costing 121, 122
market conditions 142–8
market position, analysis of
    137–42
market research 13
    aims of 18–19
    companies 27–8
    information sources 19
    interpretation of data 29–33
    interviews 16, 19
    methods 19
    planning 18–19
    primary 19–21
    questionnaires 19
    reports 28
    secondary 19, 25–8
market segments 14, 15
market share 2, 137
marketing 10–11, *16*
    aims of 1–9, 51, 137
    constraints 8–10
    mass marketing 14
    positioning 14–15
    proposals 49–51
marketing mix 13, 33–49
Maslow, Abraham 90–1
McGregor, Douglas 92

media, advertising 27, 42–3
median 29
merchandising 20
method study 86
mode 29
motivation 115
    employee 12, 84–90
    theories of 90–2
moving average total (MAT) 30,
    31

niche marketing 14–15

operations 11
organisations
    communication 7
    control structure 116
    co-operation 11–13, 17
    culture of 87
    departments 10–13, 51
    external influences 31–2, *143*
    information, importance of 17
    resources 8–9
    targets of 115
    voluntary 107, 109
output-related pay 84, 86
owner's capital 110
ownership 102–9, 113–4

packaging 20, 33–6, 48
partnerships 104, 109
payment schemes 84, 86
penetration pricing 37
performance appraisals 86, 88–9
performance related pay 86
person specifications 59, 60,
    61–3, *62*
PEST analysis 31–2, 140–1
political changes 31, 140
positioning 15, 42
presentations 49–51, 57–8
pressure groups 156
pricing
    competition-based 38–9
    cost-plus 38
    penetration 37
    skimming 37
primary research 19–25, 94–6
private companies 104–5
product mix 35–6
production 11
products
    brands 8, 33–4
    development of new 5–6, *6*

differentiation 39
features 34–5
life-cycle 41, 152
marketing new 37–8
placement 20, 50
quality of 38, 39
sampling 45
profit targets 122, 124
profitability 123, 126, 131, 132–3
profits 8, 109, 123, 124, 133
promotion, internal 60, 87–8
promotions 39–40
advertising 7, 40–3, 41–2
public relations (PR) 43–5
sales 7, 45–6
public companies 105
public relations (PR) 7, 43–5, 43, 44

qualifications, job applicants 62, 68
quality assurance 12
questionnaires 19, 21–4, 95
questions
interview 75–6, 78
market research 21–4

racial discrimination 93
rank order scales 22, 22
rating scales 22, 22
record-keeping, financial 130–33
recruitment 12
advertising 65–7
ethical issues 93–4
evaluation of 79
interviews 74–80
job analysis 60–1
job applications 67–73
job descriptions 63–5
person specifications 61–3
reasons for 60
reports
budgetary 116
market research 27–8
financial 130, 131, 132, 133
repositioning 15
research 94–6
research and development (R&D) 6, 11–12
resources 8-9, 11

'responsibility accounting' 114, 116
retailers 20, 47–8
retained profits 109, 109
revenue 11, 114
risks, business 17, 30

sales
budgets 119
channels 47, 47
direct 8, 47
forecasts 30
invoices 25
promotions 7, 45–6
revenue 11, 114
turnover 119
value 122
sampling frame 21
satisfiers and dissatisfiers, motivational theory 91
secondary research 25–8, 96
selection process 73–80
semantic differential scales 23, 23
September 11th 131, 143, 147–8
share options 86
shareholders 43, 105, 109, 110, 131, 133, 154
short-listing, job applicants 74–9, 74
sickness benefit 83
skimming 37
SLEPT analysis 140–2
SMART objectives 3, 18, 51
social trends 32, 140, 152
software
accounting 130, 136
databases 25, 57, 137
spreadsheets 57, 125–6, 125, 130, 135–6
sole traders 102–3, 109, 114
solvency 132–3
sponsorship 8, 44
spreadsheets 57, 125, 126, 130, 135–6
staff
induction 80–4
training 83–4, 89–90, 108, 134, 135
turnover 60

stakeholders 153–7
statistics
government 19, 26–7
methods 29–31
supervisors, role of 56–7
suppliers 13, 111, 155
surveys
customer satisfaction 17
market research 21–4
SWOT analysis 32–3, 51, 137–9, 141

targeting 15
targets
employee 88
organisations 115
profit 122, 124
taxes, business 109, 156
technology 32, 133–5, 140, 144, 147
terrorism, economic effect of 147–8
tests, at interviews 76
Theory X vs Theory Y, motivational theory 92
trade associations 27
training 83–4, 89–90, 108, 134, 135
triple bottom line 148–9, 153
turnover, sales 119

unemployment 145–6

value for money 38
variable costs 121, 122, 123, 124
variance analysis 115, 117–18, 127
venture capital 110
voluntary organisations 107, 109

wages 84, 90, 146, 149
wholesalers 47–8
work measurement 86
working capital 110
working conditions 87

zero budgeting 117, 119